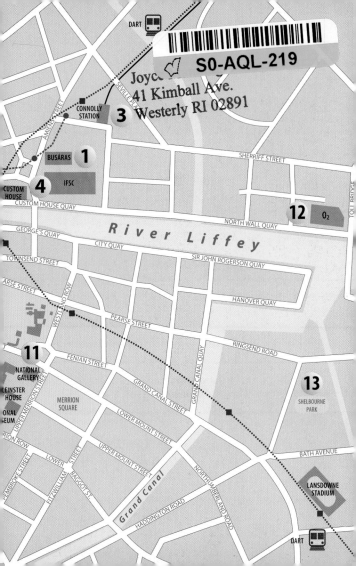

Mural by Maser outside one of Dublin's little gems,
the Andrews Lane Theatre, hidden off Dame Street.

Dublin on a Shoestring

Katherine Farmar

Ben Murnane

A. & A. Farmar

© A. & A. Farmar 2009
ISBN 978-1-906353-10-0

First edition published 1998, second edition 2002, third edition 2009

Compiled by Kathy Farmar and Ben Murnane with contributions from
Mai Byrne, Hugh Doherty, Tony Farmar, Gabriel Graham, Matthew
Magee, Des Murnane, Ruth Murnane, Derek Nagle, Colman O'Sullivan,
Sally O'Dunlaing, Kathy Tynan, Warren Yeates

Photographs courtesy of Dublin Tourism (pp 61, 197), Ben Murnane
(p.ii), Derek Speirs (p.viii), Stockbyte (p.27), Ron Yeates (p.95)

Maps by Michael Phillips

Cartoons by Tom Matthews

Cover design by Kevin Gurry

Typesetting, design and index by Bookworks

Printed by GraphyCems

Published in Dublin by
A. & A. Farmar
78 Ranelagh Village,
Dublin 6, Ireland
Tel +353 1 496 3625
afarmar@iol.ie
www.aafarmar.ie

About the editors

Katherine Farmar has studied philosophy at Trinity College, Dublin and
the University of Edinburgh. She has written for *The Irish Times* and the
Times Literary Supplement and appeared on *The Arts Show* and *The Ryan
Tubridy Show*. She blogs about comics at puritybrown.blogspot.com.

Ben Murnane was born in 1984 and graduated from Trinity College
Dublin in 2008. He is the author of *Two in a Million: A True Story
about Illness and Love* and has written for *The Irish Times*, the *Irish
Independent*, the *Evening Herald*, the *Irish Daily Mail* and RTÉ Radio.
Visit his website at www.benmurnane.com.

Introduction *Katherine Farmar, Ben Murnane*

Now is a great time to be in Dublin. The capital is young and full of young people, renowned for its welcoming atmosphere—in March 2007, the city was voted the friendliest city in Europe in a survey of 2,100 travellers—and a cultural hub of Europe. What's more, while Dublin was long held to be one of the most expensive cities to live in or visit, prices are falling rapidly and the city's rip-off reputation is changing. It has to change—as the world economy sinks, taking Ireland with it, there are bargains to be found that would have been unheard of just a year ago.

Still, a lot of shops, restaurants, pubs and hotels are clinging to the old C*lt*c T*g*r way of doing business (fleece them first, hope they don't ask questions later), and when prices are low, often the quality is too. This is where *Dublin on a Shoestring* comes in.

Dublin on a Shoestring is designed for tourists and longer-term visitors who want to have fun in the city, but don't want to ruin themselves in the process. Like most cities, Dublin has nooks and crannies that are both cheaper and more interesting than the most famous attractions—but it takes the experience of an insider to look beyond the obvious. The authors of this guide are Dubliners with years of experience in looking for fun stuff and bargains of every kind: from food to clothes to accommodation to entertainment. We've sought it out at the lowest prices we could find—without skimping on quality.

Shoestring Dublin is the Dublin of the quiet streets, the second-storey cafés, the little places tucked away in unlabelled cul-de-sacs and only advertised through word of mouth. This is the Dublin that won the #1 spot for friendliness. Use *Dublin on a Shoestring* to make your time in our great city memorable.

Contents

*James Joyce casting a sardonic eye
on the city he loved.*

Dublin for beginners

A little history

Dublin is a city of layers, with a medieval footprint that centres on Christ Church Cathedral, overlaid by a Georgian body filling the space between the canals, and Victorian and modern wings spreading north, south and west of the Liffey valley.

The first settlement in Dublin proper was a prehistoric huddle of small houses on the ridge above the lowest crossing point of the Liffey. The centre of the huddle was approximately where the Lord Edward pub is now sited opposite Christ Church Cathedral. Below this settlement was a rough wicker-work hurdle ford across the river, which since it had not yet been embanked was much wider and shallower than it is now.

From the end of the 8th century Viking raiders from Norway had periodically plundered the Irish coastline seeking treasure and captives for slaves. In 841 they established a permanent settlement in Dublin as part of a network of slave trading posts across Europe.

This Dublin perched on a ridge 12 metres or more above the Liffey, on a line from the Castle to Christ Church. Walking down the river on its ancient streets such as Winetavern and Fishamble you can easily imagine the bustle and activity as ships tied up at the wooden quays were loaded and unloaded.

In 1171 the Normans came from England, and Dublin became very much a colony. The new overlords, mostly from Bristol, built defensive stone walls (remnants of which you can see behind the Castle) and the first stone bridge in 1215. Then the centre of Dublin shifted to High St. This now seems nothing much, but throughout the Middle Ages it was an intense centre of urban activity.

For the next few centuries, despite frequent massacres and plagues, Dublin was little more than a large trading post. The real life of Ireland was still Gaelic and centred on the great clan chiefs. But as the English interests in Ireland grew, Dublin became a sort of provincial capital. Its population increased very slowly, being less than 10,000 in 1600, mostly living outside the city proper. Trinity College (founded in 1592) was deliberately placed in the fields, outside the town. St Stephen's Green was still pasture, the site of public executions and a burial place for plague victims.

The walled city

To get a sense of Dublin as a walled city of the middle ages, go to St Audeon's church (off High St, Dublin 2). There's a little park and a flight of broad steps going down called the Forty Steps. This was a main thoroughfare of medieval Dublin. It led into the city from Cook St where the ovens were banished, beyond the walls, for fear of fire. Slip through the gate and stand in Cook St where the great city wall (much restored) looms above you. Take a moment to imagine the bustling pack-horses and carts and vendors of all sorts of produce squeezing through the gate in normal times, or in wartime, the citizenry huddled behind the wall in dread of the 'wild Irish'. (The battlements, by the way, are bogus, a 19th-century fantasy.)

The glory days of Dublin began in the 17th century. Queen Elizabeth's new policy for the control of Ireland, of 'planting' as many Protestants as possible in rebellious areas, brought a new attitude. Dublin became the social, political and economic focus of these planters in Munster, Wexford and Ulster. The policy was continued by her Stuart successors. From 1660 the city began a hundred and forty years of more or less continual growth. The first stone quays embanking the river were built, confining the river like a stone corset, and whereas previous centuries had made do with one bridge (at Bridge St), now no fewer than four new bridges were thrown across the Liffey in quick succession.

Nonetheless, Stuart Dublin was still small, and overwhelmingly Protestant. There were perhaps no more than 4,000 houses.

By the 18th century the city had finally become the national centre of communications and power; it was the country's leading port, the focus of legal, medical and other professional activity, the place where the landed classes came in winter to disport themselves, financed by their country rents. To house these grandees developers built the famous squares and townscapes of Georgian Dublin. At the same time great public buildings such as the Four Courts, the Custom House and the Parliament House (now occupied by the Bank of Ireland), which once housed the Irish parliament, were erected.

By 1800 Ireland's population had grown to more than half that of England, Wales and Scotland together. The colonial regime had not been enlightened. The Catholic religion of 80 per cent of the population was still officially subject to the penal laws, and the mass of the population had few civic rights. The militant attempt in the 1790s to secure more independence for Ireland resulted in the opposite—the Act of Union of 1801 and the abolition of the Irish parliament. At war to the death with France, the English were not about to allow Ireland any freedom at all, lest hotheads encouraged France to invade Britain via Ireland. Various such attempts were in fact made, in 1796, in 1798 and in 1804. Along the Dublin coastline can be seen the Martello towers which were erected at this time as defensive fortresses. (One of these, in Sandycove, famously features in James Joyce's *Ulysses*, and now contains a Joyce museum, see page 213.)

Under the Union Dublin became a mere political branch office for London. Lawyers and clever doctors, such as Sir William Wilde (Oscar's father), rather than aristocratic office-holders, dominated social life. Catholic emancipation in 1829 did not mean that Catholics and Protestants mingled socially. The city continued to be split horizontally by class and vertically by religion. Although sectarianism was never as violent as it became in the North, as late as the 1960s every firm, every private institution—including banks, breweries, chartered accountancy practices, grocers and charities—was clearly known to be either 'Protestant' or 'Catholic' in orientation.

Although the Great Famine of the 1840s had a severe impact on Dublin, the city was in the long run more affected by the railway and steam connection established in the 1850s between London and Dublin. This enabled British manufacturers to pour goods into Ireland, finally completing the destruction of Ireland's manufacturing base. Dublin became a storage and warehouse centre for these goods.

To run what has been called the 'warehouse economy' the distributors did not need skilled workers—a large body of (Catholic) unskilled labour and a much smaller body of (largely Protestant) clerks and professional men would suffice. This economic divide was quickly represented on the ground as the clerks and the professionals left the city centre and established themselves in townships beyond the canals. The characteristic redbrick of their houses in often tree-lined roadscapes can be seen in the southside villages of Ranelagh, Rathgar and Rathmines, and on the northside in Clontarf and Drumcondra. The new suburbs were leafy and comfortable, although in an effort to keep down the rates the developers often skimped on the pavements and drains.

The inner city dwellers fared less well. Labouring wages were low and intermittent. Since the rich had fled, no one could afford rates and the city became increasingly run down. Housing was poor and getting steadily worse. The tenement slums of

Dublin—as written about by Seán O'Casey, James Stephens and others—became some of the worst in Europe, and a scandal that has only been set right within living memory. The Dubliners of Yeats' and Joyce's time inherited almost a century of economic stagnation and squabbling politics. From being the second city of the Empire, 'dear dirty Dublin' had been overtaken by Belfast in size and confidence.

All this was to change with the armed struggle for national independence that ran from 1916 to 1922. Finally, after six years of intermittent but intense fighting, Dublin became the capital city of the first country to break away from the British Empire since 1776. The city still bears the scars of the long struggle— look out for the bullet marks on the front of the Royal College of Surgeons in St Stephen's Green and on the O'Connell statue in O'Connell St.

Once more Dublin became the political centre, the national focus of commerce, and the legal and professional centre, at least for the 26 counties of the new state.

Dublin's story since 1922 is one of constant expansion as governments strove first to re-house the tenement dwellers and then to build houses for the constant flow of migrants from the country. The city's population rose from the 350,000 or so that Joyce had known, to the 650,000 of Brendan Behan's Dublin in the 1950s, to the one million or more of today. If the greater Dublin area is included, taking in the contiguous counties (with their large populations of commuters into the city) the total climbs to 1.7 million.

Reshaping the historic centre began in the 1960s, as property developers knocked down old buildings and erected office blocks. In the 1980s, Dublin Corporation completed the plan to concrete over the famous Wood Quay, the ancient Viking trading city, with two blocks known without affection as 'the bunkers'.

While planners fussed and procrastinated over what to do with the Temple Bar area, between Dame St and the Liffey, its low temporary rents made it attractive to artists, musicians, and keepers of unusual shops and restaurants during the 1980s. Then it was overhauled and gentrified by the government-created Temple Bar Properties during the 1990s. The policy now is to encourage families to the quarter with affordable prices in restaurants and hundreds of free events. The implementation of a plan to refurbish O'Connell St was finally begun in 2002, and completed in 2006 after some delays. These included the building of the controversial Spire monument (officially known as 'the Monument of Light', unofficially as 'the Spike'), restoration work on the street's older monuments, the widening of the footpaths, and the creation of a plaza in front of the GPO.

Between 2004 and 2008 Ireland saw a massive influx of immigrants from Eastern Europe, the largest group being the Poles. In a short period of time, they've left their mark on Dublin, establishing Polish restaurants, food shops, newspapers, and nightclubs, among other essentials, as well as swelling the congregations at Masses, for example at St Audoen's, in the heart of medieval Dublin, now the Polish chaplaincy; during the Polish general election in 2007, there were Polish election posters all over Dublin.

Getting your bearings

Dublin is built in the dip of a valley, where the Liffey runs from the Dublin mountains into the sea. To get an extraordinarily vivid sense of this ancient valley look south as you leave the airport on the northside. You can look straight across to the looming mountains, which are older than the Himalayas, and the city is quite invisible, buried in the valley below. And as you come into the city, note how the old (the church towers) and the new (the high-rises) contest the city space.

As in most European cities Dublin's old streets follow an irregular, often winding pattern, with the oldest (around Wood Quay) being directly traceable to pre-Viking days. The typical height of a Dublin building is four storeys; church spires are still prominent objects on the skyline, though large office buildings are beginning to compete, and the Spire, Europe's tallest free-standing sculpture, can be seen from miles away.

Upper and Lower

Many Dublin streets are divided into two, and called Upper and Lower—thus Leeson St, Baggot St, Mount St, Dorset St. Generally, the Lower is the nearer to the mouth of the Liffey, the Upper further away. This is not, however, the result of a deep plan, as the exception, Dorset St, clearly shows. It seems that the streets called Lower were simply built before those called Upper (though of course there are exceptions to this too).

Landmarks to watch out for

The oldest parts of Dublin are neatly enclosed by two canals, the Grand Canal and the Royal Canal. The old city lies inside the oval shape defined by the two canals. Down the middle of the oval runs the river Liffey, Joyce's Anna Livia Plurabelle. This runs from the Dublin mountains to the sea. Good landmarks on the north of the Liffey are (running west to east, towards the sea) the Four Courts, the Ha'penny Bridge, the Spire, Liberty Hall, the Custom House and The O_2.

South from the Liffey are the Guinness Brewery, Christ Church Cathedral, Dublin Castle, Trinity College, St Stephen's Green and the National Gallery.

For most visitors the axis across the Liffey to know runs from the top of O'Connell St to St Stephen's Green. Start at the Parnell

Monument (next to the Rotunda Hospital and the Gate Theatre) down O'Connell St, past Henry St and its shops, the GPO, over O'Connell Bridge, past Trinity College on your left and down Grafton St to St Stephen's Green.

North/south

Dubliners are convinced that there is a noticeable difference in character and style between those who live on the north of the river and those who live on the south. This difference is officially recognised by the fact that all odd-numbered post-codes are northside and even-numbered are southside. Thus in the city centre, Dublin 1 is north of the river, Dublin 2 is south (see post-code map opposite).

The cliché would have it that people from the southside are richer, softer, more arrogant, and more educated—but not necessarily more intelligent. By contrast, people from the northside are thought to be poorer, rougher, and more down-to-earth.

The stereotypical southsider is embodied in Ross O'Carroll Kelly, a beer-swilling, philandering, cash-flashing character created by journalist Paul Howard, whose adventures can be read in *The Irish Times* every Saturday.

The stereotypical northsider can be seen in the novels of Roddy Doyle, such as *The Commitments* ('the Dubliners are the blacks of Ireland, and the northside Dubliners are the blacks of Dublin . . . say it loud: I'm black and I'm proud!'), *The Van*, and *The Woman Who Walked Into Doors*. Of course, it's best to bear in mind that although these stereotypes have *some* basis in reality, they're wildly exaggerated. There are hoodlums on the southside and rich idiots on the northside, too.

What's where in the Dublin postcode districts

15
Blanchardstown, Castleknock, Clonsilla, Mulhuddart

11
Cappagh, Finglas, Glasnevin Cemetery

9
Beaumount, Drumcondra, DCU, Glasnevin, National Botanic Gardens, Santry, Whitehall, St Patrick's College

17
Belcamp, Clonshaugh, Darndale

13
Baldoyle, Howth, Sutton

5
Artane, Bull Island, Kilbarrack, Raheny, St Anne's Park

7
Four Courts, National Museum (Collins), Phibsboro

3
Clontarf, Croke Park, Dollymount, East Wall, Fairview

1
Abbey Theatre, Busáras, Custom House, Henry St, Kings Inns, O'Connell St, O₂

20
Chapelizod, Palmerston

8
The Coombe, IMMA, Islandbridge, Kilmainham, Phoenix Park

RIVER LIFFEY

2
Grafton St, Merrion Square, St Stephen's Green, Temple Bar, Trinity College

10
Ballyfermot, Park West Business Centre

12
Bluebell, Crumlin, Walkinstown

6
Ranelagh, Rathgar, Rathmines

4
Ballsbridge, Donnybroook, Ringsend, RDS, RTÉ, Sandymount, Shelbourne Park, UCD

22
Bawnogue, Clondalkin, Neilstown

6w
Harold's Cross, Kimmage, Terenure

14
Churchtown, Clonskeagh, Dundrum, Goatstown

Co. Dublin
Blackrock, Booterstown, Dalkey, Dún Laoghaire, Glenageary, Killiney, Monkstown, Sandycove, Stillorgan

24
Firhouse, Tallaght

16
Ballinteer, Knocklyon, Rathfarnham

18
Cabinteely, Carrickmines, Foxrock, Sandyford

The busy, stirring winds

I noticed now a quality of dryness in the air of Paris which I had never experienced in moist Dublin ... my brain ached, my gritty socks burned my feet and I felt a terrible absence of sea or hills. I longed for that constant view of wistful Dublin mountains and the busy winds which keep Dublin freshly stirred.

Peter Lennon *Foreign Correspondent: Paris in the Sixties*

Dublin in books and films

Books

Dublin is a literary city—and proud of it; the streets of the city are adorned with bronze inlays with excerpts from *Ulysses*, not to mention the statues of James Joyce, Oscar Wilde, Patrick Kavanagh, W. B. Yeats ... We have had to be selective in our choice of books about Dublin because there are so many of them.

The giant of giants is, of course, *Ulysses* by James Joyce, widely regarded as the great novel of the 20th century. It has been said that if Dublin was burnt to the ground you could recreate it from the pages of *Ulysses*. That's nonsense of course, but the soul of the city does pulse in its pages. It's certainly a tough read, as Joyce braids together pastiches of contemporary newspapers, the Catholic catechism, Anglo-Saxon poetry, and the Bible (among many others) in a day in the life of Dubliner Leopold Bloom. If you're not quite up to that, you might try Joyce's earlier and more accessible works, *A Portrait of the Artist as a Young Man* and the short story collection *Dubliners*.

The award-winning Roddy Doyle has written numerous novels set in the northern suburbs of Dublin, in the fictional district of 'Barrytown' (based on Kilbarrack—which is a station on the DART line if you want to follow him up). All of them are worth a look, but probably the best of them is the Booker Prize winner *Paddy Clarke Ha Ha Ha*, a look at life in Dublin in the 1960s as seen through the eyes of a ten-year-old boy.

There have been a number of novels written about Celtic Tiger Dublin; for our money, the most interesting of the bunch is Jarlath Gregory's *G.A.A.Y.: 100 ways to love a beautiful loser*.

And for lighter reading, pick up any one of the Ross O'Carroll Kelly books by Paul Howard, a series which starts with *The Miseducation Years* and goes on for eight volumes; the most recent is *Mr S and the Secrets of Andorra's Box*, and Howard is showing no signs of losing steam. Ross O'Carroll Kelly is a fiendishly clever creation—a spoiled child of the Celtic Tiger generation, gormless, snobbish, boorish and crass, and yet with a certain core of humanity that keeps him from entirely losing the reader's sympathy.

There's a pair of recent non-fiction books that should be read by anyone seeking to understand modern Ireland, and Dublin in particular. The recent economic downturn may have turned them into historical documents, but they're invaluable as accounts of what it was like to live through Ireland's sudden and rapid transformation.

The first is *She Moves Through the Boom* by Ann-Marie Hourihane, an impressionistic account of conversations and observations of a city changing as it becomes prosperous— sometimes for the better, sometimes not so much.

Donal Ruane's *Tales in a Rearview Mirror* tells 25 true stories that Ruane heard or observed while driving a Dublin cab; like *She Moves Through the Boom*, it offers a snapshot view of contemporary Dublin, but the tone is sharper and less meditative and Ruane's intentions are less serious.

And finally, here are some histories and guides worth a look:

- Asher Benson *Jewish Dublin* A series of pen portraits of some of the people and places of Jewish Dublin. Brings to life one of the city's most distinctive and vibrant small communities.

- Terence Brown *Ireland: A Social and Cultural History 1922–2001* How Ireland's writers and artists fared after Ireland gained independence.
- Vivian Igoe *A Literary Guide to Dublin* Dublin's authors, literary society and such like; a series of walk routes at the back and a guide to the cemeteries (for those who like that kind of thing).
- Adrian McLoughlin *Guide to Historic Dublin* The best handy guide for anyone interested in the physical fabric of the city, the traditions and story of the historic area between the canals.
- Christopher Moriarty *Exploring Dublin—Wildlife, Parks, Waterways* Spotting the birds, the plants and the wildlife of Dublin, along the canals, in the parks and through the colleges. Bibliography to help you explore further.
- Peter Somerville-Large *Dublin—The First 1,000 Years* Reliable, readable canter through the facts. Definitely the best one-volume introduction to the city.

Films

- *The Dead* Slow-moving and dreamy adaptation of the James Joyce story, set in early 20th-century Dublin and featuring a beautifully restrained performance by Angelica Huston under the direction of her father John Huston. This was Huston's last film, and a fitting end to any film-maker's career.
- *Michael Collins* Neil Jordan's take on the life and death of the Irish revolutionary hero, including a brief glimpse of the 1916 Rising. Try not to wince when Julia Roberts comes on screen. Her accent is terrible, but she's trying.
- *The Commitments, The Snapper, The Van* Based on the best-selling trilogy by Roddy Doyle, these three films follow the trials and tribulations of the Rabbitte family: Jimmy Rabbitte

the would-be music manager, Sharon Rabbitte the single mother, and Jimmy Senior the chip-van entrepreneur. Warm and loveable without lapsing into sentimentality, they offer an honest look at the northside of the late 1980s and early 1990s.

- *Once* An earnest and rather charming, if slight, romantic drama, which includes the Oscar-winning song 'Falling Slowly'. It's instructive to watch this immediately after *The Commitments*, which ends where *Once* begins: with Glen Hansard busking on Grafton St. The two characters he plays in the two films might as well be from different worlds.

- *Pavee Lackeen* A near-documentary about the most unfortunate members of Ireland's society: the Travellers. *Pavee Lackeen* follows a Traveller girl called Winnie through a succession of mostly-empty days; it sounds bleak, and it is, not least because it's honest about the terrible position the Travellers are in and the treatment they receive from the settled community. But there's a compelling beauty to the film as well, as just by following Winnie and her family through their lives we are given an acute sense of their humanity.

Dublin for people with disabilities

Dublin has become far more welcoming for people with disabilities. Things have improved thanks to new regulations as well as increasing awareness.

Of course, you will still encounter problems. Although all newly built and upgraded establishments must by law be fully accessible, there are plenty of old buildings which are just as inaccessible as ever. Some establishments are wheelchair accessible but without wheelchair-accessible toilets.

Because one wheelchair user's needs may be very different to another's, the best advice is to plan ahead and check all facilities in advance—even those billed as wheelchair-friendly or offering full access for disabled customers.

If you have a guide dog, be aware that guide dogs by law must be permitted wherever the general public is: on buses and trains as well as in restaurants, bars, theatres, etc. Most venues won't ever kick up a fuss but some still seem to think admission for guide dogs is at their discretion. It isn't.

Citizens Information, Lo-Call 1890 777 121, web www.citizensinformation.ie, can give you general information regarding facilities and equipment or personal rights and entitlements. If staff there cannot help you directly they will refer you to the relevant organisation that can. You can also drop into any of the **Citizens Information Centres** located around the city, which provide a face-to-face, free and confidential service. A quick phone call will give you the location of your nearest one, or you can find it through the website. The Lo-Call (charged at a local rate from any landline in Ireland) Information Phone Service is available Mon–Fri 09.00–21.00. From abroad tel +353 21 452 1600.

The **Irish Wheelchair Association**, Blackheath Drive, Clontarf, Dublin 3, tel 818 6400, web www.iwa.ie, provides services to mobility impaired people throughout the Republic of Ireland. Anyone with a disability considering moving to Ireland long-term can apply for membership of the association; its range of services covers everything from assisted living to counselling and housing to equipment sales and repair. Another very useful service they offer is wheelchair hire.

Fáilte Ireland, the National Tourism Development Authority, has a scheme for validating and providing information on accommodation for people with disabilities—see www.discoverireland.ie/where-to-stay/VAS.aspx. The scheme defines four levels of accessibility and has contact details for all places listed.

The list is growing but not yet extensive, particularly in the shoestring category. You can phone Fáilte Ireland with enquiries at 1850 230 330 or contact them through the website www.discoverireland.ie. Information and a list of Dublin accommodation approved by the scheme can be found on the **Dublin Tourism** website at www.visitdublin.com/disabled. The general accommodation listings on www.visitdublin.com, also indicate which places are accessible.

In *Dublin on a Shoestring* we have indicated where wheelchair access is possible, but not all such places are fully accessible—as mentioned, toilets may not be—so do check. Joined-up thinking is often lacking—one Dublin drinking establishment has a beautiful, pristine wheelchair users' toilet . . . located up a flight of steps.

For a more complete picture of wheelchair accessibility in Dublin restaurants, pick up a copy of the *Jacob's Creek Restaurant and Event Guide*, produced by the **Restaurants Association of Ireland**. Available for €6 from bookshops, it lists some 300 restaurants countrywide and over 100 in Dublin, indicating which are accessible. Restaurants are also graded according to how expensive they are. For more info contact the RAI, tel 677 9901, email info@rai.ie. A forum discussion at www.boards.ie/vbulletin/showthread.php?t=2054894844 may be of interest as well. It lists wheelchair-accessible hotels, shops, pubs and more.

Getting to and from Ireland

BY AIR Following a change in EU law in 2008, responsibility for meeting the needs of air travellers with disabilities now rests with the airport authorities rather than the individual airlines. Confusingly, however, you must still inform the airline of your needs when booking (they then pass this information on to the airport authorities). Online check-in is often not available to anyone requiring special assistance. So, arrive in good time and make sure you know the procedures and protocols of your particular airline. **Aer Lingus**'s Special Assistance phone number is 0818 365 011; **Ryanair**'s 249 7761.

Dublin Airport can be extremely crowded, and is not always easy to negotiate independently, particularly for the sensory impaired. All services and facilities, though, are fully accessible to disabled people. If you have any queries, contact the Dublin Airport Authority's Customer Relations Department, tel 814 4717.

BY SEA If you are a wheelchair user and are travelling by ferry, give your ferry company at least three working days' notice. Most areas of all vessels are now fully accessible and specially adapted cabins are available as well. The terminal buildings at both of Dublin's ports (Dublin Port and Dún Laoghaire) are also fully accessible. To contact **Dublin Port** tel 887 6000 or email info@dublinport.ie; **Dún Laoghaire Harbour** can be reached at tel 280 8681 or through the website www.dlharbour. ie. If you are travelling with **Stena Line** and have any accessibility or assistance queries contact Eamonn Hewitt, tel 204 7617, email eamonn.hewitt@stenaline.com; if you're with **Irish Ferries** contact Sheila Gleeson, tel 855 2222, email sheila.gleeson@irish-ferries.com. Irish Ferries' website has a fairly comprehensive section on accessibility and facilities for disabled people: www. irishferries.com.

Getting around Dublin

BY BUS Over half of **Dublin Bus** routes are now fully wheelchair accessible, compared to a mere 16 a few years ago when the previous edition of *Dublin on a Shoestring* was researched. This includes all the late-night **Nitelink** services. These routes

A Piece of the Aran Islands

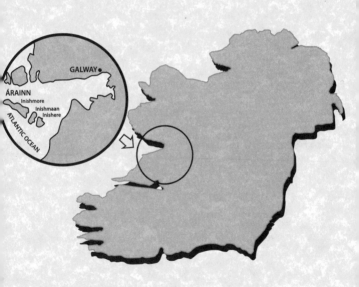

ÁRAINN
Inishmore
Inishmaan
Inishere
ATLANTIC OCEAN
GALWAY•

Lía Árann

Each of these pieces has been carefully chosen handcrafted and polished from the Lower Carboniferous Limestone of the Aran Islands which stretch across the mouth of Galway Bay on the west coast of Ireland.

This limestone is formed from the solidified muddy sediment of a tropical sea that covered this part of the globe over 300 million years ago. It preserves a wealth of fossil remains - shellfish, sea lilies, coral, extinct animals and plants which were abundant in that sea. When magnified the details of these are fascinating!

Crafted by
Máirtín Ó Conceanainn
Eoghanacht,
Kilronan, Inishmore,
Árainn, Co. Galway
Phone: 099-61411
Email: roundhouse@eircom.net
www.liaarann.com

comprehensively cover the city and stretch well into the greater Dublin area. The timetables at www.dublinbus.ie indicate which routes are accessible.

Every accessible bus has a priority space for a wheelchair user, which can also be occupied by a pram/buggy. Only one wheelchair or pram/buggy can occupy this space. When the bus stops at your stop, the driver will 'kneel' the bus and extend the ramp for wheelchair access. Let the driver know when you're getting on where you intend to get off.

Dublin Bus can be contacted at tel 873 4222 or email info@dublinbus.ie.

BY TRAM The **Luas**, Dublin's light rail system, is fully accessible to all passengers. If you have any questions, however, or would like assistance with your journey, contact Luas Customer Care, Freephone 1800 300 604, email info@luas.ie. Luas can arrange for a member of staff to accompany you on the tram, should you wish.

BY TRAIN Trains—DART, mainline and suburban—require a portable ramp to enable wheelchairs to enter the carriages. These are available at all staffed stations and on board some trains. Phone at least 24 hours in advance to inform Iarnród Éireann of your needs and arrive at the station with half an hour to spare so that staff will be able to provide whatever assistance is required.

There are wheelchair-accessible toilets at several DART stations and most mainline termini have them. Most DART stations and many other stations have ticket office loop systems for the hearing impaired.

Iarnród Éireann/Irish Rail produces a useful free booklet, *Guide for Rail Passengers with Disabilities*, which includes general information as well as contact numbers and facility details for every train station in the country. The booklet can be downloaded from the company's website at www.irishrail.ie/your_journey/disabled_access.asp. It is also available at all staffed stations and through the Access and Liaison Officer, Connolly Station, Amiens St, Dublin 1, tel 703 2634, email access@irishrail.ie. Braille and audio versions are available too. The Access and Liaison Officer can also be contacted with any other queries you may have, about any access or facility issues.

BY TAXI If you can transfer from your wheelchair, most taxis should be able to transport you with your wheelchair stowed in the boot. A better option is a wheelchair-accessible taxi and, over the past few years, there has been a big increase in the number of these operating in Dublin. It is an offence for a driver at a taxi rank operating a wheelchair-accessible taxi to refuse to pick up a disabled passenger. However, availability of these taxis can be very limited at certain times, so book a day or more in advance if possible. You'll almost always have to give an hour or two's notice in any case, and you may have to try a number of companies before you find one with an available vehicle.

Dublin taxi companies operating accessible vehicles

Blue Cabs, tel 802 2222	Near Cabs, tel 836 7411
Cab 2000, tel 890 0900	Taxi 7, tel 460 0000
City Cabs, tel 872 7272	Terenure Taxis, tel 490 1111
Co-Op Taxis, tel 676 6666	VIP-ACE, tel 478 3333
National Radio Cabs, tel 677 2222	Xpert Digi Taxis, tel 667 0777

A service designed specifically for disabled people is **Vantastic**, Freephone 1800 242 703, web www.vantastic.ie. It provides fully accessible door-to-door transport for people with disabilities in the Dublin area, and fares are about 20 per cent cheaper than taxi rates. Most of Vantastic's work is with registered members who use the service to get to work, clinics and so on, but you can sign up for an account even for a one-off journey. You'll need to give up to 48 hours' notice to avail of this service and, of course, all bookings are subject to van availability. Membership forms can be downloaded from the website or phone the number above; membership costs just €5, a once-off payment which is then discounted off the cost of your first trip. Vantastic also has accessible vehicles for hire and offers accessible tours and trips (see page 225).

ACTS (Accessible Community Transport Southside) is another service providing door-to-door transport for people with mobility difficulties. They operate in south Dublin, from Dún Laoghaire to Tallaght, with fares about a third cheaper than the equivalent taxi rates. For further details and an application form tel 292 1573/292 1574 or email gerryacts@eircom.net.

Going to the country by bus

If you intend travelling by bus from Dublin to other parts of the country, you will almost certainly require assistance. The central bus station, Busáras, Store St, Dublin 1, is where all the **Bus Éireann** national routes depart from. Unfortunately, while the station itself is fully accessible, the coach-style buses used on most routes are not.

Passengers travel high off the ground above the large luggage compartments. You will have to fold your wheelchair and stow it with the luggage under the bus, and bring someone to assist you with embarking and disembarking via the steep steps. Since these are provincial bus routes which penetrate every rural area in the country, the stops on the route can be awkward to negotiate—they can appear at the side of almost any road, and it's not unheard of for them to be blocked by illegally parked cars.

For general information on **Bus Éireann** services tel 836 6111 or see www.buseireann.ie.

Other useful organisations and links

Accessible Ireland www.accessibleireland.ie
Lists accommodation, restaurants, tourist attractions, etc, and gives details of their accessibility. The number of establishments featured is small but growing. Sign up and share your own thoughts.

Assist Ireland www.assistireland.ie, Lo-Call 1890 277 478
Provided by the Citizens Information Board, this online resource has information on assistive technology and a directory of products available from Irish suppliers. It also has a helpful travel section.

Disabled Drivers Association of Ireland www.ddai.ie, tel (094) 936 4054/ (094) 936 4266

Enable Ireland www.enableireland.ie, tel 872 7155
Support for children and adults with disabilities and their families.

Irish Deaf Society www.deaf.ie

National Council for the Blind in Ireland www.ncbi.ie, tel Lo-Call 1850 334 353

National Disability Authority www.nda.ie, tel 608 0400
The lead state agency on disability issues.

Outside the Box www.rte.ie/radio1/outsidethebox
An interesting RTÉ radio programme about disability issues. Listen online at this address.

Gay Dublin

While Dublin's gay scene cannot be compared to those of, say, London or San Francisco, it is nonetheless vibrant, broad and growing. It was, of course, given a big boost back in 1993 thanks to the legalisation of sexual activity between consenting males over 18.

Websites

The website of the magazine *Gay Community News,* www.gcn.ie, is a good place to start exploring gay Dublin. Its bright pages are crammed with information. The magazine itself comes out monthly and is also full of news, features and listings. It's free, and is available from such bars as The George, The Dragon and The Front Lounge (see below); you can also pick it up at the IFI in Temple Bar and Books Upstairs on College Green.

Another good site for listings, features, and general information and contacts is **QID**, www.queerid.com (also found at www.gaydublin.ie). QID fashions itself as Ireland's gay social networking site. You can get your own profile, blog, and send private messages for free.

www.google.ie/gaydublin is a good link to check out, with a map showing the city-centre locations of various 'gay places'.

Gay pubs and clubs

There are several specifically gay pubs in Dublin, the oldest of which is **The George**, 89 Sth Great George's St, Dublin 2, tel 478 2983. Reliably crowded the closer you get to the weekend, it caters to a mixed if mostly male crowd of a range of ages, with a younger and often alternative bent during college term time. If you're feeling cheap, get in before 22.00 to avoid paying cover. A student ID will get you cheaper entry midweek. You can ask for a pass out if you're leaving, just in case you want to return later. Sundays are supposed to be the best nights (particularly so on bank holiday weekends), with Bingo and a reasonable if not awe-inspiring drag show running from around 22.00.

Further up the same street is George's larger and younger brother, **The Dragon**, at 64–65 Sth Great George's St, Dublin 2, tel 478 1590 catering to an even more male-dominated crowd, with a weekend emphasis on gym-going types and the jeans-and-T-shirts crowd in general. Saturdays are best but involve a cover charge after 23.30.

The Front Lounge, 33 Parliament St, Dublin 2, tel 670 4112 is half a mile away off Dame St. Starting as merely gay friendly, it was completely and unilaterally annexed by gay customers several years ago, and shows no sign of being released quite yet. A more relaxed, dance-floor free alternative to George and The Dragon, it draws a mixed crowd, and is the only gay venue where the cocktails aren't a crime against humanity. Its Tuesday karaoke can be enjoyable. Plays host to a lesbian invasion once a month, when Dublin's Sapphic population unites to have a few jars before heading on to KISS (see below).

PantiBar, across the river at 7–8 Capel St, Dublin 1, tel 874 0710 is a smaller and more unpredictable place. Run by Miss Panti, one of Dublin's better-known drag queens, its shows can be excellent, but the venue can often be found half empty. The crowd is generally a little older than in the other venues though younger on Wednesdays during college term. Of course venue unpredictability is complemented by better value—cover charges at Panti are unheard of, drinks prices are cheaper and specials are frequent.

If you're looking for a gay club, make a beeline for the listings on the above websites and **www.indublin.ie**, to find a place that suits your taste and pocket.

With Ireland's relatively strict licensing laws and early closing times, all of the venues above and below open until legal closing time (02.30 Monday to Saturday and 01.00 Sunday at time of going to press) most nights of the week. So it's variety of venue and a change of crowd that you get by going to a club night, rather than the ability to dance till dawn.

Gay nights

Regular gay nights include the usually quiet **VIQ**, Mondays at Sin, Sycamore St, Temple Bar, Dublin 2, tel 633 4232—make sure to loiter in The Front Lounge around 23.00 to get free tickets in. **Glitz** is on Tuesdays at Break for the Border, 2 Johnston Place, Lr Stephen St, Dublin 2, tel 478 0300, and hosts a consistently young crowd bopping to a mix of trash and pop-dance, though the mix has become heavier of late. The dubiously titled **Bukkake** is on bank holiday Sundays at the Purty Kitchen, 34–35 East Essex St, Temple Bar, Dublin 2, tel 677 0945, hosting a varied crowd on multiple floors. The otherwise quiet lesbian scene in Dublin reaches its monthly zenith at **KISS**, in the Tivoli Theatre, 135 Francis St, Dublin 8, tel 454 4472, usually held one Friday every month. Keep an eye on the above listings to find out when exactly.

Gay festivals

Dublin now plays host to several celebrated gay festivals, among them **aLAF** (A Lesbian Arts Festival), www.alafireland.com, running annually since 2002; the **International Dublin Gay Theatre Festival**, www.gaytheatre.ie, held every May (see page 171); and Gaze, the **Dublin International Lesbian & Gay Film Festival**, www.gaze.ie, held over the August Bank Holiday weekend. Keep an eye on *Gay Community News* and QID to see what's happening.

Other basic stuff

Stuff we thought you might find useful, but couldn't think where else to put.

Accidents and emergencies

If you cannot find a garda (police officer), dial 999 from your mobile or the nearest payphone (no charge). You will be asked whether you are reporting a fire, medical or police emergency. You will also be asked to give a clear indication of your location so make sure you can describe exactly where you are by a local landmark (such as a pub—they always know where they are) so that the emergency service can find you. If you're using a payphone the location should be clearly written up in the phone booth; check this before you dial and if not identify a local landmark (e.g. a pub). The main accident and emergency departments are at the following hospitals:

Beaumont Hospital Beaumont Rd, Dublin 9, tel 809 2714
Mater Hospital Eccles St, Dublin 1, tel 803 2000
St James' Hospital James St, Dublin 8, tel 410 3000
St Vincent's Hospital Elm Park, Dublin 4, tel 209 4358
Tallaght Hospital Dublin 24, tel 414 3500.

Once you get to a hospital you will have to be prepared to wait. The standard A&E charge is €66 unless you have a medical card, a referral note from a GP, or a European Health Insurance Card (which replaces the E111 form). If you're a European traveller eligible for the EHIC scheme, you should apply before you leave your own country; the card is valid for two years.

ATMs (cash machines)

There are numerous 24-hour Automatic Telling Machines (ATMs) in the city centre outside banks, e.g. in Dublin 2: 100 Grafton St, 39 St Stephen's Green, 7 Dame St; in Dublin 1: O'Connell Bridge, 37 Upr O'Connell St, as well as in some shops, e.g. Dunnes Stores, and convenience stores. Look out for signs.

Bank holidays

There are nine bank holidays. They fall on 1 January, 17 March (if falling on a weekday, otherwise next weekday), Easter Monday, the first Monday in May, June and August, the last Monday in October, Christmas Day if on a weekday, otherwise the next Tuesday, St Stephen's Day (26 December) if on a weekday, otherwise the next weekday. Good Friday is not a bank holiday, though many businesses treat it as such, and no alcohol is sold.

Dental

Emergency dental care is available at the Dublin Dental Hospital in Lincoln Place, Dublin 2 (just next to the back entrance to Trinity College), tel 612 7200 (Mon–Fri, 09.00–17.00; call after hours and you can leave a message; for urgent treatment call 612 7257). The emergency charge of €66 must be paid in advance and covers x-rays and subsequent treatment for three months.

For standard dental work it is possible to opt for treatment at the Dental Hospital by a student under supervision. This saves 25 per cent of the not-extortionate charges.

Directory enquiries

See telephones page 29.

Drugs

The use and supply of illegal drugs carry severe penalties—more so for supply than for use. Some drugs that are legal in other countries are not legal here—e.g. the khat plant (which has an amphetamine-like effect) is legal in the UK but not in Ireland. Likewise, the sale of unprocessed psilocybin mushrooms ('magic mushrooms') was made illegal in 2006.

Any garda is entitled to detain and search you on reasonable suspicion that you are in possession of or involved in the supply of illegal drugs. You can be detained without charge for up to seven days, and can be strip searched.

Fax

Faxes can be sent from shops that sell stationery and photocopying services.

Internet access

Free wireless internet access is available in all of Dublin's public libraries (see page 188), which also offer access to internet terminals to all card-carrying library members. Many hostels and hotels offer free wireless internet to their guests; the St Stephen's Green Shopping Centre has free wireless for any passer-by. Paid wireless is available in various spots throughout the city centre— most Eircom payphones are wireless hotspots, and many cafés, bars, hotels and restaurants offer wireless through either Eircom or BitBuzz. For a list of Eircom hotspots, see www.eircom.ie/hotspots; for a list of BitBuzz hotspots, see www.bitbuzz.com.

Muggings, robberies

The relaxed atmosphere in town is certainly nice but there *are* muggings and robberies in the street particularly after the pubs close.

Keep away from murky streets at night, from groups of youths (who will probably do more damage to themselves than you, but it's wise to keep clear); keep valuables tightly under control; keep bags and wallets out of sight (don't, for instance, be lulled by the friendly atmosphere into leaving valuables on a table in the pub while you go to the toilet); don't flash cash at an ATM machine; don't wear 'rob-me' jewellery; if you are out late at night, stay in groups; be aware that young men are more likely to be attacked at random than young women.

*Leinster House, once the seat of Ireland's premier Duke,
now houses the Irish parliament.*

If you are robbed or injured, report the crime to the Gardaí. If you need to replace passports or have money sent from home, call the **Irish Tourist Assistance Service** (ITAS), tel 478 5295, who will help you to contact embassies, banks, etc., or you can try the **Crime Victims Helpline** at 1850 211 407, Mon 10.00–19.30, Tues–Fri 10.00 –1700, Sat 14.00–16.00

Newspapers and magazines

There are three daily Irish broadsheets: *The Irish Times*, the *Irish Independent* and the *Irish Examiner*, and one evening tabloid, the *Evening Herald*. The *Times* regards itself as the paper of record; its reputation is of a solid, middle-class, middle-age, unflashy AB journal. The whole daily paper appears on its website, www.irishtimes.com, free to view (for stories less than a year old, at least). The *Independent* has higher sales and a slightly rougher reputation; its website is at www.independent.ie. The *Examiner* has good political and books coverage.

If you're looking for international newspapers, or local papers from other parts of Ireland, try Eason's of O'Connell St, Dublin 1, or Read's of Nassau St, Dublin 2. For free reads, some pubs and cafés carry copies of newspapers for the customers to read, or you can try a public library (see page 188 for details).

For news about and affecting Dublin's immigrant communities, check out the weekly paper *Metro Éireann*, which often gets the relevant stories first, weeks before the mainstream papers. It can sometimes be hard to find; try a library if can't find it in the shops.

There are two free daily newspapers available in Dublin: the Dublin edition of *The Metro*, and *Herald AM*, owned and run by the same people who publish the *Evening Herald*. These are mostly distributed to commuters, and if you're travelling after rush hour you may have to settle for a used copy.

One of the best Dublin-based magazines is free: *Totally Dublin*. It can be found in pubs, cafés and shops all over the city. *Totally Dublin* includes listings, but the focus is on in-depth articles and reviews and idiosyncratic commentary. It's a substantial read, and so cool it'll give your fingers frostbite.

If you don't mind actually paying for your magazines, there are four local titles worth mentioning: *Hot Press* combines commentary on music with outspoken political articles. *The Phoenix* is Ireland's answer to *Private Eye*, with satirical coverage of Irish and international politics. *The Dubliner* is a general culture/lifestyle magazine, good for zeitgeist commentary and for highlights of upcoming events that you might otherwise miss. And *The Gloss* is a women's magazine with a little more thought and intelligence than the norm.

Opening hours
Banks Mon–Fri 10.00–16.00 (Thurs 17.00).
Post offices Usually Mon-Fri 09.30–13.00, 14.30–17.30
Pubs Mon–Wed 10.30–23.30 Thurs–Sat 10.30–0.30 Sun 12.30–23.00 with variations for individual pubs.
Public and business offices 09.00–17.00.
Restaurants 12.00–14.30 for lunch, dinner 18.30–23.00. Cafés, café-restaurants all day.
Shops Mon–Sat 09.00 or 09.30–6pm Thurs 20.00 in the city centre and some shopping centres; Sun (many, but by no means all) 12.00–18.00. 24-hour convenience stores are increasingly common.

Telephone
Telephone services are in the process of being deregulated so you'll see various brands of public telephone kiosks. Phone booths mostly take phone cards rather than cash; pubs usually have a telephone available for public use, and these generally take cash. Phone cards are available from newsagents in denominations ranging from 10 units (where 1 unit represents a 3-minute

call) to 50 units. Local calls from payphones cost a minimum of 30c for a local call, although pubs and other places may charge 50c. Local calls from a private phone cost 5c per minute.

Telephone directories are not easy to get hold of outside private homes; the public phone in the nearby pub *might* have one, but it will be extremely tatty and very likely missing crucial pages; the local library will have a set, and the library in the Ilac Centre, Henry St, Dublin 1 has a fine collection of overseas directories.

For **directory enquiries** within Ireland call 11811 or 11890, for international numbers call 11818 or 11860.

Mobile phone top-ups are on sale in many newsagents and convenience stores; watch out for the signs attached and have the exact notes available as the machines usually don't give change.

AREA CODES The telephone area code for Dublin is 01. When dialling from outside Ireland dial +353 before and drop the '0' from the area code. As almost all phone numbers listed in this book are Dublin area, we have not included the 01 area code; numbers outside Dublin have the area code in brackets. There is no need for an area code before numbers beginning with 1890, 1850 or 0818.

Post

Postage stamps are obtainable from post offices—marked Oifig an Phoist. Some post boxes have 'Litreaca' written at the slot for the post—this is the Irish for 'Letters' or 'Post.'

Shopping bags

There is a government levy on plastic carrier bags. When you go shopping, you may be asked if you want a plastic bag; if you say 'yes', you'll be charged 22c for each bag you use (this money goes directly to the Department of the Environment). Some shops (especially clothes shops) give out free paper bags instead, but it's safest to have a reusable bag of your own to carry your shopping. Supermarkets sell sturdy reinforced plastic or cloth bags for around €2.

Smoking

Since March 2004 it has been illegal in Ireland for anyone to smoke in enclosed workplaces, including restaurants and pubs. This is why there are so many cafés with tables on the pavement outside, despite the unsuitable climate. If customers want to smoke, they have to sit outdoors. Do *not* try to sneak a cigarette in a pub, café, or restaurant. Most pubs and bars that don't have outdoor areas where you can smoke provide ashtrays outside their entrances; smoke there, or not at all. And the plus side is that a mutual smoke in a force 6 gale is a great way to meet new friends!

Time

Although the sun rises in Dublin some 20 minutes later than in London, the time used is the same. Summer time, when the clocks are put forward an hour, runs from the last Sunday in March to the last Sunday in October.

Tipping

Tipping is much more casual in Dublin than other European or American cities. The main place for tipping is in restaurants and hotels. Nowadays many up-market restaurants automatically add a 'service charge' to the bill; however, this often goes to the restaurateur, so the staff still hope for a tip of 10 per cent or more. Hairdressers, taxi-drivers and others appreciate a tip of 10 per cent or so but don't feel you have to.

Toilets

There are some public toilets in Dublin, marked MNÁ (for *women*) and FIR (for *men*). Dubliners generally prefer to use the toilets in pubs, cafés and hotels. Toilets in large department shops are open to the public.

Traffic

Road usage by both motorists and pedestrians is erratic and often individualistic. The most obvious example is at traffic lights, where the orange light, intended as a warning to slow down, is often treated as a signal for the driver to hurry across so as not to be caught by the red. Seeing a gap in the traffic, pedestrians will happily surge across the road regardless of the state of the lights.

Weather

Average temperatures in summer are between 14°C and 18°C, and in winter between 4°C and 8°C. There is considerable variance around these figures: in what the newspapers call a heatwave temperatures can reach 30°C. It is, however, rarely very cold, and there might be no rain, especially in summer, for two or three weeks in succession. Generally Irish rain is unaggressive—but it *will* rain, so be prepared.

Websites

There are a handful of truly essential websites to keep bookmarked during your stay in Dublin. www.irishtimes.com, www.independent.ie and www.rte.ie are best for news, being the sites of *The Irish Times*, *Irish Independent* and RTÉ (the national broadcaster) respectively. As well as text news stories, RTÉ's site also has an extensive archive of streaming radio and video.

For entertainment listings, no site beats www.entertainment.ie, which covers everything from what's on TV tonight to what bands are going to be playing in Whelan's in three months' time.

www.boards.ie is a very lively general discussion board that covers every conceivable topic of interest to anyone living in Ireland. It's brimming with information, although as with all message boards, the advice on offer is best taken with a pinch of salt and weighed against other, less subjective sources.

Finally, if you're planning on staying in Dublin for a longer period, you might find yourself in need of

- **www.nixers.com**, an essential resource for finding a job; or
- **www.daft.ie**, an equally essential resource for finding a place to live; or
- **www.citizensinformation.ie**, which has comprehensive and searchable information on public services and the law in Ireland.

Somewhere to sleep

Somewhere to stay

Dublin offers a huge choice of good value, high-standard accommodation in hotels, guesthouses, B&Bs, tourist hostels, self-catering apartments and university campuses. The number of available tourist beds in the city has increased dramatically over the past few years, giving visitors more than ever to choose from. However, it can still be difficult enough to find a place to stay if you have not booked in advance. Now is in fact a great time to stay in the city because hotels, B&Bs and hostels are lowering their rates dramatically to entice visitors.

Most premises that are approved by Fáilte Ireland/Irish Tourist Board display the shamrock sign and are included in the computerised booking system used by tourist offices throughout the country.

A complete listing of all **Dublin Tourism** members is available on **www.visitdublin.com**—registered and approved hotels, guesthouses, B&Bs/townhouses, hostels and self-catering accommodation in Dublin city and county. Complete with photographs, it outlines basic details of prices and facilities. You can book here too, often at a special discount.

Our recommendations (listed by area starting on page 42) range in price from approximately €10 pps (per person sharing) per night in a tourist hostel to—at the very top end—about €99 in high-quality guesthouses (which are like small hotels) or good value hotels. These are only standard rates; multi-night deals may be available that push the price down further, and the value in **hotels** in particular at the time of publishing goes above and beyond anything we can detail here—with some places lowering their prices by up to 85 per cent and beds going from as low as €20! Particularly midweek or off-season, it is always worth ringing up even the more expensive hotels, or checking their websites, to see what's on offer. 1800hotels.ie, Freephone 1800 468 357 within Ireland, international tel +353 1 797 9063, is a service that can give you free, quick advice about what deals are available, in hotels from two- to five-star, to save you ringing all around town.

Breakfast

Hostels generally include a light continental breakfast in the price, whereas B&Bs and guesthouses go for the full Irish—fruit juice, cereal, bacon, eggs, sausages, black pudding, brown bread, toast and tea or coffee. Usually 'full Irish breakfast included' means you can have any combination of the constituent elements—eggs on toast, bacon and eggs, etc. Vegetarian options are generally available.

Cheap **single rooms** can be difficult to find. Off-season or midweek it is usually possible to get a fair price for single occupancy of a larger room. However, at peak times expect to pay a substantial supplement and sometimes even the full price of a double if you are not sharing. **Family rooms** are widely available.

Increasingly hotels are offering a room only rate and making up their money with high-priced 'extras' like breakfast. You could get a hotel bed for €25 per person but if you're going to spend €12 each on breakfast then you might be better off going for the more personal service of a B&B, with breakfast included, for €35. B&Bs also tend to have either on- or off-street free parking.

The other thing you get in **B&Bs**, that you generally won't get anywhere else, is a genuinely local service. Usually you're staying in a family home—your hosts are people who've lived in Dublin, often for decades, and know it better than the backs of their hands. They'll have entertaining stories to tell and typically endless advice about where to go and what to see. There are not many B&Bs within short walking distance of the city centre but most are only a quick bus ride away. Style and size vary hugely, but standards (in most cases monitored by Fáilte Ireland) are very high, and the proprietors are usually friendly and welcoming. Guesthouses range from being like large B&Bs to small hotels.

Dublin's **hostels** have long since shed their old image of scruffy, communal living and strict rules and curfews. Many have private en suite rooms—some doubles—as well as the usual dormitories. All our recommended hostels supply bed linen for free; some have towel hire with a deposit that is returned, but you'll usually have to bring your own towels, soap and so on. Guests of all ages are welcome, including families with children. As a rule, the more people you share a room with, the less you pay per head. So, while a twin or double room in a hostel may cost as much as in a B&B in the suburbs, a night in a city centre dormitory can cost as little as €10, depending on the time of year.

The hostels recommended here are cheerful and busy, and although not luxurious in style, they are clean and cosy enough for most tastes. All offer secure facilities for luggage—particularly important when you're sharing with strangers—either free or at a small charge (€1–2 a day) and all keep comprehensive information on local events. All have self-catering kitchens and most have laundries; almost all have WiFi at least in common areas and with one or two exceptions it's free. Some have computers with internet access for guest use, foreign exchange facilities, deals with local car parks and other perks. Group deals and special group packages are often available. Women-only dorms are available in many hostels, though they may only be offered at less-busy times of the year. You normally require photo ID to check in to a hostel.

All in all, hostels offer the best value around, from the most basic to the best equipped. A list of just over 80 affiliated, tourist board-approved hostels throughout Ireland is available from **Independent Holiday Hostels of Ireland**, tel 836 4700, web www.hostels-ireland.com. As well as the online listing/search feature, their guide is available online as a PDF and in all affiliated hostels (seven in Dublin) and in tourist offices. It's generally free though tourist offices may have a small charge (50c). Most of the hostels can be booked through the IHH website.

Self-catering studios, apartments or houses are a good option, particularly for a small group or a family. From about €450 per week, you can get a very comfortable centrally located, one-bedroom apartment for two people; in the suburbs this can go down to about €350. If you are prepared to stay a short bus ride away from the city centre, there are plenty of options to sleep groups of four or more from about €600 weekly. A good selection of the above is listed on the Dublin Tourism website, **www.visitdublin.com**. The standard let is from Saturday to Saturday, but some owners are prepared to let for weekends—nightly rates are rare. You can also contact the **Dublin Self-Catering Accommodation Association**, tel 269 1535, which has a listing of Fáilte Ireland-approved properties in Dublin. They will advise you what is available at any particular time and then you book directly with the owner. A few of the hostels/B&Bs below offer self-catering apartments by the night with breakfast in the establishment. See the entries for Abbey Court (page 42), Litton Lane (page 45), Mount Eccles Court (page 46) and Tavistock House (page 57). See also River House Hotel, page 50 and Gogarty's, page 49.

From June to September **university accommodation**—both B&B and self-catering—becomes available. The three main university campuses with accommodation—Dublin City

University (DCU), University College Dublin (UCD) and Trinity College Dublin (TCD, also occasionally and confusingly known as Dublin University)—are located in the north, south and centre of the city respectively. The Royal College of Surgeons in Ireland (RCSI), also in the city centre, has rooms available during the summer at its Mercer Court apartments.

Camping in any of Dublin's fine parks is neither allowed nor advisable—the parks are not safe at night. The two official campsites nearest to the city, although still a long way from the centre if you are backpacking, are listed on page 59. If you plan on camping around the country have a look at the site **www. camping-ireland.com**.

All parks listed are Fáilte Ireland approved or for Northern Ireland they are graded. There's also a guide available for €5 from the site operators, the Irish Caravan & Camping Council—check in the tourist offices or email info@camping-ireland.com for a copy.

Wheelchair access to older buildings is sometimes awkward if not impossible, but many of the modern hotels, as well as some hostels, have wheelchair access. More and more hotels have specially adapted rooms; so do some hostels—we've indicated which establishments are accessible below. B&Bs don't usually have wheelchair access facilities, but guest rooms on the ground floor may be accessible with some assistance. Always book in advance and check the exact nature of the facilities offered.

If you have a credit card, it's possible to **book online** either from Ireland or overseas through www.visitdublin.com. There's a booking fee of €2.95. To book by phone see the numbers in the box below—there's a €5 booking fee for this service, which is not operated by Dublin Tourism. You also pay a non-refundable deposit of 10 per cent of the total charge, paying the balance to the premises on arrival. If you book directly with the provider by phone you may be able to negotiate the price, and there is no booking fee, but of course you have to pay for whatever calls you make. Also, Dublin Tourism often offer special rates which may not be available if you go to the provider directly.

If you're already in Ireland you could call in to a **tourist office** for free information. For a booking fee of €4 (or €7 for self-catering bookings) a travel advisor will make reservations for you. You pay a 10 per cent deposit and receive detailed directions to your chosen abode for the night (very valuable to the weary traveller!). At the Dublin Tourism Centre on Suffolk St, Dublin 2, you can also use the self-service, touch-screen unit to book with a credit card during office hours (09.00–17.30; later in summer). The booking fee is the same as on www.visitdublin.com, and of course the 10 per cent deposit also applies, with the balance payable in the normal way on arrival at the accommodation.

Credit cards are accepted in most premises, apart from B&Bs, which usually accept a deposit sent in advance as a booking. Visa and MasterCard are the most widely accepted cards though American Express is accepted in some places. Laser is accepted in more and more places. A room booked by credit card is usually held until noon of the day after the arrival date. In the event of a no-show, it will then be released and the card charged for one night's accommodation. However, cancellation policies vary so it is wise to check. Also check if there is a cut-off time for arrivals as guesthouses and B&Bs are usually family-run and do not have night porters—it is wise to phone ahead even if you are arriving during the day to ensure that there will be someone on the premises to let you in. In high season, B&Bs may stipulate that you check in at a reasonable hour, or at least telephone to confirm that you are on your way. Hostels and hotels tend to have 24-hour reception.

The **Dublin Tourism Centre**, in a converted church on Suffolk St, offers the most extensive services, including a café, a bookshop and various accommodation- and ticket-booking facilities; however, it tends to become very crowded in the summer months. The full reservation system is also available at all other Dublin Tourism offices. The other city centre office is at 14 Upr O'Connell St, Dublin 1, and is much smaller and generally quieter.

More tips

- On special occasions like rugby weekends and St Patrick's Day, the whole city goes insane and prices go through the roof and towards the moon. Book well in advance or give up all hope of getting a good deal. Rates listed here generally exclude these brief periods of madness.
- The best value rates, especially for hostels and hotels, are usually available online when you book in advance through the provider's website. You can save significantly by going this route.
- Some B&Bs and guesthouses are now offering cheaper room-only rates (i.e. without breakfast) to try and compete with the budget hotels. It can't do any harm to ask.
- Smoking is not allowed inside B&Bs or hostels. Most hotels have smoking rooms, which you should request when booking. Some smaller hotels don't differentiate between smoking and non-smoking, and simply allow smoking in any of the rooms.
- Pets are only allowed in one approved accommodation provider in Dublin—Tavistock House, Ranelagh, Dublin 6, page 57.

The unique Irish style of greeting . . .

. . . a little nod allied to a slight inclination of the head, as if trying to touch the left shoulder with the right cheek, together with a wink . . . usually accompanied by 'Hawaya' (How are you?) or 'Hayadone' (How are you doing?) or 'Hazagone?' (How is it going?). This requires years of training.

From Dublin: le guide Autrement

Tourist information and bookings

By phone or online from anywhere in the world.

For Tourist Information:
Within Ireland: 1850 230 330
From the UK: 0800 039 7000
From any other country: +353 66 979 2083
Fáilte Ireland—the National Tourism Development Authority: www.discoverireland.ie

To book accommodation:
Within Ireland: 1800 363 626
From the UK: 0800 2580 2580
From any other country: +353 669 792 082
Dublin Tourism—to book approved accommodation online: www.visitdublin.com

Tourist offices in the city

These are walk-in centres only. To receive tourist information over the phone see the box above.

Dublin Tourism
Suffolk St, Dublin 2
Open Mon–Sat 09.00–17.30 (June–Sept 19.00), Sun/bank hol 10.30–15.00 (July–Aug 17.00)

14 Upr O'Connell St, Dublin 1
Open Mon–Sat 09.00–17.00

Arrivals Hall, Dublin Airport
Open Mon–Sun 08.00–22.00

Dún Laoghaire Ferry Terminal, Co Dublin
Open Mon–Sat 09.30–17.30 (closed 13.30–14.45)

Listings by postcode area

The postcode map is on page 9. Entries within each area are in alphabetical order.

CITY CENTRE: DUBLIN 1 The area north of the river surrounding O'Connell St has an air of jaded grandeur, having long since fallen from its 18th-century status as Dublin's most sought-after address. It has traditionally been home to budget accommodation as it includes several points of entry to the city: Dublin Port (North Wall), Busáras (central bus station, Store St) and Connolly Train Station (Amiens St). In the last decade it has undergone considerable residential and commercial development, particularly around Capel St and the International Financial Services Centre, becoming home to many young professionals as well as the burgeoning immigrant population. A walk along Gardiner St will, however, still take you past a lively mixture of small hotels, comfortable guesthouses and large tourist hostels. Many of these rely almost solely on the passing trade, although the better ones tend to book up in advance.

Dublin Bus no 41 costs €2.20 from the airport to the city and terminates on Lr Abbey St, near Gardiner St and much of the accommodation in Dublin 1.

Abbey Court Hostel 29 Bachelor's Walk, Dublin 1, tel 878 0700, web www. abbey-court.com

Right beside O'Connell Bridge, Abbey Court is one of the easiest hostels to locate in the city, as well as being one of the most secure—and one of the cleanest. Accommodation ranges from four-, six- and 10-bedded dorms to private double/twin rooms. Some rooms en suite (with power showers), with additional toilets/showers on each corridor. Well-equipped self-catering kitchen plus a large dining area and patio barbecue area. In summer there's a terrific atmosphere on the walk out front and you can get a discount off a cruise on the Liffey. There's free use of the safety deposit boxes and no charge for the left-luggage room, as well as free WiFi and two cosy TV lounges in which to sit and chill. Breakfast is served in the Apache Pizza next door where there are also good discounts. Also has a selection of good value apartments beside the hostel.

€19–23 pps 10-bed dorm, €24–28 pps 6-bed dorm, €27–31 pps 4-bed room, €39–44.50 pps private double/twin room. Weekly rate €105 (dorm). Self-catering apartments €30–44.50 pps. Continental breakfast included.

Abraham House 82–83 Lr Gardiner St, Dublin 1, tel 855 0600, web www. abraham-house.ie

Relaxed and friendly hostel with helpful staff; a restored Georgian townhouse 10 minutes' walk from Temple Bar or Grafton St and two minutes from Busáras or Connolly Station. The building is a bit rough around the edges inside but it is clean and undeniably has some character. Accommodation consists of large and smaller dorms as well as private rooms. All rooms en suite and there are free left-luggage facilities as well as free WiFi.

€10–26 pps dorm, €30–46 pps private room. Continental breakfast included.

Anchor Guesthouse 49 Lr Gardiner St, Dublin 1, tel 878 6913, web www. anchorguesthouse.com

Offers 22 en suite rooms between the original Georgian building and a new extension, ranging from quad to single. The older rooms are a bit more spacious and homely. Popular with those who might normally book a hostel thanks to the low B&B rates in the very central location. Limited free parking and free WiFi in the sitting room. TVs, radios and phones in all rooms.

€35–50 pps, €55–70 single. Weekly rates negotiable. Cooked breakfast (not full Irish) included.

The Belvedere Hotel Great Denmark St, Dublin 1, tel 873 7700, web www. belvederehotel.ie

Fairly stylish, modern hotel only two minutes from O'Connell St. There's not much of an atmosphere but comfort is in abundance. Spacious rooms with all the usual three-star hotel facilities plus free broadband, which you should request when booking. The Belvedere bar hosts all kinds of events—from tango to comedy (see page 152).

€59–169 per room, €20 triple supplement. Breakfast not included (full Irish €9.95). Wheelchair access.

Castle Hotel 3–4 Great Denmark St, Dublin 1, tel 874 6949, web www.
thecastlehotelgroup.com

One of Dublin's oldest hotels, just off Parnell Square in a
mid-18th-century building, and owned by a terrific character called—
unbelievably—Fionn MacCumhaill. Completely refurbished in 2009;
gorgeous traditional decor and friendly atmosphere and welcome,
plus some of the best value in town for the comfort you get in the
central location. Little touches like chocolates on the pillow when you
arrive! A babysitting service is available on request and there's free
WiFi. Walton's Hotel, beside the Castle and part of the same group,
was recently incorporated into the Castle. Walton's famous music
shop—set up by Martin Walton, Michael Collins's bodyguard—is still
there, thankfully.

€99 per double room, €139 executive double room/triple room,
€69 single. Full Irish breakfast included.

Clifden Guesthouse 32 Gardiner Place, Dublin 1, tel 874 6364, web www.
clifdenhouse.com

Restored Georgian townhouse with 15 rooms. Comfortable,
well-equipped accommodation and friendly service. Close to the very
centre of town, all rooms en suite. Free parking in their own secure car
park at the back. Phone, TV and tea/coffee facilities in all rooms. There's
also a huge room that's perfect for families.

€35–55 pps, €35–60 single. Full Irish or continental breakfast
included. Rates from €30 single/pps without breakfast. Weekly rates
available.

Hotel St George 7 Parnell Square, Dublin 1, tel 874 5611, web www.
thecastlehotelgroup.com

A recently renovated boutique hotel in the same group as the
Castle (see above); 50 rooms in a converted Georgian building with the
same impressive style. Breakfast is served in the restored basement
room that would have housed the original kitchen in Georgian times.

€99 per double room, €139 executive double room/triple room, €69
single. Full Irish breakfast included.

Isaacs Hostel 2–5 Frenchman's Lane, Dublin 1, tel 855 6215, email hostel@
isaacs.ie, web www.dublinbackpacker.com

This was the first Tourist Board-approved hostel in Dublin and it's
a favourite with backpacker types looking for atmosphere and chat.
Excellent range of services and facilities including a great café serving
breakfast and lunch. The basement area has a sauna, pool table, TV

room and one of the cheapest laundries in Dublin. Like its sister Jacob's Inn (below) it's constantly bustling with budget travellers, though Isaacs is a little more traditional in look and style, with smaller rooms that are not en suite. Lots of entertainment provided including movies every night and musicians can stay for free if they do a session! Free WiFi.

€10–15 pps dorm, €20–30 pps private room, €30–50 single. Weekly rate €84–99 (dorm). Light breakfast included.

Jacobs Inn Hostel 21–28 Talbot Place, Dublin 1, tel 855 5660, email jacobs@jsaacs.ie, web www.dublinbackpacker.com

Beside Busáras, this modern, purpose-built hostel has dorms that sleep up to 12 people as well as double and family rooms. It's huge, sleeping up to 400, and very clean and spacious; larger bedrooms in the older sections—the new rooms are more snug. Male, female and mixed sex rooms, all en suite. Lift to all floors. All the usual hostel facilities, plus a restaurant open for breakfast and lunch, and a lot happening in terms of entertainment—including movies every night. A free tour of the city also starts from here (and Isaacs). Free WiFi. This is also the only hostel in Dublin that is part of Fáilte Ireland's Validated Accessible Scheme.

€10–20 pps dorm, €20–50 pps private room. Weekly rate €91 (dorm). Light breakfast included. Wheelchair access; some rooms specially adapted.

Jurys Inn Custom House Custom House Quay, Dublin 1, tel 854 1500, web www.jurysinns.com

A very popular hotel with holidaymakers and business people on budgets, situated on the waterfront, beside the International Financial Services Centre. Only a short walk from O'Connell St or The O₂. All the usual facilities of a three-star hotel. No great atmosphere but good, solid modern comfort; the rooms can sleep up to three adults or two adults and two children. Early booking essential, especially for the best rates.

€89–120 per room. Breakfast not included (full Irish €12, continental €9.95). Wheelchair access; some rooms specially adapted.

Litton Lane Hostel 2–4 Litton Lane, Dublin 1, tel 872 8389, web www.irish-hostel.com

Just off Bachelor's Walk, Litton Lane is housed in a former recording and rehearsing studio once used by the likes of U2, Van Morrison, Sinéad O'Connor and David Bowie. The hostel makes the most of its historic associations—the walls are painted with funky, colourful murals of rock icons. Mix of eight- and 10-bed dorms, private rooms with cable TV and self-catering apartments. The self-catering kitchen is small but suits the size of the hostel and is not often crowded thanks to the choice of local eateries. Free WiFi, left-luggage and indoor bike storage.

€12.50–30 pps dorm, €25–40 pp in a private room. Weekly rate €90–105. Self-catering apartments €75–150 per night. Continental breakfast included.

Marian Guesthouse 21 Upr Gardiner St, Dublin 1, tel 874 4129, web www. marianguesthouse.com

Very friendly family-run guesthouse off Mountjoy Square and a short walk from the centre of town. Six rooms, five of them en suite, all with TV. Free parking in private car park.

€30–35 pps, €40 single. Full Irish breakfast included.

Marlborough Hostel 81–82 Marlborough St, Dublin 1, tel 874 7812, web www.marlboroughhostel.com

Next door to the Pro-Cathedral, this very central hostel is not the liveliest or the largest, but its relaxed and friendly style is part of the appeal. The two restored Georgian buildings house four-, five-, six- and eight-bed dorms. Each bed comes with its own free-to-use, secure luggage locker. A €10 refundable deposit is required on entry. There's a games room and a self-catering kitchen, plus barbeque facilities, bike parking and free WiFi.

€12–30 pps dorm. Weekly rate €105–125. Continental breakfast included.

Mount Eccles Court Hostel 42 Nth Great George's St, Dublin 1, tel 873 0826, web www.eccleshostel.com

A long-running family-owned hostel popular with backpackers. It spans three converted buildings (originally a school) on one of Dublin's most intact Georgian streetscapes and it is somewhat run-down. However, the splendid proportions of the original architecture and the warm welcome make up for what it lacks in modern decor. Mix of private rooms/self-catering apartments and dorms, some en suite. Free WiFi in reception.

€10–17 pps dorm, €35–45 pps private room/apartment. Weekly rate €80 (dorm). Light breakfast included. Self-catering apartments €90–110.

CITY CENTRE: DUBLIN 2 Home to Temple Bar and some of Dublin's best and busiest bars, hotels, shops and restaurants, as well as cultural institutions, Dublin 2 is much livelier at night than its neighbouring area across the river. This is great for anyone who wants to dance the night away and then safely walk back to their lodgings, but the same liveliness can be a pain if, when you eventually turn in, the noise from the streets keeps you awake. If you are a light sleeper, these places are not for you. Much of the accommodation in Dublin 2 is very expensive, but there is still plenty of choice for the budget traveller, and the options are increasing.

Ashfield House 19–20 D'Olier St, Dublin 2, tel 679 7734, web www. ashfieldhouse.ie
Very central, modern hostel located between the river and Trinity College, and an ideal base for going out at night. Relaxed atmosphere with spacious common area. The building was a hotel, an army and navy store, a restaurant and then a church, and in 1995 became a hostel. All rooms en suite. There is a self-catering kitchen on the ground floor where guests converge to cook, eat or just hang out. Free WiFi and free luggage storage.
€22–26 pps dorm, €35–42 pps triple room, €38–42 pps double/twin room. Continental breakfast included. Wheelchair access on one side of building; one room specially adapted.

Avalon House (hostel) 55 Aungier St, Dublin 2, tel 475 0001, web www. avalon-house.ie
Almost 300 beds set out in private rooms and dorms of every shape and size—all within ornate Victorian walls. Most rooms en suite. Spotlessly clean and professionally run, with great, friendly service and a great buzz. Avalon House has its own café on the ground floor which is open to the public and very popular; the espresso was voted the best in Dublin by *The Irish Times*. There's a cinema in the basement as well as a games room and a TV room. Offers very good information about the city and its ongoing events, as well as tailor-made group services. Free WiFi.
€10–20 pps dorm, €32–37 pps private room. Weekly rate €77–99. Continental breakfast included.

Barnacles Temple Bar House (hostel) 19 Temple Lane, Temple Bar, Dublin 2, tel 671 6277, web www.barnacles.ie

Perfectly situated for all the entertainment the city has to offer. Rooms all en suite; these are small but attention to detail compensates. Bright, stylish decor with ample under-bed secure storage as well as wardrobe space for each guest, and reading lights above every bed. All the standard facilities. Very security conscious, like most premises. Well-equipped kitchen for preparing gourmet meals; cosy common room with TV, stereo and open fire from which to watch the world go by outside. Free WiFi.

€15–29.50 pps 10/11-bed dorm, €20–39.50 pps 4/6-bed dorm, €32–48.50 pps double/twin room. Light breakfast included.

The Fleet Street Hotel 19–20 Fleet St, Temple Bar, Dublin 2, tel 670 8124, web www.fleethoteltemplebar.com

Boasts more character than most places in Temple Bar, having once housed Bewley's café and bakery—Harry Clarke's stained glass windows are preserved throughout the building. It consists of 71 reasonably well-equipped single, double and twin rooms and the service is friendly and helpful.

€59–129 per room. Breakfast not included.

Kilronan House 70 Adelaide Rd, Dublin 2, tel 475 5266, web www.kilronanhouse.com

Very comfortable, long-established three-star guesthouse that prides itself on being a cut above the rest. Only a few minutes from the centre of things yet away from the bustle on a quiet street. Elegant and well-equipped bedrooms. Free WiFi and free parking available.

€37.50–84 pps, €50–75 single. Full Irish breakfast included.

Kinlay House 2–12 Lord Edward St, Dublin 2, tel 679 6644, web www.kinlaydublin.ie

One of the best of the longer established hostels in Dublin, and particularly popular with groups. Choice of rooms from single up to 24-bed dorms all housed in a very large, old building with a gothic feel. Many rooms en suite. Free WiFi and a big TV in the dining area, plus a super-comfy TV lounge. Accommodation is fairly basic but excellent facilities include a shop selling food, toiletries, bus tickets and more; as well as the usual laundry, self-catering kitchen, laptop safes, etc.

€18–24 pps 16–24-bed dorm, €22–33 pps 4–6-bed room, €30–42 pps double/twin/triple room. Weekly rates available. Continental breakfast included.

Leeson Inn 24 Leeson St, Dublin 2, tel 661 2002/662 2002, web www.leesoninndowntown.com

Opulent accommodation in a very elegant restored Georgian house. Hotel-style though not officially a hotel as there is no bar or restaurant on the premises. Onsite parking on request and free WiFi in reception. Top location, although the area changes dramatically on weekend nights. Basements transform into nightclubs and the street becomes thronged with queues of desperadoes in search of some action.

€59–149 per double room, €139–159 triple, €149–169 quad, €49–99 single. Breakfast not included (full Irish €10).

Mercer Court, **Royal College of Surgeons Campus Accommodation** Lr Mercer St, Dublin 2, tel 478 3022/478 3022, web www.mercercourt.ie

Close to St Stephen's Green and Grafton St, Mercer Court offers 100 en suite private rooms from late June to late September, complete with TVs and phones. Free overnight car parking and free tea and coffee in the lobby throughout the day, plus onsite laundry. Good special deals too.

From €35 pps, €45 single. Continental breakfast included.

The Oliver St John Gogarty 18 Anglesea St, Temple Bar, Dublin 2, tel 671 1822, web www.gogartys.ie

Attached to one of Temple Bar's most popular pubs, this hostel really is in the middle of the action. Mixture of dorms from four-bed to ten-bed plus private twin rooms; most rooms en suite. TV room and a self-catering kitchen, plus a bar and restaurant attached. There are self-catering apartments onsite as well. The hostel has free luggage storage and the apartments have free WiFi.

€12–38 pps dorm, €32–49 pps twin room. Continental breakfast included. Self-catering apartments €150–290 per apartment (sleeps six). Breakfast not included with apartments.

O'Neill's Victorian Pub & Townhouse 36–37 Pearse St, Dublin 2, tel 671 4074, web www.oneillsdublin.com

Comfortable and cosy B&B-style accommodation above one of Dublin's oldest family-run pubs. Quad, triple, double, twin and single rooms, all with TV and all en suite with power showers. Good location near Trinity College, though the busy street outside may present sleeping problems for some.

€35–65 pps, single from €45. Full Irish breakfast included.

River House Hotel 23–24 Eustace St, Temple Bar, tel 670 7655, web www.riverhousehotel.com

A small hotel on the doorstep of the city's cultural quarter/prime nightlife district. Twenty-nine bedrooms, all en suite—single, double, twin and triple, plus two bedroom-only apartments that sleep seven. Also has its own bar and a recommended nightclub. Pleasant atmosphere, good service and a substantial breakfast, but the noisy location may be a problem for some. TV, radio, hairdryer, phone and tea/coffee in each room.

€30–70 pps, €40–70 single. Apartments €200–400 per night. Full Irish breakfast included.

Trinity College Campus Accommodation College Green, Dublin 2, tel 896 1177, web www.tcd.ie/accommodation

A 400-year-old oasis in the city centre with hundreds of rooms to let each summer. The rooms vary greatly in style—some are housed in the charming old buildings around the squares of the college; others are in the modern apartment blocks on the edge of the campus and overlook the very un-charming Pearse St. The best views are in the Graduates' Memorial Building overlooking the Campanile. Single rooms up to apartments that sleep seven. Available from mid-June to mid-September in 2009 and from 2010 from the end of May to mid-September. Discounted access to sports centre and free parking at weekends.

€81 per double room with shared bathroom, €125 twin en suite, €60.50–74.50 single, €149–223.50 for a 2/3-bedroom apartment. Continental breakfast included (upgrade to full Irish €4 per night). Wheelchair access; some rooms specially adapted.

NORTH CITY: DUBLIN 3, 7 AND 9 These residential areas to the north of the city are only a short bus ride from the centre and are full of reasonably priced, good-quality B&Bs as well as hostel and campus accommodation.

Annagh House 301 Clontarf Rd, Dublin 3, tel 833 8841, web www.annaghhouse.ie

An opulent refurbished Victorian home with a wonderfully friendly and chatty hostess, this B&B lies on the seafront just a few kilometres from the city centre. Four rooms, all en suite with tea/coffee-making facilities and TV. Wide-ranging breakfast menu includes a vegetarian option and a low-carb option—other dietary needs catered for where possible. Free off-street parking and free WiFi. Dublin Bus no 130.

€35–50 pps, €50–65 single. Full Irish breakfast (or alternative) included.

Applewood 144 Upr Drumcondra Rd, Dublin 9, tel 837 8328

Delightful apple-themed B&B built on an orchard, with a landscaped back garden for guest use and a full and varied breakfast menu. In a prime location between the city and the airport. Three en suite double rooms and a single room with private bathroom. All have TV and tea/coffee facilities. Free off-street parking. Dublin Bus nos 3, 11, 11A, 11B, 13A, 16, 16A, 33, 41, 41B, 41C, 41N, 746.

€30–35 pps, €35–40 single. Full Irish breakfast (or alternative) included.

Autumn Leaf 41 St Lawrence Rd, Clontarf, Dublin 3, tel 833 7519, email autumnleaf@eircom.net

Very welcoming B&B in an attractive restored Victorian home located in a lovely quiet neighbourhood close to the sea. Two double rooms and two triples; TV and tea/coffee in rooms. Free off-street parking. Vegetarian and coeliac-friendly breakfast options available. Dublin Bus nos 31N, 130.

€35–45 pps, €50–60 single. Full Irish breakfast (or alternative) included.

Cartan House 44 Iona Rd, Glasnevin, Dublin 9, tel 830 5906

A very pleasant and friendly B&B down a quiet street but with plenty of good restaurants and pubs nearby. Three en suite rooms and one standard, all well equipped. Dublin Bus nos 3, 11, 11A, 11B, 13A, 16, 16A, 33, 41, 41B, 41C, 41N, 746.

€35–38 pps, €50 single. Full Irish breakfast included.

Dublin City University Campus Residences DCU, Ballymun Rd/ Collins Ave, Glasnevin, Dublin 9, tel 700 5736, web www. summeraccommodation.dcu.ie

Offers 1,000 bedrooms, double and single, in modern apartment blocks from mid-June to mid-September. Rooms are either en suite or share a bathroom between two. Campus bar, restaurant and sports complex (with a discounted rate) open to guests. Free broadband in all rooms. Dublin Bus nos 11, 11A, 11B, 13, 13A, 19A, 40N, 46X, 116.

€49–71 per double room without breakfast, €36–51 single; €65–89 per double inc. buffet breakfast, €45–60 single. Wheelchair access.

Dublin International Youth Hostel 61 Mountjoy St, Dublin 7, tel 830 1766, web www.dublininternationalhostel.com

An enormous hostel housed in a former convent and the only Dublin member of An Óige, the Irish Youth Hostel Association. The accommodation consists mainly of dorms, though some private rooms are available. Excellent facilities include free WiFi, a games room, comfortable common areas, laundry and parking. The sense of a busy community makes it ideal for those travelling alone looking to meet up with others. Dublin Bus nos 10, 38.

€21–24 pps 6/8/10-bed dorm, €23.50–27 pps 4-bed room, €26–28 pps double/triple room, €35–40 single (generally €2 discount for IYHA members). Continental breakfast included.

Egan's House (guesthouse) 7 Iona Park, Glasnevin, Dublin 9, tel 830 3611, web www.eganshouse.com

Located halfway between the city centre and the airport, in a quiet suburb. Elegant, well-equipped rooms, with armchairs or sofas to allow guests to lounge in private in front of their own TV. There's a public lounge on the ground floor where guests can enjoy a glass of wine by the open fire (Egan's have a wine licence). Free WiFi and free parking outside. Dublin Bus nos 3, 11, 11A, 11B, 13A, 16, 16A, 33, 41, 41B, 41C, 41N, 746.

€19–79 pps, €39–89 single. Full Irish or continental breakfast included.

Hydra House 61 Iona Rd, Glasnevin, Dublin 9, 830 6253

A beautiful, welcoming B&B down a quiet side street with two en suite rooms and two standard, all with TV and tea/coffee. Cosy with an open fire and extremely friendly owners. The house itself is a veritable gallery of framed treasures: nature paintings, old photos, rugby posters; in parts the walls are almost completely covered. Free on-street parking. Dublin Bus nos 3, 11, 11A, 11B, 13A, 16, 16A, 33, 41, 41B, 41C, 41N, 746.

€30–35 pps, €50 single. Full Irish breakfast included.

Loyola B&B 18 Charleville Rd, Phibsboro, Dublin 7, tel 838 9973, email loyola18@eircom.net

Gorgeous Victorian house 1km from the city centre; four bedrooms, two en suite. A great garden, especially for kids. The hostess is very accommodating and friendly. All the rooms have TV, clock radios and hairdryers. Welcomes long-term stay. Free off-street parking. Dublin Bus nos 10, 38, 38A, 38B, 38C, 39, 39A, 39B, 39C, 39N, 39X, 120, 121, 122.

€35–40 pps, €40–50 single. Full Irish breakfast included.

Regency Hotel Whitehall, Dublin 9, tel 837 3544/Freephone 1800 930 007, web www.regencyhotels.com

The Regency is the grande dame of Dublin budget hotels, boasting more character and class than most. She's a little tired looking on the outside now but still buzzing with life and all sorts on their way to and from the airport and the city. The leisure centre is free for guest use, with a 17-metre pool, kids' pool, Jacuzzi, steam room, sauna and gym. There is also a spa on site. They don't really have standard rates so depending on the time of year you can get very good deals. Dublin Bus nos 3, 13A, 16, 16A, 33, 41, 41B, 41C, 41N, 746.

€89–300 per room, single from €79—check website for lower rates and packages. Full Irish breakfast included. Wheelchair access; three rooms specially adapted.

Sea Breeze 312 Clontarf Rd, Dublin 3, tel 833 2787

Comfortable, very homely and welcoming B&B on the seafront, with buses every 10 minutes into the city. Three rooms, all en suite with TV; tea/coffee-making facilities just outside the rooms. Free on-street parking outside. Dublin Bus no 130.

€40 pps, €45–50 single. Full Irish breakfast included.

Sunnybank Hotel 68–70 Botanic Rd, Glasnevin, Dublin 9, tel 830 6755, web www.sunnybank.ie

Small, family-run hotel with a bar and its own Chinese restaurant, just a short bus ride from the city centre and a short walk to the National Botanic Gardens and the historic Glasnevin Cemetery where many of the greats of Irish history ended up. All rooms en suite. Not exceptionally stylish but good value if you prefer a hotel option. Dublin Bus nos 13, 19, 19A, 40N.

€40–45 pps, €45–50 single. Full Irish breakfast included. One bedroom with wheelchair access.

Tinode House 170 Upr Drumcondra Rd, Dublin 9, tel 837 2277, web www.tinodehouse.com

Top-quality B&B in a comfortable and stylish Edwardian home on the main airport road, close to the city centre. Four rooms, all en suite and with TV and tea/coffee facilities. Excellent and varied breakfast menu and a patio and orchard which serve as a very pleasant beer garden. Free WiFi. Dublin Bus nos 3, 11, 11A, 11B, 13A, 16, 16A, 33, 41, 41B, 41C, 41N, 746.

€35–45 pps, 55–70 single. Full Irish breakfast (or alternative) included.

NORTH CITY: NEAR THE AIRPORT As Dublin Airport is not very far from the city centre, there is really no need to book special accommodation there. However, if you are worried about missing your flight or if you simply want extra time in bed, staying in the area between Drumcondra and Santry will give you a far shorter journey to the airport. B&B signs can be seen along most of the main roads between the city and the airport. Here are two different options.

Bewley's Hotel Dublin Airport Baskin Lane, Swords, Co Dublin, tel 871 1000, web www.bewleyshotels.com

Bewley's is ideal if you feel like spending your last night in Dublin in relative luxury at relatively little expense. There's free WiFi throughout the hotel. A free airport shuttle bus runs every 20 minutes. Unfortunately, there is no bus direct from the city centre, but to avoid a taxi fare you could get a bus to the airport (16A, 41, 41B, 41N, 746) and then the Bewley's shuttle to the hotel.

€99 per room standard rate but rooms from €59. Breakfast not included (full Irish €12). Wheelchair access; some rooms specially adapted.

The Emmaus Centre Lissenhall, Swords, Co Dublin, tel 870 0050, web www.emmauscentre.ie

Ten minutes from the airport by taxi/car, Emmaus is run by the Christian Brothers and the Sisters of the Holy Faith. The centre is used as a spiritual retreat and conference centre but also welcomes guests on their way to or from the airport or the city. Take a walk through the 10-acre, tree-filled grounds, of which there are wonderful views from the rooms; all rooms are en suite with complimentary toiletries and internet access. Children are not allowed, however. Take Dublin Bus no 33 from Lr Abbey St; get off at the second stop after the Estuary Round-about—Emmaus is located down Ennis Lane, which is on your left.

€30–35 pps, €35–40 single. Buffet breakfast included. Wheelchair access; some rooms specially adapted.

SOUTH CITY: DUBLIN 4, 6 AND 8 Much of the accommodation in the south city is concentrated in the expensive Ballsbridge area, though it is well worth looking elsewhere. Dublin 4, Dublin 6 and 8 all have their own charms and are very close to town, some parts within walking distance of the centre.

Ardagh House 1 Highfield Rd, Rathgar, Dublin 6, tel 497 7068, web www. bandbdublin.net

Large family-run guesthouse with a big garden. Nineteen rooms, all en suite with TV and tea/coffee facilities. Quite luxurious but friendly and fairly laidback; good place for families. Free parking and free WiFi. Ten minutes' walk from the Cowper Luas stop (Green line) or Dublin Bus nos 14, 14A, 15, 15A, 15B, 15N, 128.

€40–55 pps, €60–80 single. Full Irish breakfast (or alternative) included.

Bewley's Hotel Ballsbridge Merrion Rd, Ballsbridge, Dublin 4, tel 668 1111, web www.bewleyshotels.com

Beside the RDS and five minutes' walk from Sandymount DART Station. The hotel is a beautiful redbrick building in a lovely leafy setting. Excellently equipped rooms—each has an iron and ironing board, trouser press, hairdryer, safe and free broadband internet, as well as the usual TV and tea/coffee-making facilities. Free WiFi in communal areas and some rooms. Dublin Bus nos 4, 4A, 5, 7, 7A, 7N, 8, 45.

€99 per room. Breakfast not included (full Irish €9.50). Wheelchair access; some rooms specially adapted.

Colette Carter, 32 Annesley Pk, Ranelagh, Dublin 6, tel 496 6039, 087 677 7075, email colettec@bigfoot.com

Victorian house, recently refurbished with great style in a lovely, quiet location close to Ranelagh village with its great pubs and restaurants. Offers two en suite rooms—a double and a twin—each with TV, alarm radio and hairdryer. Very homely, relaxed and welcoming. Special diets, including coeliac and vegetarian, catered for at breakfast by the hostess who is a cordon bleu cook. The Beechwood Luas stop (Green line) is five minutes' walk away, St Stephen's Green is 20 minutes' walk.

€45 pps, €55 single occupancy. Full Irish breakfast included.

D4 Hotels Pembroke Rd, Ballsbridge, Dublin 4, tel 668 4468, web www.
d4hotels.ie

A collection of three hotels offering value in Dublin's poshest district: the Ballsbridge Court, Ballsbridge Towers and Ballsbridge Inn. All are three-star, very well kitted out, stylish and luxurious. These also happen to be some of the friendliest hotels in Dublin. The Inn has a unique downstairs food hall including a pizza place that is open till 02.00 Friday and Saturday, and the Towers has an 18-seater cinema that you can bring your own movies to! Free WiFi on the ground floor and free broadband in bedrooms. Three minutes' walk from Lansdowne Rd DART Station; Dublin Bus nos 4, 4A, 5, 7, 7A, 7N, 8, 45, 63, 84.

€99–109 per room standard rate, but rooms from €39 at certain times. Breakfast not included. Wheelchair access; some rooms specially adapted.

Donnybrook Lodge 131 Stillorgan Rd, Dublin 4, tel 283 7333, web www.
donnybrooklodge.net

Pleasant, homely guesthouse which offers very good value for its Dublin 4 address. Beside UCD, with buses to the city centre stopping just outside the door every few minutes. Single, double, twin, triple and quad rooms, all en suite. Free WiFi in all rooms as well as a courtesy computer in the lounge. Free off-street parking. Dublin Bus nos 2, 3, 10, 10A, 46A, 46B, 46D, 46N, 63, 84, 84X, 145.

€35–€47.50 pps, €55–65 single. Full Irish breakfast (or alternative) included.

Four Courts Hostel 15–17 Merchant's Quay, Dublin 8, tel 672 5839, web www.fourcourtshostel.com

This large, very well-equipped hostel is served directly by Dublin Bus nos 16A and 748 (Airlink) from the airport; it's also near the Four Courts Luas stop (Red line) and within 10 minutes' walk of O'Connell Bridge. While perhaps not the warmest in terms of traditional atmosphere, it is very clean, modern and secure, with every facility you could want: games room, reading room, car park, lift to all floors, free WiFi, Sky Sports . . . Many of the rooms overlook the Liffey and the architectural splendour of Gandon's Four Courts. It's also easy to find on the quays due to the hideous green exterior.

€17–29 pps dorm, €29–38 pps private room, €50–60 single (€4 supplement pp Fri-Sat). Weekly rate €99 (dorm). Continental breakfast included. Two fully wheelchair-accessible rooms.

Jurys Inn Christchurch Christchurch Place, Dublin 8, tel 454 0000, web www.jurysinns.com

The original in the budget Jurys Inns chain. Great location (if you don't mind church bells)—directly opposite Christ Church Cathedral and around the corner from St Patrick's. All the facilities of a three-star hotel with good, solid modern comfort though no great atmosphere. Rooms can accommodate up to three adults or two adults and two children. Early booking essential, especially for the cheapest rates.

€99–149 per room (cheaper rates available in advance online). Breakfast not included (full Irish €12, continental €9.95). Wheelchair access; some rooms specially adapted.

Phoenix Park House 38–39 Parkgate St, Dublin 8, tel 677 2870, web www.dublinguesthouse.com

A warm and friendly, family-run guesthouse/small hotel right beside Phoenix Park. Three minutes' walk from Heuston Train Station and the Heuston or Museum Luas stops (Red line). The rooms are large and all en suite with TV and tea/coffee-making facilities. Vegetarians are catered for. Dublin Bus nos 25, 25A, 25N, 26, 66, 66N, 67, 67A, 68, 69, 69X.

€33–49 pps, €60–75 single. Full Irish breakfast (or alternative) included.

St Aiden's 32 Brighton Rd, Rathgar, Dublin 6, tel 490 6178, web www.staidens.com

A mix of modern and period rooms in a family-run guesthouse; a nice quiet location in the pleasant village of Rathgar. All rooms en suite with TV, tea/coffee-making facilities and phones. Good breakfast menu and a selection of books and videos for guest use. There's a playground nearby for children and discounted access is offered to a local health centre. Free on-street parking and free WiFi. Kosher friendly. Dublin Bus nos 15, 15A, 15B, 15N.

€35–47.50 pps, €45–60 single. Full Irish or continental breakfast included.

Tavistock House 64 Ranelagh Rd, Dublin 6, tel 498 8000, web www.tavistockhouse.com

A Victorian home on the city side of the bustling suburb of Ranelagh. Close to the Ranelagh Luas stop (Green line) and within walking distance of St Stephen's Green. Fourteen rooms, all en suite, six of them self-catering. As comfortable as any hotel, but retains a welcoming, friendly atmosphere. Free WiFi and babysitting service available. Also the only tourist accommodation in Dublin with facilities for pets. Dublin Bus nos 11, 11A, 11B, 44, 44B, 44C, 44N, 48A.

€45–50 pps, €55 single. Self-catering suites €155–165 per night (sleep up to 4 people). Full Irish breakfast (or alternative) included.

UCD Village Campus Accommodation Belfield, Dublin 4, tel 269 7111/716 1046, web www.ucdvillage.ie

Well-equipped, modern apartments with basic self-catering facilities, located in the landscaped setting of Ireland's largest university. Rooms are let either individually or as complete apartments and are open to guests from June to the end of August. The accommodation is near all campus facilities which include a bar, restaurant and café. The sports centre, tennis courts and running track are also open to guests at a discounted rate. Over two dozen Dublin Bus routes serve UCD, including nos 46A, 145 and no 10, which goes inside the campus.

€30 single room with shared bathroom, €40 single en suite. Breakfast not included. Wheelchair access.

Waterloo House 8–10 Waterloo Rd, Ballsbridge, Dublin 4, tel 660 1888, web www.waterloohouse.ie

Very luxurious guesthouse within walking distance of St Stephen's Green. Offers 17 en suite bedrooms in two restored Georgian houses. Some king size rooms with garden views and fireplaces. Lift, free WiFi and free car parking, as well as a computer with internet access for guest use and a free *Irish Times* for your perusal in the morning.

€49–90 pps, €79 single. Full Irish breakfast (or alternative) included. Wheelchair access.

Waterloo Lodge (guesthouse) 23 Waterloo Rd, Ballsbridge, Dublin 4, tel 668 5380, web www.waterloolodge.com

The generally cheaper alternative to Waterloo House; in the same great location (almost directly across the road) but considerably less plush and less of an atmosphere. Group rates and extended-stay discounts generally available. Free WiFi and free car parking.

€29.50–90 pps, €55 single. Full Irish or continental breakfast included.

OUT OF TOWN: DÚN LAOGHAIRE This busy ferry port is full of good-value B&Bs for anyone just off the boat from Holyhead. As it is linked to the city centre by the DART and Dublin Bus nos 7, 7A, 7N, 8, 45, 46A, 46N and 746, it is quite convenient for getting in and out of town. There are also lots of lovely places to stay in all of the seaside areas between here and the city. The hostel below is near the port.

Marina House 7 Old Dunleary Rd, Dún Laoghaire, Co Dublin, tel 284 1524, web www.marinahouse.com
    Small-scale, friendly hostel in a restored stone building by the sea. Close to the DART (closer to Salthill & Monkstown Station than Dún Laoghaire). The accommodation is mostly four-bed dorms, with one eight-bed and one 10-bed, and one private double/twin room. Most of the rooms are en suite. There's a lovely garden off the first floor. WiFi available (not free). Dublin Bus nos 7, 7A, 7N, 46A, 746.
    €20–27 pps dorm, €25–30 pps private room. Weekly rates €100–120 pps dorm, €175 pps private room. Continental breakfast included.

CAMPING OUT OF TOWN
Camac Valley Tourist Caravan & Camping Park Naas Rd, Clondalkin, Dublin 22, tel 464 0644, web www.camacvalley.com
    Thirty-five minutes southwest of the city on the N7, Camac Valley encompasses a 15-acre site with facilities including showers, toilets, full laundry, TV, a snack shop, an internet café, a playground, waste disposal and 24-hour security. They also operate a catch-and-release fishing lake with free rod hire. Dublin Bus no 69 from Aston Quay to Camac Valley.
    €9–10 per backpacker per night; €19–26 for two adults/family with a tent, caravan or motor-home. Designated pitches for wheelchair users and wheelchair-accessible showers and toilets.
North Beach Caravan & Camping Park North Beach, Rush, Co Dublin, tel 843 7131, web www.northbeach.ie
    While not as large or well-equipped as Camac Valley, this is nevertheless a pleasant spot overlooking the beach and the sea beyond. Nice walks nearby and facilities include showers, laundry and a public telephone. Internet café nearby. Open from April to

September only. Dublin Bus no 33 from Lr Abbey St to Rush; get off at stop round the corner from the Strand Bar, cross the road and follow the signs for North Beach.

€10 per adult per night, €5 per child.

Somewhere to live

The rental sector in Dublin has grown in the last decade or so, with the completion of numerous apartment developments. This has led to a major improvement in the quality of the accommodation available. Rents are now falling—some 12 per cent in the last year although this is from a very high base. It still won't be easy, but your search for somewhere to live should now be less gruelling than in recent years.

Rents

Bed in a room shared with 3 others in Dublin 1 (bills included)	€75 pw
1 single-bed flat in Dublin 3	€145 pw
Bedsit in Dublin 1	€160 pw
1 double-bed flat on the Sth Circular Rd, Dublin 8	€220 pw
Single room in a house on Lr Leeson St, Dublin 2	€400 pm
2-bed apartment in Dublin 2	€1,100 pm
3-bed house in Cabra, Dublin 7	€1,200 pm
3-bed house in Clondalkin, Dublin 22	€1,250 pm

Places in the centre of Dublin are always going to be in demand and hence dearer than elsewhere. As a rule, the only way to get cheaper rent is to move well out into the suburbs and/or house-share with several people.

Temple Bar buzzes at night.

Somewhere to sleep

Your rights

A legal leasing arrangement clearly defines your obligations and entitlements. Although every tenant is entitled, by law, to a rent book or a written letting agreement, it is common enough for agreements to be either exclusively verbal, or at least not entirely above board.

Threshold, 21 Stoneybatter, Dublin 7 (Dublin Bus nos 37, 39, 70 from Hawkins St, Dublin 2), tel 635 3651, web www.threshold. ie, is a charity working to prevent homelessness and provides free and independent advice and advocacy on housing matters. They produce a free comprehensive guide to renting translated into 13 languages. There is a lot of useful information on their website as well. The organisation can provide you with a model rent book suitable for most lettings (cost €2 plus postage).

Even if you don't think you'll have any difficulty finding (and holding on to) a suitable place to live, it is worth browsing through Threshold's material simply for helpful tips. If you need to discuss a particular problem or if you have a specific query, the staff there are extremely well-informed and sympathetic. You can call and arrange to see someone at the Stoneybatter centre; the service is by appointment only. The only problem is you may find it difficult to get through on the phone—they are very busy.

Rent supplement

If you are claiming social welfare, on a FÁS scheme, have a disability, or are working part-time and finding it difficult to make ends meet, you may qualify for help towards your rent. Apply to the Community Welfare Officer at your local health centre, which you can locate through **Citizens Information**, Lo-Call 1890 777 121, web www.citizensinformation.ie. The amount granted is calculated to leave a minimum 'after rent' income. Assistance is occasionally also given towards deposits on rented property. Assessment is quite rigorous, however, and you can be refused rent allowance, for example if your flat is considered unnecessarily large or expensive. The method and timespan for payments vary considerably from office to office, so be prepared for some unsympathetic responses from landlords who, when asked to complete the required application form, are less than delighted to help. Unfortunately for all concerned, many offices are slow in making the payments, leaving landlords temporarily out of pocket. On the other hand, many landlords in the lower rental bracket are quite used to dealing with rent allowance payments and are happy to plan around them.

Emergencies

If you find yourself in a serious housing emergency in Dublin, there are a few organisations which may be of use to you. If you are having landlord/tenant problems regarding your letting arrangement, whether it is written or verbal, then Threshold is the place to go for advice. If you need specific legal advice, your local **Citizens Information Centre** may be able to help (see contact info for Citizens Information above), but Threshold is the best place.

If your emergency leaves you with literally no roof over your head and no money to do anything about it, the place to go is **Focus Ireland**, an organisation helping those who have been made homeless. Go to their coffee shop and advice centre at 14A Eustace St, Dublin 2, tel 671 2555. It is open Mon–Fri 10.00–17.00 (closed 15.00–16.00); Sat, Sun and bank hol 11.00–15.00. If you need help outside these hours Freephone 1800 724 724—this line is open 24 hours. The coffee shop/advice centre offers the services of a trained crisis worker, as well as a low-cost meal (€1.60 for a main course), to anyone in need. Focus Ireland also have a range of day services for homeless people.

Somewhere to sleep

Somewhere to sleep

Finding a flat or bedsit

Online, you can search both the area and the price-range you want quickly and easily, without the need for legwork or the services of an estate/accommodation agent. However, this doesn't mean your search should be conducted entirely in cyberspace. Some of the best flats and bedsits are still passed on between friends, so ask anyone you know in Dublin if they have heard of anywhere suitable. Check the notices in local shop windows, and on their notice boards inside. Keep a look out for the 'To Let' signs in the neighbourhood you want to live in.

August, September and October are traditionally the worst months of the year for flat-hunting, as students are returning to every part of Dublin in search of a cheap place to live. Ninety per cent of student-affordable accommodation is already gone by the end of August. It is slightly easier to find somewhere in May and June when students disappear for the summer holidays, but even then it is rarely a simple and never an enjoyable task.

WEBSITES The major websites for letting are www.daft.ie and www.myhome2let.ie (the rental section of the more general www.myhome.ie). Also try www.let.ie. You can usually find pictures of the properties along with contact information and facilities details. Another site, with a special focus on student-suitable accommodation, is www.findahome.ie. College Cribs, www.collegecribs.ie, lists places aimed at students and 'young people' and hence generally in the affordable category. www.letbynet.com is a free advert site with lettings all over Ireland and Britain. General classifieds site www.gumtree.ie has extensive accommodation listings too.

ESTATE AGENTS The major estate/letting agents also have websites, where you can check out their lists of property for rent—e.g. www.gunne.ie, www.mannion.ie, www.dng.ie, www.lowe.ie, www.wyse.ie, www.remax-ireland.com, www. huntsman.ie, www.homelocators.ie, www.dublinlettings.com. As a rule, though, these organisations tend to focus on the higher end of the rental market. Your best online bets when it comes to cheaper accommodation are www.daft.ie, www.gumtree.ie and www.collegecribs.ie.

Looking for a place through an estate agent or an accommodation agent, the most important thing is to be absolutely clear about what is on offer—e.g. whether or not there is a charge to tenants and, if there is, what you are entitled to for this fee. Estate agents are required by law to be licensed and bonded and most also belong to professional institutes with their own rules of conduct. The exact legal position regarding other accommodation agencies is not as clear, so it is important to be aware of the type of organisation you are dealing with. If you do pay anything out to one of these companies, always get a receipt and check first whether you are entitled to a refund if they fail to find you a suitable place within a reasonable time.

When viewing a property, always arrive early for appointments and bring some cash for booking a deposit. Regardless of your place in the queue, most landlords will respond better to someone with money in hand. Don't forget to get a receipt if you do part with any money.

NEWSPAPER ADS The *Evening Herald* is the best newspaper for small ads and has columns for houses to let, apartments and flats to let, and house/flat sharing. Buy it as soon as it hits the shelves—around 12.00 daily, except on Sundays—and start making appointments to view immediately. Competition is fierce, and it is not unusual to have to queue even to get a look at a place. *Buy&Sell*, both in print and online at www.buyandsell.ie, doesn't have as extensive an accommodation list as the *Herald*, but it carries a selection of generally reasonably priced places. The print edition is published on Mondays, Wednesdays and Fridays.

Student accommodation

Most of the major colleges have their own campus accommodation, which varies in style and price. There is, however, only enough on-campus accommodation for a small proportion of each university's students, so demand is very high. Information is sent out when places are offered and the criteria governing who qualifies for rooms varies from college to college. Even overseas students are not guaranteed places—though the colleges are usually very helpful to students unfamiliar with Dublin, and keep listings of accommodation that is available to their students. Lists of off-campus accommodation for DCU, DIT, NCI, RCSI and UCD, as well as some of the smaller/private colleges, are available online at www.findahome.ie (sometimes a college password is required). Contact your college of choice for more info.

College Cribs, www.collegecribs.ie, is a very helpful site which allows you to instantly search for student accommodation near your place of education. You may also want to check out Student Accommodation Services, who offer purpose-built student apartments in the city, with rooms at €100/€105 per week. Depending on the location the rooms are either en suite twin or single with a shared bathroom. See www.studentaccommodation.ie or tel 703 8900.

UCD opens an office in its student centre from mid-July to mid-September where students can look up newspaper listings and make free calls to landlords. One of the great things about services like these if you're new to Dublin, is that you get the opportunity to meet people to house-share with. For information on Trinity accommodation phone the SU welfare officer on 646 8437.

Sharing

Sharing a house or a flat makes a lot of sense if you find that even a one-bedroom flat is out of your price range.

As in other cities, house or flat shares are often advertised by students living together who need a quick replacement for someone who's left. They generally don't expect a huge commitment from a new tenant as they'll probably only remain for the academic year themselves. First-time home buyers also often take in tenants to help with mortgage payments.

Young working people, not yet in the market to buy a house, often share for a few years. There are always plenty of ads for house/flat shares in the daily papers and online from people who, for example, have rented a three-bedroom place between two on the assumption that they can advertise for a third person to share. Keep an eye on the above websites as well as http://ie.easyroommate.com; on sites like this and www.gumtree.ie and www.letbynet.com, you can advertise your needs for free as well as search for a place.

Hostels/short-term accommodation

If you cannot get a place before you move, and you do not have friends to stay with temporarily, you will need somewhere affordable to sleep while you search. Hostels (see page 36) are about the best option, and many now welcome long-term stay, though it may depend on the time of year. Some are more flexible than others, so it is worth trying to strike a deal.

It also may be possible to stay in a house or apartment short term while you look for somewhere longer term. Check out the short-term listings on the likes of www.daft.ie and www. gumtree.ie.

Lodgings/digs

Another short-term possibility for anyone new to Dublin is to take lodgings ('digs') in a family home, where you can get a warm room in somebody's house with breakfast provided and sometimes an evening meal. Depending on the arrangement (whether you're staying five or seven days a week, how many meals you're getting, etc), this will typically cost €100–150 per week.

Digs can be found on some of the above websites, in particular www.collegecribs.ie, which allows you to search for them; newspaper listings are also worth a look. The universities compile lists of digs for their students that are made available before term starts. This is ideal accommodation for anyone who does not feel capable of fending entirely for themselves in a new city, and the sheltered atmosphere of an established family home provides a certain extra security.

Daily life

Getting around

Into the city centre

FROM THE AIRPORT **Aircoach** (known to Dubliners as 'the blue bus') is run by a private company that offers two routes, the Leopardstown route and the Donnybrook route. Both are loops, and both stop at the Gresham at the top of O'Connell St (handy for the hostels in nearby Gardiner St) and at Trinity College (good for Dame St, Temple Bar and with a little walking, Christ Church). If your destination is on the Luas Green line (see page 74) the neat trick used by locals is to get off at Trinity and walk up Grafton St to the Luas stop in St Stephen's Green. Beyond that you'll have to be careful—one Aircoach route will take you as far as Leopardstown, the other goes no further than Ballsbridge, looping round the RDS. Aircoach also runs a route to Bray/Greystones, see www.aircoach.ie.

The buses are scheduled to run 24 hours a day, 7 days a week, every 15 minutes from 05.00 to 00.00 and every hour from 00.00 to 05.00—and on the whole they do. Fares are €7 one-way and €12 return to and from the city centre to the airport, and €8 one-way and €14 return to and from suburban stops.

Student Travel Card

If you are a full-time student, you may wish to invest in a Student Travel Card (see the website www.studenttravelcard.ie). The card costs €12, and entitles you to a wide range of discounts on travel with Bus Éireann, Dublin Bus, Luas, and DART rail services.

Daily life

Dublin Bus runs a number of lines from and to the airport, as follows:

The **Airlink** lines (dedicated airport buses): route no 747 to O'Connell St and Busáras (the central bus station) roughly every 30 minutes from 05.45 to 22.50 Mon–Sat, 07.15 to 23.30 Sunday. Fares are €6 one-way, €10 return for an adult and half that for a child. Route no 748 goes to Heuston Railway Station, roughly every 30 minutes from 06.50 to 21.30 Mon–Sat, 07.00 to 22.05 Sun. Fares are €6 one-way, €10 return for an adult and half that for a child.

There are also **ordinary Dublin Bus lines** that pass through the airport. These are not dedicated airport buses as such, and stop along the way with depressingly high frequency; on the other hand they are cheaper, as their fares are standard Dublin Bus fares. They are not really suitable if you have a lot of luggage, as they have limited luggage space and may not allow passengers with too many bags to board. These routes include:

Route 746 from Dún Laoghaire, which goes through Donnybrook and O'Connell St, roughly every hour from 08.00 to 20.30 Mon–Sat, 10.30–17.30 Sun.

Route 102 to Swords, Portmarnock and Sutton, roughly every two hours from 05.45 to 20.05 Mon–Sat, 09.35–22.30 Sun.

Route 58X to Drumcondra, O'Connell St, Nassau St, Donnybrook, Stillorgan, Deansgrange, Shankill, once a day Mon–Fri only at 17.10.

Route 41 to Lr Abbey St roughly every 15 minutes from 06.00 to 23.30 Mon–Fri, roughly every 20 minutes from 06.45 to 23.25 Sat, roughly every 30 minutes from 07.15 to 23.15 Sun.

Route 16 to O'Connell St, Harold's Cross, Terenure and Rathfarnham roughly every 20 minutes from 08.45 to 23.10 Mon–Fri, 07.40 to 22.20 Sat, roughly every 30 minutes 08.30 to 22.40 Sun.

FROM THE PORTS There are two ferry ports in Dublin. The port of arrival normally depends on the ferry company you sail with.

Dublin Port, sometimes referred to as 'the North Wall' (served by **Irish Ferries and Stena Line)** is at Alexandra Road, near the city centre. Served by Dublin Bus numbers 53 and 53A, it is about 10 minutes' walk from O'Connell Bridge.

Dún Laoghaire Port (usually served by **Stena**) is about 10 km to the south of the city centre, but is served by the DART train as well as Dublin Bus routes 7, 8, 45 and 46A, making it reasonably convenient to the city. Dún Laoghaire Port has its own tourist office which opens for information and reservations every time a ferry comes in. It is located in the terminal building.

FROM THE RAILWAY STATIONS If you are coming to Dublin by train from the south or west you will arrive at **Heuston Station** (the old Kingsbridge), on the south bank of the Liffey. The city centre is a short Luas (Red line), bus or taxi ride away—a good number of buses pass near the station, most of them headed for the suburbs; for the city centre, the 90 is the one you're looking for—or a 15-minute walk down the quays.

If you are coming from the north, north-west or south-east you will arrive at **Connolly Station**, Amiens St, on the north bank of the river. It is sometimes referred to as 'Amiens Street Station', its old name, or (incorrectly) as 'Connolly Street Station'. Connolly is a short walk (5 minutes) from O'Connell Bridge.

FROM BUSÁRAS, THE CENTRAL BUS STATION Busáras is the main bus terminal for all **Bus Éireann** buses, i.e. those serving all regions outside Dublin. It is across the road from Connolly Station—5 minutes' walk from O'Connell Bridge.

Daily life

Daily life

Around the city

WALKING The first thing to keep in mind is that central Dublin is quite a small area and walking around the city is the best way to get to know it. It is possible to walk from one side to the other in less than 30 minutes. The Dublin Transportation Office has a website that offers directions and journey plans for pedestrians and cyclists at **www.dto-journeyplanner.ie**; it's more detailed and more useful than Google Maps, as it allows users to specify their start points or end points by the railway or Luas station they're nearest to, or by landmarks such as the Spire, Trinity College or the Royal Hospital Kilmainham.

However, for spontaneous exploration, a good **street map** is a must for the independent traveller, as Dublin's streets are laid out in the ad hoc, organic European style, and signposting tends to be erratic at best. The best and most comprehensive map available is the ***Dublin City and Districts Street Guide*** published by the Ordnance Survey. Available through most bookshops, it is a little unwieldy, being a spiral-bound A4-sized book rather than a folded map, but it's well worth having if you're staying in the city for a while. It contains a full street index, a bus reference guide and lots of useful information. Extending right out as far as the surrounding counties which it covers in some detail, it is extremely useful for figuring out the suburbs as well as for finding the right roads out of the city for further travel.

For a smaller guide to have in your pocket while you're walking around the city, the ***Collins Streetfinder*** is the best. It isn't as comprehensive as the Ordnance Survey map, and doesn't cover all the suburbs, let alone the surrounding counties, but as long as you stay within the city proper and don't stray into the wilds of Greater Dublin, you should be fine.

Dublin manners

It is surprising how, in public places, perfect strangers will place their hands, almost tenderly, on your shoulder or even on your waist, in order to move you out of their way or after having jostled you. Physical contacts which, in other countries, would be practically shocking, are here nothing out of the ordinary.

From Dublin: le guide Autrement

CYCLING As cars very firmly rule the roads in Dublin, **cycling** is an option for the brave but careful: cycle lanes are shared with buses and taxis. Cycling has some marvellous advantages, though, if you have the stomach for it. It's probably one of the fastest ways to get around the city as most traffic jams can be avoided or bypassed on a bike and you can stop wherever you like. Security for your bicycle is a problem in the city centre where bicycle theft is big business, so be very careful to leave your bike somewhere highly visible and use as many U-locks as you can afford to secure it. Just in case, get it insured. Also, for your own safety, wear a helmet and some high visibility clothing.

If you're only in Dublin for a short stay, **renting a bike** is a cheap and easy option. Lots of outlets around the city rent bikes, particularly in the summer months when demand from tourists is high and when the weather is a little more likely to suit this mode of transport. Some hostels also offer this service to guests. The **Golden Pages** classified telephone directory (online at www. goldenpages.ie) is a good source for bike sales and hire outlets.

If you are buying a bike, there are a lot of shops in the suburbs, particularly on the north side, so it pays to shop around a bit. A great source for secondhand bikes is the **Garda auction** held twice a year (March and September) at **Kevin St Garda Station** near St Stephen's Green in Dublin 2. Here, all of the unclaimed stolen bikes which the police have held for more than a year are auctioned off for half nothing to the public. For further details, contact the Kevin St station at 666 9400.

One good outlet for secondhand bikes on the north city is **Cycleways** at 185–6 Parnell St, Dublin 1 (directly opposite the Ilac Centre), tel 873 4748. They also sell new bikes, cycle clothing and equipment and operate a bike park.

For bike repairs, another useful address in town is **Square Wheels Cycleworks**, a funky looking place in Temple Lane South in Temple Bar, tel 086 081 4417. They also sell secondhand bikes and have a secure bike park with very reasonable rates.

LUAS The quickest and most comfortable public transport service in Dublin is the snazzy new Luas system. Named after the Irish word for 'rapid', this simple light rail system has two lines. The **Red line**, on the northside, runs parallel to the river from Connolly Station and Abbey St in the city centre via the National (Collins) Museum and then out as far as Tallaght. The **Green line**, on the southside, runs south from St Stephen's Green out to Sandyford. If you stay mostly in the centre, it's the Red line you will see the most of; it's the quickest and easiest way to get from the centre to the Four Courts and the National Museum at Collins Barracks.

Trams on both lines take an average of about 2 minutes to travel from one stop to the next. The frequency of trams varies from every 4 minutes (during rush hour on the Green line) to every 20 minutes (during late nights on the Red line). Every station has a constantly updated digital display indicating when the next tram is due to arrive.

The first Red line tram departs Tallaght at 05.30 on weekdays, 06.30 on Saturdays, and 07.00 on Sundays and bank holidays. The first Green line tram departs Sandyford at 05.30 on weekdays, 06.15 on Saturdays, and 06.45 on Sundays and bank holidays. The last trams of the night leave at 00.30 on weekdays, Saturdays and bank holidays on both lines, and at 23.30 on Sundays on both lines.

Although the Luas is the fastest and most comfortable mode of transport within Dublin city, it gets very crowded at peak hours, when commuters squeeze in. So if you have a lot of luggage, or a baby buggy, or a wheelchair, or a pressing need to sit down, it's better to avoid travelling on the Luas between 07.30 and 09.30 in the morning and between 17.00 and 18.30 in the evening. What's more, fares between 07.45 and 09.30 are 10 cent higher per ticket.

At other times, when the trams are less crowded, passengers on the Luas are in general very courteous and accommodating to disabled, elderly, pregnant, or overburdened passengers, and will even give up their seats to those they see as needing them more.

Tickets can be bought at the ticket machines at each station. If you plan to use the Luas a lot, you can save money by buying prepaid tickets at 26 official outlets, each one very near one of the stations. (For a full listing of outlets, see the Luas website at **www.luas.ie**.) The cheapest fares are got by the **Smartcard**. This has a minimum start-up fee of €10, which includes €4 of travel credit, which can be topped up at Luas ticket machines, either with cash or credit or debit cards. Travelling with a Smartcard is quick and neat—no queuing for tickets. You just tag on before getting on the tram by holding your card up to one of the Smartcard validators at the station. Tag off at your destination—if you forget you will be charged as if you had travelled to the end of the line. The validator's display will tell you how much credit you still have on your Smartcard. Your Smartcard will tag off automatically after 90 minutes.

Daily life

Daily life

Fares for an adult travelling on the Luas range from €1.25 to €2.30 for a single journey (€2.90 to €4.30 for a return), depending how far you want to go. Various Flexi and Combi tickets are available that offer unlimited travel on the Luas for one, seven, or 30 days; Combi tickets also apply to travel on the Dublin Bus network. See www.luas.ie for full details of tickets and fares.

We don't advise that you try to fare-dodge on the Luas; ticket inspections are frequent, and if you're caught without a valid ticket or a tagged-on Smartcard, you'll be subject to a 'standard fare' fine of €45. You can be issued this fine if you have no ticket; if your ticket applies to travel in a different direction; if your ticket applies to travel in a different zone; if your ticket requires ID and you don't have your ID; or if you are travelling with a Smartcard that is not tagged on.

Luas etiquette

Every public transport system has its own quirks, which require a particular code of behaviour on the part of those who use it, so that everyone's journey is as pleasant as possible. Here are some tips for those travelling on the Luas for the first time:

- Do not stand in front of the Smartcard validators (the chest-high blue things with little yellow caps at either end of the station). Travellers who use Smartcards will curse your name.
- Give up your seat if you see someone coming along who is elderly, disabled, pregnant, or burdened with heavy bags. (Or at least is more elderly, disabled, pregnant, or burdened with heavy bags than you are.)
- Use the spaces behind the seats to stow your bags, not the aisle.
- If you're sitting in an aisle seat with an empty window seat beside you and somebody comes along wanting to sit down, it's easier for them if you move into the window seat rather than shifting your legs sideways—unless you're getting off at the next stop.

Luas etiquette

- When the tram is crowded, if you're standing near the doors, make way for passengers who are getting off at the next stop; when the tram's arrived, it may sometimes be polite to step onto the platform temporarily to let them off (there's almost always time to get back on again, so you won't get stranded).

- If you have a portable music device, like a Walkman or iPod, don't leave the volume turned up all the way. The other passengers probably don't share your taste in music. The same goes for mobile phones; your conversation is probably fascinating to you, but that doesn't mean anyone else cares.

- The terminus at St Stephen's Green gets very crowded when trams arrive and disgorge their passengers, and the placement of railings to keep Luas passengers from overwhelming the pavements doesn't help. But you can help. Let passengers off the tram before you try to board; don't stand still on the platform and get in people's way while they're streaming off the tram; if you use a Smartcard, have it ready for the validator before you get off the tram; be patient and don't push or shove the other passengers.

- If you're waiting for a tram at St Stephen's Green and wondering whether the next tram goes to Sandyford, or which side of the platform to get your tram from, don't wonder: the answers are always, respectively, 'yes' and 'it doesn't matter', and the same applies to any other Luas terminus. Each Luas line goes on a straight journey from terminus to terminus, with no branches and no crossover of lines.

- If you're at a non-terminus station and wondering which is the right side to wait, check the signs (the display which tells passengers when the next tram is arriving also states which direction it's heading in) or ask another passenger.

BUS Buses are a great way to see the city, and with a little gentle eavesdropping you can learn something about real Dubs. All parts of Dublin and the surrounding suburbs have at least one Dublin Bus route going through them and many areas have several. Outer suburban routes extend to parts of Cos Kildare and Wicklow and to the very north of Co Dublin. When choosing where to stay or live in Dublin, try to find somewhere served by several bus routes.

Most bus stops carry the **timetables** for the main routes that stop there. The easiest way to check timetables is on www.dublinbus.ie: you can search either the route number or the area you want to go to. However, at the moment, only the time of departure from the terminus is listed, not the likely time of arrival at each stop, so the timetable is only a guide to the frequency of the service. Canny bus-users estimate the likely wait by the number of people waiting—a crowd probably means a bus hasn't been by in a while. There is a plan to have real-time GPS digital displays at bus stops, letting you know exactly how far away the next bus is, but this is several years off. In the meantime if you're standing at a stop with no idea when a bus will arrive, you can use **Bustxt** from any Irish mobile phone network—text 'BUS' followed by the route number (e.g. 'BUS 145') to 53503 and you will receive the times of the next three buses in each direction. But again, these are only the times of departure from the terminus. Texts cost 30c and network charges may apply as well.

Not all stops are listed on timetables, so if in doubt ask the driver or another waiting traveller. Once on the bus, if you're not sure where to get off, ask the driver to let you know when the bus is at your destination. The driver will be happy to oblige.

Scheduled bus services operate from 05.00 (depending on the route) throughout the day with the last bus leaving the city centre at 23.30 (but see Nitelink below). The frequency of services varies widely depending on the route and the time of day, but on average there's a 10-minute wait between buses, with fewer services off-peak and on Saturdays, and fewer again on Sundays. Bank holiday buses operate on Sunday times.

The **Xpresso** service, designed with commuters in mind, is an express version of the outer suburban routes which bypasses many of the intermediate stops. Xpresso buses are recognised by the 'X' added to their usual route number. Tickets paid for on the bus cost a little more than on scheduled services but weekly and monthly tickets (see below) can be used on them for no extra charge.

Nitelink is a Dublin Bus late night service. All Nitelink services have a number of intermediate pick-up points and an 'N' after the usual route number. There are a total of 24 routes serving the suburbs on Friday and Saturday nights, with a standard fare of €5, departing from College St, Westmoreland St or D'Olier St, all in Dublin 2. Services start at 00.00 and go on till 04.00; most services are every half hour though some are every hour or every two hours. If you live along one of the routes, this is a good, cheap alternative to a taxi.

Daily life

Queuing and using the buses like a Dubliner

It probably doesn't seem that there's a queue at the stop. This is because there isn't. There is a collection of individuals waiting for the same event.

- When the bus arrives, the first person to get on is not the first person who arrived at the stop but the person nearest to the door when it opens. Everyone else gets on in whatever order eventually establishes itself.
- Pushing and shoving is frowned on but moving in front of people isn't, unless the bus is so crowded that very few people will be let on.
- Smoking is not allowed anywhere (not that that stops some people).
- Sticking chewing-gum on the seats is not technically illegal but it damn well ought to be.
- Talking loudly is not polite unless your conversation is fascinating and unusual.
- And finally: say thank you to the driver as you get off. Most Dubliners do and the drivers like it.

Daily life

Tickets and fares Standard Dublin Bus fares for an adult range from €1.15 to €4.50 depending on how long your journey is; for journeys taking place in the city centre, there's a shopper's fare of 80c. Fares generally increase by 5–20c every January.

Unless you're using a prepaid ticket, you should have the exact fare in coins as bus drivers cannot give you change, nor do they accept notes. If you don't have exact change and you pay more than the fare, you'll be given an extra ticket which can be redeemed for cash at Dublin Bus's central office at 59 Upr O'Connell St, Dublin 1.

Dublin Bus has a wide range of daily, weekly, monthly, and annual 'Rambler', 'Short Hop', and 'Travelwide' tickets, which can save you a lot of money if you use the bus frequently (as well as saving the hassle of fumbling for change as you get on). Some of them are combination bus/Luas or bus/train tickets, which are particularly good value. If you have a student ticket, or a monthly or annual ticket, you will need special photo ID which can be obtained either at the Dublin Bus central office at 59 Upr O'Connell St, or by post (in which case you will need to insert your own photograph). If you use a monthly or annual ticket and are caught by an inspector without the corresponding photo ID, this will be counted as fare-dodging, and you will be fined.

Some prepaid tickets operate as smartcards, which work in a similar way to the Luas Smartcards (page 75), but rather than having a set amount of credit, they are valid for a set number of journeys or days. (Dublin Bus and the city's other public transport providers are working on creating an integrated ticketing system with a single smartcard to be used on all services, but they're not quite there yet.)

Prepaid tickets are available from most city centre newsagents (a Dublin Bus sign is displayed outside) as well as directly from Dublin Bus Head Office. For full details of the ticket offers and the locations of ticket agents, see the Dublin Bus website at www.dublinbus.ie.

Dublin Bus Head Office
59 Upr O'Connell St, Dublin 1, tel 873 4222, web www.dublinbus.ie
Open Mon 08.30–17.30, Tues–Fri 09.00–17.30, Sat 09.00–14.00, Sun 09.30–14.30
    Phone line open for information and customer service: Mon–Sat 08.30–18.00

TRAINS Trains in Dublin can be divided roughly into three groups: Intercity (see page 85), Suburban and DART.
    Dublin is the main hub of the national railway service, with trains radiating out to all parts of the country. Internally it has its own rapid-transit system in the DART (Dublin Area Rapid Transit), which has been a boon to commuters since its inception in 1984. The DART travels north–south through the Dublin suburbs, from Howth in the north part of the county to Greystones in the south.
    For visitors the journey up and down the DART line is a great way to see the glories of Dublin Bay, and the variety of the city from Roddy Doyle's Kilbarrack to Killiney—look out for the famous white Sorrento Terrace overlooking the bay, home to Bono and Neil Jordan.
    A single adult fare varies from about €1.35 to about €4.30, depending on how far you travel. As with Dublin Bus and the Luas, there are prepaid tickets available that will save you money if you are a frequent train traveller. For full details, plus complete timetables, see the Iarnród Éireann website: **www.irishrail.ie**

Daily life

TAXIS Taxis are not exactly shoestring transport, but if there are a few of you and you want to get home quickly in relative comfort, they are a very welcome option. Thanks to deregulation and a vast increase in the number of licence plates issued (about which the taxi drivers continue to kick up a fuss), it is now far easier to catch a cab.

Except maybe on a Friday or Saturday night, you shouldn't have trouble hailing a cab on the street in the city; they pass by fairly frequently and you know one is available if the sign on the roof is lit up. If you know exactly when you'll want to leave, it is still wise to book a cab in advance. For the numbers of several Dublin taxi companies, see page 18; you could also search in the Golden Pages directory—**www.goldenpages.ie**. Most taxis take a maximum of four people but there are vans available that carry up to seven at no extra charge per person.

Taxi ranks are located at various points around the city centre, including O'Connell St, Dublin 1 and College Green (outside Trinity College main entrance) and St Stephen's Green in Dublin 2. During the week, even late in the night, there will usually be a long line of cars waiting for your business. It is good manners to go to the taxi at the top of the queue but of course you can choose whichever cab you like.

If you are travelling up to a distance of 30 km any cab must take you, so don't entertain any rubbish from drivers saying they don't go out that far.

The following fares apply, both in Dublin and throughout the country. All fares should be calculated on the meter unless you've pre-booked a taxi in which case you may waive your right to this. There is no charge for any baggage. Carrying animals other than guide dogs is at the discretion of the driver but if he/she does allow it there is no charge.

Minimum fare: for distances of 1 km or 170 seconds, minimum fare of
€4.10 from 08.00 to 20.00; €4.45 from 20.00 to 08.00 or on Sundays
or bank holidays.

Tariff A: next 14 km or 40 mins, €1.03 per km or 36c per min from 08.00
to 20.00; €1.35 per km or 48c per min from 20.00 to 08.00 or on Sun/
bank hol.

Tariff B (comes into effect after Tariff A distance travelled): next 15 km or
42 mins, €1.35 per km or 48c per min from 08.00 to 20.00; €1.57 per
km or 55c per min from 20.00 to 08.00 or on Sun/bank hol.

Tariff C (all times, applies for whole journey): over 30km or 85 mins, €1.77
per km or 63c per min.

For each additional passenger, €1. Booking fee €2.

Complaints must be made in writing to the Taxi Regulator. You
can download the form on the website **www.taxiregulator.ie**,
or request one by phoning Lo-Call 1890 60 60 90. This is also
the number to call with any general information queries. The
Gardaí still deal with lost property. Call the Garda Carriage
Office on 666 9850.

   Hackney cabs offer a call-out service only: they do not
have roof signs and cannot be hailed on the street or hired at
a rank; they can't use the bus lanes whereas taxis can. They
can be booked for both the outgoing and return journey; they
don't operate on a meter so you must agree the fare in advance.
Hackneys are especially useful around peak times such as
Christmas—so many people are partying and not driving and so
booking a cab is often essential.

   Most drivers like it when you make light conversation, and of
course they will offer their own opinions, wanted or unwanted,
on every topic under the sun. Tipping is common enough but
not expected.

Getting out of Dublin

The normal Dublin bus and train services actually extend quite far into the countryside and tend to get cheaper per mile the further you go, so always check if your destination is served by either of them. If it isn't, you have lots of other options for leaving the fair city.

Dublin Bus operates tours to north and south county Dublin, to the outlying attractions of the hills and the coastline. (See page 225.)

In such a small country, it is never too expensive to get around anyway and provincial buses are amazingly good value. The provincial buses all depart from Busáras, the central bus station, and virtually every obscure corner of the island is covered by the **Bus Éireann** (Irish Bus) fleet (website at **www. buseireann.ie**). The main towns and cities are served by regular and frequent bus schedules, and even the furthest away backwaters generally get a good, if roundabout service. Tickets and information can be got at Busáras or from the Bus Éireann desk in the Dublin Tourism Centre. The information line for all provincial services is 836 6111 during normal business hours.

A number of **private bus companies** compete with Bus Éireann on the provincial routes. Most are based outside Dublin and have local operations as their main business, but many of them also run regular scheduled services to and from Dublin. They mostly operate from the quays around O'Connell Bridge and sometimes offer cheaper fares than the equivalent Bus Éireann routes. Information on these services is usually passed on by word of mouth as many of the companies are not in the Dublin area phonebook, so if you are planning a trip to anywhere outside Dublin, ask friends or your accommodation provider at the other end to advise on the best option. The Dublin Tourism Centre also keeps information on many of these services.

Getting a **train** is much more expensive than the buses in most cases and not much faster. The other disadvantage to travelling by train is that the network is not really all that extensive, and while it covers most city to city journeys, it goes no further. To see most of the west of Ireland, for example, you'll still have to transfer to a bus at some point. That said, trains are typically more comfortable and more pleasant, so if you're headed for a major town and you feel a bit flush, go for it.

There are two main stations for the Intercity trains: Heuston Station which serves Cork, Galway and Limerick, and Connolly Station which serves Sligo, Wexford, Rosslare and Belfast . These services tend to be quite good and relatively regular, although drastically reduced on Sundays.

For information on all **Iarnród Éireann (Irish Rail)** services, call into any station, call the Iarnród Éireann central office at 703 4070 (Monday to Friday, 09.00–17.00) or check their website at www.irishrail.ie.

Hitchhiking is not really practised in the Dublin area but becomes more acceptable further out into the country. In a lot of rural areas, it is common for local people to thumb a lift, but usually this will be from a fellow local who is known to them and therefore does not constitute any risk. In summer, backpackers hitchhiking are a regular sight in or going towards the more popular tourist destinations, and getting a lift is usually easy enough. However, crime takes place in rural Ireland like everywhere else. Unless you are travelling with someone else, hitching is never worth the risk. **Never hitchhike alone.**

Daily life

Daily life

Shoppping without a gold card

When it comes to shopping on a shoestring you need to be prepared to use energy and ingenuity. Follow our tips and you'll be well-dressed, well-fed, well-read and well . . . you get the picture.

Note: all opening times are only a guide as they tend to change seasonally, with later opening times in summer in particular—and some independent shops just open whenever they feel like it.

Clothes

A bit of rummaging may be required to find bargains but it's still worth the effort. The main shopping areas are O'Connell St, Henry St and Mary St in Dublin 1 and Grafton St and St Stephen's Green in Dublin 2. Even with the sales, however, if you don't venture beyond the plastic frontages of these streets, you'll be sorely disappointed. Be prepared to stalk the backstreets, tracking down low-price finery. You'll be well rewarded for your canny combing of charity shops, secondhand shops and the cheaper end of the high street market.

CHARITY SHOPS The end of the boom years means that even those with money may be slower to part with their designer gear than they were in the past. Still, charity shop chic is quite a common phenomenon and the rewards for those with a keen eye are enormous. Whole outfits can be put together for under €20 if you're lucky. This is not in the interests of recycling: the less you spend on each garment, the more goodies you'll have to squash into your wardrobe. Not only can you find fairly ordinary next-to-new clothes, but also brand names and luxury garments for a fraction of the original price.

Synonymous with charity shopping, **Oxfam**, with its main branches on Sth Great Georges St, Dublin 2 and in Rathmines, Dublin 6, commands a good selection of standard charity shop fare. Next to its George's St branch is **Enable Ireland**, which is a slightly more up-market version on the same theme. These shops suffer from their location near the student vultures of Trinity College, DIT and DBS and many of the best clothes are snapped up seconds after they arrive. For this reason, it is well worth heading north of the Liffey to the home of one of the best-stocked and least well-known charity shops in Dublin, **CASA** (the Caring and Sharing Association). Beside CASA on Capel St is **Gorta**, which also has a branch on neighbouring Liffey St, once again beside another charity shop—**Barnardos**.

A ten-minute walk up Parnell Sq and onto Dorset St will bring you to the **Mater Hospital Shop**, another well-organised and well-stocked charity shop which occasionally has designer outfits at reasonable prices and is frequently overlooked. Close by is **Mrs Quin's Charity Shop**, which also stocks shoes, books and a large selection of bric-a-brac, and operates under the slogan 'Don't Bin It Mrs Quin It'.

Barnardos web www.barnardos.ie/our_shops.html
     33 Lr Liffey St, Dublin 1, tel 873 0937
     Open Mon–Sat 09.30–17.30
     206 Lr Rathmines Rd, Dublin 6, tel 497 4717
     Open Mon–Fri 10.00–17.15, Sat 10.00–17.00
CASA web www.casa.ie/shops
     26 Capel St, Dublin 1, tel 872 8538
     Open Mon–Fri 10.00–17.30
     4 Mary St, Dublin 1, tel 874 8013
     Open Mon–Fri 10.00–17.00, Sat 09.30–17.00, Sun 12.00–17.00
     56 Marlborough St, Dublin 1, tel 873 5104
     Open Mon–Fri 10.00–17.30, Sat 10.00–17.00
     59 Upr Dorset St, Dublin 1, tel 894 3170
     Open Mon–Sat 10.00–17.30

Daily life

Enable Ireland web www.enableireland.ie
> 25 Capel St, Dublin 1, tel 873 3867
> 28 Lr Camden St, Dublin 2, tel 478 0647
> Unit 8, Sth Great George's St, Dublin 2, tel 478 2763
> *Open* Mon–Sat 09.30–17.30

Gorta web www.gorta.org/gorta-shops
> 136 Capel St, Dublin 1, tel 874 8044
> 32 Lr Liffey St, Dublin 1, tel 873 1155
> *Open* Mon–Sat 09.30–17.30

Mater Hospital Shop web www.materfoundation.ie/mater-charity-shop.html
> 17 Lr Dorset St, Dublin 1, tel 878 7801
> *Open* Mon–Sat 10.00–16.00

Mrs Quin's Charity Shop web www.mrsquins.ie
> 21 Lr Dorset St, Dublin 1, tel 087 139 4321
> *Open* Mon–Sat 09.30–16.45
> 9A Bridge St, Ringsend, Dublin 4, tel 087 139 4348
> *Open* Mon–Sat 10.00–17.00

Oxfam web www.oxfamireland.org/shops
> 2 Wicklow House, Sth Great George's St, Dublin 2, tel 478 0777
> *Open* Mon–Sat 10.00–18.00, Sun 14.00–18.00
> 204 Lr Rathmines Rd, Dublin 6, tel 496 4181
> *Open* Mon–Sat 10.00–17.30

SECONDHAND Dublin's secondhand/vintage shops can tend to be a little pricier than they should be, so bargain hunters would be well advised to retain a sense of healthy scepticism and to keep a keen eye out for plain rubbish. A garment's presence in a cool secondhand clothes shop does not guarantee its place in fashion history's roll of honour. As with charity shops, bear in mind that even if an item doesn't look particularly promising to begin with, a little imagination and careful customisation can often work wonders.

The Temple Bar area, despite attempts at gentrification, is still something of a bastion of secondhand chic. **Eager Beaver** has a huge range of relatively cheap and functional trousers, jackets, jumpers and shirts, often with a nod to the '60s and '70s, as well as a few more glamorous items, all spread over two floors on Crown Alley. They offer a ten per cent student discount, so bring your ID card if you have one. Just down the road on Upr Fownes St, you'll find **Flip**, which provides a more customised and well presented stock of trendy trousers, jackets, jeans, shirts and dresses, both new and secondhand (though they can tend to be a little bit more expensive). Also on Upr Fownes St is **Sé Sí** ('he/she' in Irish), with a mix of clothes and accessories and quirky little things, including handmade jewellery and vintage bags—most stuff is new but there is some secondhand.

At the time of writing, **Epoch Boutique**, formerly of Crow St, is in the process of opening a new premises. They stock vintage and great quality recycled clothes and are probably the only place in Dublin that do what they do, at least to such a standard. Have a look at their website to discover their new home—**www. epochboutique.ie**.

Outside of Temple Bar, but still in the same general Dublin 2 area, head up to the Market Arcade and you'll encounter **Wild-child**, possibly the best secondhand outlet in the city centre. Wildchild caters for both guys and girls and stocks a wide range of secondhand and new funky retro clothes and shoes. (There's a vintage furniture store, **Wildchild Originals**, worth checking out too—ask in store or visit **www.wildchildoriginals.com**.)

Across the road from the Market Arcade, on Castle Market, make sure you check out **Harlequin**. As its name suggests, it has a vibrant and eclectic mix. It has a great selection of men's shirts in the basement and the occasional bargain rail is always worth a look.

Finally, a fun place for the seriously fashion-conscious to visit is **The Loft Market** on Fridays, Saturdays and Sundays, on the top floor of the Powerscourt Centre, Dublin 2. They do art, vintage clothes, bags, jewellery and shoes—there's a collection of different designers all in the one space. The prices range from quite cheap to quite expensive and you can even meet designers and get stuff made to order.

Eager Beaver 17 Crown Alley, Temple Bar, Dublin 2, tel 677 3342
    Open Mon–Sat 10.00–18.00 (Thurs 19.30, Fri 19.00), Sun 12.00–18.00
Flip 4 Upr Fownes St, Temple Bar, Dublin 2, tel 671 4299
    Open Mon–Wed 10.00–18.00, Thurs 11.30–19.30, Fri 11.00–19.00, Sat 10.00–18.00, Sun 13.00–18.00
Harlequin 13 Castle Market, Dublin 2, tel 671 0202
    Open Mon–Fri 11.00–18.00 (Thurs 19.30), Sat 10.30–18.00, Sun 13.00–17.00
The Loft Market Top Floor, Powerscourt Centre, 59 Sth William St, Dublin 2, tel 671 7000, web www.myspace.com/theloftmarket
    Open Fri 12.00–18.00, Sat 11.00–18.00, Sun 12.00–18.00
Sé Sí 11 Upr Fownes St, Temple Bar, Dublin 2, tel 677 4779
    Open Mon–Wed 11.00–18.00, Thurs–Fri 11.00–18.30, Sat 11.00–19.00, Sun 12.00–18.00
Wildchild 24 Market Arcade, Dublin 2, tel 633 7748, web www.wildchild.ie
    Open Mon–Fri 11.00–19.00 (Thurs 20.00), Sat 10.00–18.00, Sun 13.00–18.00

Market Arcade Sth Great George's St, Dublin 2, web www.georgesstreetarcade.ie
Open Mon–Sat 09.00–18.30 (Thurs 20.00), Sun 10.00–18.00
The charming Market Arcade, connecting Sth Great George's St and Drury St, is an old Victorian covered market and is characterised by the wonderful mix of shops and a variety of stalls which run down its centre. It was built in the 1880s as part of the first purpose-built shopping centre in the city and is worth a visit by itself. There are secondhand shops aplenty here and you can also avail of the opportunity to get your nose pierced or have a cup of tea or a bagel in between ambling up and down through the market.

Daily life

NEW CLOTHES Dunnes Stores is still a reliable source of cheap, sensible, mass-produced basics such as T-shirts, underwear, etc. Join the rest of the Irish population at one of the many branches, the main ones in town being in St Stephen's Green Shopping Centre, Dublin 2 and in the Ilac Centre, Dublin 1. The store locator at www.dunnesstores.ie is actually very useful as it not only gives you the location, contact details and opening times of each branch, but also lets you know what's stocked in each store. **Guineys** on Nth Earl St, Dublin 1 is also worth a browse especially for jackets, jeans, bed linen, towels and various household items. There are two more branches along the same stretch on Talbot St.

Penneys, of O'Connell St and Mary St, Dublin 1, and many of the major shopping centres in the city, offers the best current trends and 'youth fashion' on the cheap, particularly if you're on the lookout for an exciting outfit at the last minute with limited financial resources. The next step up price-wise and highly recommended for the more fashion forward is **H&M** on Mary St, Dublin 1, Sth King St, Dublin 2 and in the Dundrum Town Centre. It provides a huge selection of funky, high fashion clothes as well as more conservative yet still stylish fashion and accessories for the slightly older generation. There's a branch of **Zara** beside H&M on Sth King St, as well as on Henry St and in the Dundrum Town Centre. **A-Wear** on Grafton St and Henry St is also notable for high fashion pieces and accessories for relatively cheap high street prices.

Upstairs in the St Stephen's Green Centre, a visit to the huge, strip-lit, **TK Maxx** for knockdown prices on designer shoes and clothes and sportswear and shoes is a must. Because of its 'bazaar' quality you can be fairly sure that your outfit will be original but this is not a shop for the light-hearted bargain hunter.

Daily life

The massive influx of the British chain stores has made shopping for low-cost women's clothing something of a giddy treat. **Dorothy Perkins** and **Debenhams** can be found in the Jervis Centre and on Henry St, Dublin 1, respectively. **Clerys Department Store** on O'Connell St, Dublin 1 houses **Miss Selfridge, Sisley, Topshop, Karen Millen, Bay Trading Co., Long Tall Sally, Wallis, Warehouse, Espris** and **Dolcis Shoes**—to name but a few—within its doors.

More tips for saving money

- Haggle. This won't cut much ice in the big chain stores unless the product in question is damaged, but smaller places are often quite willing to take a few euro off the price if you ask nicely.
- Always check out the more expensive clothes shops during sales and watch out for and always browse through sales racks in all shops. Real bargains live here.
- If you have a student card, use it.
- Walk the extra mile. Dublin is not an especially big city and the centre is highly concentrated. Unless you live in the outer suburbs or plan to visit them often, it shouldn't be necessary to use buses all the time. No matter what the papers say, it is generally very safe to walk the streets.
- Shop in out-of-the-way places. You will waste a lot of money if you spend it all on Grafton St. As a rule, side streets are cheaper than main streets, the northside is cheaper than the southside, and market stalls are cheaper than shops.
- Do research. Given student discounts and the cost of alcohol, it can be cheaper to spend your evening at the theatre than in a nightclub. Some clubs are free in before a certain time, some offer discounts to students, some wouldn't let students in if they had a million euro in their pockets. Consulting the relevant magazines and websites can save you a lot of hassle.

As you make your way up to Henry St a handful of relatively cheap and cheerful women's shops such as **Extrovert** belt out chart hits in competition with each other. It is worth elbowing your way through the mass of teenage girls to see what's on offer in these shops. However, the sizes are a wee bit on the small side and, unsurprisingly, they do lean towards the cheaper, nylon-based materials. Don't forget the various branches of **Oasis** which stock clothes, shoes, bags and accessories but tend to be a little overpriced.

DIY jewellery

If you've ever felt like making your own necklace, **The Crown Jewels**, Castle Market, Dublin 2, tel 671 3452 is the place to go. You'll find beads and pendants in all shapes and sizes, from three cents to €8 for a Venetian pendant, with the strings to hang them on.

....

River Island, downstairs in the Arnotts Department Store on Henry St, plus a flagship store on Grafton St and a new branch in the Ilac Centre, stocks an amazing range of high fashion clothes, shoes and accessories for both sexes (but it is a little pricey). Further down the street in the Jervis Centre, **Topshop** also sells similar up-to-the-minute high street fashions and accessories but it too can get a bit pricey (there is also a very well stocked flagship store on St Stephen's Green which is well worth a rummage particularly if you have a student card for the 10 per cent discount). **Arnotts** is home to a wide range of high fashion shops stocking clothes, shoes and accessories for men and women, though it does lean towards the designer end of things. There's also an Arnotts in the Jervis Centre, where Debenhams used to be—a little bit of the Irish getting their own back on the invading UK stores.

Of a different style, in Temple Bar, **Urban Outfitters** is worth your attention—a shop which seeks not only to clothe you but to accessorise an entire lifestyle. It seems to be targeted to appeal to the 20–30s quirky, intelligent urban-dweller demographic. It's fairly expensive but worth a browse. They have 10 per cent off for students.

If you feel like venturing beyond the city centre, it is well worth your time hopping on the Luas from St Stephen's Green and heading to the **Dundrum Town Centre**. Of late all of Dublin's other 'satellite' shopping centres—Liffey Valley, the Blanchardstown Centre, The Square in Tallaght—have been eclipsed by the sheer hipness (hipivity?) of Dundrum. If you get off the Luas and don't know where to go, simply follow the gaggles of teenage girls on their way to the mothership . . . Here you'll find a dazzling array of chain stores including **Marks & Spencer, Zara, BT2, Monsoon, French Connection, H&M, Pepe, Jane Norman** and **Bershka** amongst (many) others. There are also branches of **Harvey Nichols** and **House of Fraser** which are worth a browse.

Men haven't exactly got a huge amount of choice when it comes to Dublin's fashion mainstream. The range of shops is more limited and very few occupy the cheap and cheerful spot that certain chains do for the girls. **Penneys** and **Dunnes** have men's departments that as with the women will cover the basics like underwear, T-shirts and everyday tops and trousers. For a current, high fashion fix, **H&M** and its men's range cannot be beaten on price or style. **Topman**, part of Topshop in the Jervis Centre and with a stand-alone store on Grafton St, comes a close second, though as with the women's section it can be expensive (also like the women's branches it has a 10 per cent student discount). **Next** of Grafton St and the Jervis Centre are worth a look; they provide a non-sporty, casual yet stylish look. The Next chain also stocks reasonably priced women's clothes and has recently undergone a high fashion makeover in that regard. For the chaps, **Unique Discount Menswear** on Liffey St specialises in honest value and fairly trendy clothes that should be checked

*Grafton Street, Dublin's favourite place for shopping,
for busking or just hanging out.*

out. **Jack & Jones** on Trinity St provides a great selection of funky and laidback menswear with a nod to a skater-ish style.

For the man in search of a new suit, the Dundrum Town Centre is your one-stop shop. For something basic and functional, there's **Marks & Spencer**; a step up in price and style is provided by **Zara**; and if you want to go all out, head to **Massimo Dutti**, stocking an excellent range of fine Italian pieces—not cheap by any means but good value for the quality of what you're getting.

A-Wear web www.awear.com
    47 Henry St, Dublin 1, tel 872 4644
    Open Mon–Fri 09.30–18.30 (Thurs 21.00), Sat 09.30–19.00, Sun 11.00–18.00
    92 Grafton St, Dublin 2, tel 472 4960
    Open Mon–Tues 09.30–19.00, Wed–Fri 09.30–20.00 (Thurs 21.00), Sat 09.30–19.00, Sun 10.00–19.00
    —also in the Dundrum Town Centre, tel 299 1210, and other satellite shopping centres
Debenhams 54–62 Henry St, Dublin 1, tel 814 7200, web www.debenhams.com
    Open Mon–Sat 09.00–19.00 (Thurs 21.00, Fri 20.00), Sun 11.00–19.00
    —also in several satellite shopping centres
Dorothy Perkins Jervis Centre, Mary St, Dublin 1, tel 878 1016, web www.dorothyperkins.com
    Open Mon–Wed 09.00–18.30, Thurs 09.00–21.00, Fri–Sat 09.00–19.00, Sun 11.00–18.30
    —also in several satellite shopping centres
Dunnes Stores
    Ilac Centre, Henry St, Dublin 1, tel 873 0211
    Open Mon–Sat 09.00–18.30 (Thurs 20.00), Sun 12.00–18.30
    St Stephen's Green Centre, Dublin 2, tel 478 0188
    Open Mon–Tues 08.30–19.00, Wed 08.00–19.00, Thurs–Fri 08.30–20.00, Sat 08.30–19.00, Sun 11.00–19.00
Extrovert 21 Henry St, Dublin 1, tel 873 5186
    Open Mon–Sat 09.30–18.30 (Thurs 21.00), Sun 11.00–18.00

Daily life

Guineys web www.michaelguiney.com
    11–12 Nth Earl St, Dublin 1, tel 872 4377
    Open Mon–Sat 09.00–19.00 (Thurs 20.00), Sun 12.00–18.00
    83 Talbot St, Dublin 1, tel 874 7211
    93 Talbot St, Dublin 1, tel 878 6788
    Open Mon–Sat 09.00–18.00, Sun 13.00–17.00
H&M Ilac Centre, Henry St, Dublin 1, tel 299 1505, web www.hm.com/ie
    Open Mon–Wed 09.00–18.30, Thurs 09.00–21.00, Fri–Sat 09.00–19.00,
    Sun 11.00–18.30
    Sth King St, Dublin 2, tel 804 4729
    Open Mon–Sat 09.00–19.00 (Thurs 21.00), Sun 11.00–18.00
    —also in the Dundrum Town Centre, tel 299 1502, and other satellite
    shopping centres
Jack & Jones web www.jackjones.com
    Ilac Centre, Henry St, Dublin 1, tel 872 9902
    Open Open Mon–Wed 10.00–18.00, Thurs–Fri 10.00–19.00, Sat 09.30–
    19.00, Sun 13.00–17.00
    6–9 Trinity St, Dublin 2, tel 820 0198
    Open Mon–Fri 10.00–18.00 (Thurs 19.00), Sat 10.00–18.30, Sun 13.00–17.00
    —also in the Dundrum Town Centre, tel 216 9988, and other satellite
    shopping centres
Next web www.next.co.uk
    Jervis Centre, Mary St, Dublin 1, tel 878 1406
    Open Mon–Wed 09.00–18.30, Thurs 09.00–21.00, Fri–Sat 09.00–19.00,
    Sun 11.00–18.30
    67 Grafton St, Dublin 2, tel 679 3300,
    Open Mon–Fri 09.30–19.00 (Thurs 21.00), Sat 09.30–18.00, Sun 11.00–
    18.00
    —also in the Dundrum Town Centre, tel 205 1310, and other satellite
    shopping centres
Oasis web www.oasis-stores.com
    Clerys Dept Store, Dublin 1, tel 817 3280
    Open Mon–Sat 10.00–18.30 (Thurs 20.00), Sun 12.00–18.00
    3 St Stephen's Green, Dublin 2, tel 671 4477
    Open Mon–Sat 09.30–18.30 (Thurs 20.30), Sun 14.00–18.00
    41–43 Nassau St, Dublin 2, tel 677 4944
    Open Mon–Sat 09.30–18.30 (Thurs 20.30), Sun 14.00–18.00
    —also in the Dundrum Town Centre, tel 296 7371, and other satellite
    shopping centres

Daily life

Penneys web www.primark.co.uk
Lr O'Connell St, Dublin 1, tel 656 6666
Open Mon–Wed 08.30–20.00, Thurs 08.30–21.00, Fri–Sat 08.30–19.00,
Sun 11.00–19.00
47 Mary St, Dublin 1, tel 872 7788
Open Mon–Fri 09.00–20.00 (Thurs 21.00), Sat 08.30–19.00, Sun 11.00–19.00
—also in the Dundrum Town Centre, tel 215 7202, and other satellite shopping centres

River Island web www.riverisland.com
Arnotts Dept Store, Henry St, Dublin 1, tel 0818 333 073
Open Mon–Sat 10.00–18.30 (Thurs 22.00), Sun 12.00–18.00
Ilac Centre, Henry St, Dublin 1, tel 872 3991]
Open Mon–Wed 09.00–18.30, Thurs 09.00–21.00, Fri–Sat 09.00–19.00,
Sun 11.00–18.30
102–103 Grafton St, Dublin 2, tel 0818 333 074
Open Mon–Sat 09.00–19.00 (Thurs 21.00), Sun 11.00–18.00
—also in the Dundrum Town Centre, tel 296 8541, and other satellite shopping centres

TK Maxx Unit 103 St Stephen's Green Centre, tel 475 7080, web www.tkmaxx.com
Open Mon–Sat 09.00–19.00 (Thurs 21.00), Sun 11.00–18.00
—also in satellite shopping centres

Topman 41 Grafton St, Dublin 2, tel 679 3481, web www.topman.com
Open Mon–Sat 09.00–18.30 (Thurs 21.00), Sun 12.00–18.30
—also part of Topshop in the Jervis Centre, Mary St, Dublin 1, tel 878 0477, Clerys Department Store, Lr O'Connell St, Dublin 1, tel 878 6000, and in satellite shopping centres

Topshop web www.topshop.com
Clerys Dept Store 18–27 Lr O'Connell St, Dublin 1, tel 878 6000
Open Mon–Sat 10.00–18.30 (Thurs 21.00), Sun 12.00–18.00
Jervis Centre, Mary St, Dublin 1, tel 878 0477
Open Mon–Wed 09.00–18.30, Thurs 09.00–21.00, Fri–Sat 09.00–19.00,
Sun 11.00–18.30
6–7 St Stephen's Green, Dublin 2, tel 672 5009
Open Mon–Sat 09.30–19.00 (Thurs 22.00), Sun 11.30–18.00
—also in satellite shopping centres

Unique Discount Menswear
Ilac Centre, Henry St, Dublin 1, tel 872 8835
19 Upr Liffey St, Dublin 1, tel 873 3823
Open Mon–Sat 09.30–18.00 (Thurs 20.00), Sun 12.00–18.00
St Stephen's Green Centre, Dublin 2, tel 478 2600
Open Mon–Sat 09.30–18.00 (Thurs 20.00), Sun 11.00–18.00
Urban Outfitters 4 Cecilia St, Temple Bar, Dublin 2, tel 670 6202, web www.urbanoutfitters.com
Open Mon–Sat 10.00–19.00 (Thurs, Fri 20.00), Sun 12.00–18.00
—also in the Dundrum Town Centre, tel 296 2140
Zara
Henry St, Dublin 1, tel 804 5900
Open Mon–Sat 09.30–19.00 (Thurs 21.00, Fri 20.00), Sun 11.00–19.00
40–43 Sth King St, Dublin 2, tel 675 3420
Open Mon–Sat 10.00-19.00 (Thurs 21.00, Fri 20.00), Sun 11.00–19.00
—also in the Dundrum Town Centre, tel 291 0700, and other satellite shopping centres

Daily life

Shopping centre and department store opening hours

Arnotts Dept Store 12 Henry St, Dublin 1, tel 805 0400, web www.arnotts.ie
Open Mon–Sat 10.00–18.30 (Thurs 22.00), Sun 12.00–18.00
Clerys Dept Store 18–27 Lr O'Connell St, Dublin 1, tel 878 6000, web www.clerys.com
Open Mon–Sat 10.00–18.30 (Thurs 21.00), Sun 12.00–18.00
Dundrum Town Centre Dundrum, Dublin 16, tel 299 1700, web www.dundrum.ie
Open Mon–Fri 09.00–21.00, Sat 09.00–19.00, Sun 10.00–19.00
Ilac Centre Henry St, Dublin 1, tel 704 1460, web www.ilac.ie
Open Mon–Sat 09.00–18.30 (Thurs 21.00, Fri/Sat 19.00), Sun 11.00–18.30
Jervis Centre Mary St, Dublin 1, tel 878 1323, web www.jervis.ie
Open Mon–Wed 09.00–18.30, Thurs 09.00–21.00, Fri–Sat 09.00–19.00, Sun 11.00–18.30
St Stephen's Green Shopping Centre tel 478 0888, web www.stephensgreen.com
Open Mon–Sat 09.00–19.00 (Thurs 21.00), Sun 11.00–18.00

Shoes

The only way to survive shoe shopping in Dublin without spending frightening amounts of money is to join a religious order that forbids the wearing of shoes. Failing that, **Barratts** and **Korky's** of Grafton St and Henry St stock relatively low-cost, low-quality footwear that will at least be fashionable. **Penneys** (page 98) is also fantastic for cheap, high fashion yet low quality shoes for both men and women. **Schuh** on O'Connell St stocks a massive amount of quirky as well as fashionable shoes and trainers for men and women at fairly affordable prices. **Arnotts** (page 99) has an extensive selection of shoes at varying prices. It's also worth checking out **Zerep** of Liffey St and Grafton St, particularly for men's footwear. **Office** on Grafton St and Henry St is good for all varieties of shoes, men's as well as women's heels and boots; they have a 10 per cent student discount too. **Foot Locker**—with branches on Grafton St, O'Connell St and Henry St—houses a great selection of designer brand sneakers and trainers for men and women at a range of prices. A visit to the last vestiges of the Dublin street trade is also worthwhile—you may be able to pick up a bargain (see *Liberty Market*, page 101).

If you feel like seeing how the other half lives, take a stroll around **Brown Thomas** on Grafton St which stocks just about everything you will need when you finally get that solicitor's letter regarding the will of the unknown distant relative who's just bequeathed you their massive fortune.

Barratts web www.barratts.co.uk
   Ilac Centre, Henry St, Dublin 1, tel 872 8688
   Open Mon–Sat 09.00–18.00 (Thurs 21.00), Sun 12.00–18.00
   1 Henry St, Dublin 1, tel 872 4033
   Open Mon–Wed 09.30–18.30, Thurs 09.30–20.30, Fri 09.30–19.00, Sat 09.00–18.30, Sun 12.00–18.00

80 Grafton St, Dublin 2, tel 671 0644
Open Mon–Sat 09.00–19.00 (Thurs 21.00), Sun 12.00–18.30
—also in several satellite shopping centres

Foot Locker web www.footlocker.com
49 Lr O'Connell St, Dublin 1, tel 804 9400/804 9417
28 Henry St, Dublin 1, tel 872 1417/872 7293
11 Grafton St, Dublin 2, tel 677 8162/677 8212
44 Grafton St, Dublin 2, tel 677 8919/671 0021
Open Mon–Sat 10.00–18.30 (Thurs 20.00), Sun 12.00–18.00
—also in several satellite shopping centres

Korky's
Ilac Centre, Henry St, Dublin 1, tel 873 0722
Open Mon–Fri 09.30–18.30 (Thurs 21.00), Sat 09.00–19.00, Sun 12.00–18.30
4 GPO Buildings, Henry St, Dublin 1, tel 873 1359
47 Grafton St, Dublin 2, tel 670 7943
Open Mon–Sat 10.00–19.00 (Thurs 20.30/21.00), Sun 12.00–18.30

Liberty Market Meath St, Dublin 8, tel 280 8683
Open Thurs–Sat 10.30–16.00
The Liberty Market on Meath St, offers probably the most authentically 'shoestring' shopping experience in the city. The area requires a certain vigilance and there will be a lot of rubbish to sift through, but for emergencies or essentials you can get sorted out here at utterly dirt-cheap prices. Between the traders here and around Thomas St you can get everything from toilet paper, washing powder and deodorant to bric-a-brac, household items and new and secondhand shoes and clothes. Part of the reason everything is so cheap is that all the expenses are shared by a huge number of traders.

Office web www.office.co.uk
6 Henry St, Dublin 1, tel 874 8250
Open Mon–Fri 09.30–18.30 (Thurs 21.00), Sat 10.00–19.00, Sun 12.00–18.00
7 Grafton St, Dublin 2, tel 670 9960
Open Mon–Sat 10.00–19.00 (Thurs 21.00), Sun 12.00–18.00
—also in the Dundrum Town Centre, tel 296 3381, and Liffey Valley Shopping Centre, tel 620 3975

Daily life

Schuh web www.schuh.ie
> Jervis Centre, Dublin 1, tel 873 0433
> *Open* Mon–Fri 09.30–18.00 (Thurs 21.00), Sat 09.30–18.30, Sun 12.00–18.00
> 47–48 Lr O'Connell St, Dublin 1, tel 872 3234
> *Open* Mon–Wed 09.30–18.30, Thurs 10.00–20.30, Fri 09.30–19.00, Sat 09.30–18.00, Sun 12.00–18.00
> —also in the Dundrum Town Centre, tel 296 2932, and Liffey Valley Shopping Centre, tel 626 2199

Zerep
> 12 Upr Liffey St, Dublin 1, tel 874 6536
> 57 Grafton St, Dublin 2, tel 677 8320
> *Open* Mon–Sat 09.00–18.00 (Thurs 20.00), Sun 13.00–17.30

Books

Dubliners are rightly proud of their city's literary heritage; bronze plaques with quotations from *Ulysses* can be found embedded in the pavements, there are statues to James Joyce, W. B. Yeats, Patrick Kavanagh, and Oscar Wilde, and every April, the city's public libraries organise the 'One City, One Book' project, devised to encourage residents to read and talk about a great book together. So it's not surprising that Dublin has a wide range of bookshops, both general and specialist, new and secondhand.

For the best bargains, **Chapters** and **Read's** are the shops to go to for new books (though **Hodges Figgis** is worth checking out when there's a sale on), while the **Oxfam Bookshop** and **The Secret Book and Record Store** offer the most interesting and best value secondhand books; on top of these more conventional outlets, every Saturday and Sunday from 11.00 to 18.00 there is a book market in **Temple Bar Square** with four regular traders.

GENERAL NEW BOOKS

Books Upstairs 36 College Green, Dublin 2, tel 679 6687, web www. booksupstairs.com

Located as it is across the road from Trinity College, it's not surprising that Books Upstairs has a distinctly intellectual bent. It's an especially good place to go for play texts, or GLBT-interest books, or left-wing magazines such as *Red Pepper,* or books about Irish history.

Open Mon–Fri 10.00–19.00, Sat 10.00–18.00, Sun 14.00–18.00

Chapters Ivy Exchange, Parnell St, Dublin 1, tel 872 3297, web www. chapters.ie

With new books on the ground floor and secondhand books upstairs, Chapters has a vast and mostly very cheap stock. The range is a little eccentric, which means there are lots of little gems hidden among the less promising fare.

Open Mon–Sat 09.30–18.30 (Thurs 20.00) Sun 12.00–18.30

Dubray Books 36 Grafton St, Dublin 2, tel 677 5568, web www. dubraybooks.ie

Flagship branch of a home-grown bookshop chain. Dubray Books is smart and slick and centrally located, and its stock is pretty good. Easy to get to and easy to get round, it is the bookshop equivalent of pizza Margherita. It also sells very nice greeting cards and wrapping paper.

Open Mon–Sat 09.00–19.00 (Sat 18.00) Sun 11.00–18.00

Eason's 40 Lr O'Connell St, Dublin 1, tel 858 3800; Irish Life Centre, Talbot St, Dublin 1, tel 872 7010. web www.eason.ie

Also branches in Busáras and Heuston Station, and in the shopping centres in Dundrum, Liffey Valley, and Blanchardstown.

A nationwide chain. Eason's branches vary widely in size and quality, with the O'Connell St branch being the most impressive; as well as selling books, newspapers, magazines and stationery, it also has an outlet for Tower Records (see page 108) and a café. As a newsagent, also, its original vocation, it has no equal: the range of magazines and newspapers available in the O'Connell St branch is wider than any you'll find elsewhere.

Open O'Connell St Mon–Sat 08.30–18.45 (Thurs 20.45, Fri 19.45), Sun 12.00–17.45; Irish Life Centre Mon–Sat 09.00–18.45

Daily life

Hodges Figgis 56–58 Dawson St, Dublin 2, tel 677 7454
The oldest bookshop in Dublin, with a history reaching back to the
18th century. Hodges Figgis is a little bigger than its neighbour over
the road, and has the edge in the broadness of its stock. The heavily
discounted titles clustered in the basement and frequent sales cutting
prices on a wide range of titles are well worth a browse.
Open Mon 09.00–19.00, Tues 09.30–19.00, Wed–Fri 09.00–19.00 (Thurs
20.00), Sat 09.00–18.00, Sun 12.00–18.00

Hughes & Hughes St Stephen's Green Shopping Centre, Dublin 2, tel 478
3060, web www.hughesbooks.com
If you've come to Dublin from another country, Hughes & Hughes is
most likely the first bookshop you saw on your arrival, since they have
six branches at Dublin Airport (not to mention a branch apiece at Cork
Airport and Shannon Airport). The city centre branch is rather more
bookish than the cheerfully gaudy outlets in the airports; for the most
part the focus is on obvious bestsellers, but they harbour occasional
surprises that make it worth a look, and the staff recommendations are
better than such things usually are.
Open Mon–Sat 09.30–19.00 (Thurs 20.00), Sun 11.00–18.00

Read's Nassau St, Dublin 2, tel 679 6011
Read's started out as a newsagent that also sold books, and its
book section grew until it was the biggest part of the shop. This is a
bookshop of the 'pile 'em high and sell 'em cheap' school.
Open Mon–Fri 08.30–18.30 (Thurs 19.30), Sat 09.00–18.30, Sun 11.00–
18.00

Waterstone's Dawson St, Dublin 2 , tel 679 1415 & Jervis Centre, Mary St,
Dublin 1, tel 878 1311, web www.waterstones.com
Two branches of the UK chain; the Dawson St branch has a decent
café on its upper floor. Waterstone's has changed from the days when
it was an eccentric but exciting new presence in book retail, but
although it's become a little less adventurous now, and it has more
competitors than ever, it's still one of the best general booksellers
around.
Open Dawson St Mon–Fri 09.00–19.00 (Thurs 20.00), Sat 09.00–18.30,
Sun 11.00–18.00
Open Jervis Centre Mon–Sat 09.00–18.30 (Thurs 21.00, Fri 19.00), Sun
11.00–18.30

Cultivate Centre

If you're an eco-freak, a tree-hugging hippie, or just a concerned citizen wanting to reduce your impact on the environment, pay a visit to the Cultivate Centre on West Essex St. They have a venue that hosts the annual Convergence Sustainable Living Festival (as well as miscellaneous events throughout the year) and an enclosed city garden; their shop sells seeds and gardening tools, recycled stationery, organic food, environmentally-friendly cleaning supplies, books and magazines on sustainability, and miscellaneous whatnots to help you tread more lightly on the Earth. Just strolling the aisles can be an inspiring experience.

Cultivate Centre, 15–19 Essex St West, Dublin 2, tel 674 5773, www. sustainable.ie *Open* Mon–Sat 10.00–17.30

Daily life

SECONDHAND

Cathach Rare Books 10 Duke St, Dublin 2, tel 671 8676, web www. rarebooks.ie
Specialises in antiquarian books and early editions of Irish classics.
Open Mon–Sat 09.30–17.45

Oxfam Bookshop 23 Parliament St, Dublin 2, tel 670 7022, web www. oxfamireland.org/shops
The range, as you might expect, is variable, but the prices are generally as low as book prices get in Dublin, which is lower than you might think.
Open Mon–Fri 10.00–18.00, Sat 10.30–18.00, Sun 13.30–17.00

The Secret Book and Record Store 15A Wicklow St, Dublin 2, tel 679 7272
One of the most charming and delightful shops in Dublin, the Secret Book and Record Store is at the end of a long grey corridor lined with (at the time of writing) gig posters and *Calvin & Hobbes* cartoons, which gives you a sense of what kind of shop it is: quirky, individual, and full of surprises. *Does not accept credit or debit cards*.
Open Mon–Sat 11.00–18.30 (Thurs 19.30)

Stokes Books 19 Market Arcade, Sth Great George's St, Dublin 2, tel 671 3584
Don't be fooled by the neglected air of the shelves outside the main shop: Stokes' books are both interesting and well-cared-for, especially if you go inside rather than sticking with the stuff on general display.
Open Mon–Sat 11.00–18.00

The Winding Stair 40 Ormond Quay, Dublin 1, tel 872 6576, web www.
winding-stair.com
Selling both new and secondhand books, The Winding Stair
proudly declares itself to be the only shop in Dublin selling anarchist
books *po Polsku*, and plays vinyl jazz records on a 1970s-vintage player.
The shop is not very big, but it packs an astonishing diversity of
interesting stock into its small space, as well as several shed loads of
charm. There is a (non-shoestring) restaurant upstairs.
Open Tues–Sun 12.00–17.00

RELIGIOUS
Bestseller 41 Dawson St, Dublin 2, tel 677 3272
Run by the National Bible Society of Ireland. More Bibles than you
could shake a stick at, and a good selection of general Christian books.
Open Mon–Fri 09.15–17.00 Sat 10.00–16.00
Veritas 7–8 Lr Abbey St, Dublin 1, tel 878 8177, web www.veritas.ie
Run by the Irish Catholic Bishops' Conference, and so has fewer Bibles
and more rosaries than Bestseller; the Catholic emphasis narrows the
shop's range slightly, but they make up for it by having more titles
within that range.
Open Mon–Fri 09.00–18.00, Sat 09.00–17.30

FOREIGN LANGUAGE
Both **International Books**, (18 Sth Frederick St, Dublin 2, tel
679 9375, web www.internationalbooks.ie) and the **Modern
Languages Bookshop** (39 Westland Row, Dublin 2, tel 676 6103,
email modlang@indigo.ie) stock a small but respectable range
of books in languages other than English, as well as English-
language books for those learning English as a second language.
The focus is mostly on textbooks and dictionaries, but you can
also find, for instance, the Harry Potter books in Italian, or *Le
Petit Prince* in the original French. International Books also has
a range of foreign-language DVDs.

International Books Open Mon–Sat 09.00–17.30
Modern Languages Bookshop Open Mon–Fri 08.30–17.30, Sat 09.30–17.30

COMICS & GRAPHIC NOVELS
Crow Corner Crow St, Dublin 2, tel 087 273 8376

Selling exclusively secondhand comics, Crow Corner is the place to go for back issues of old comics (and some more recent ones), and for good value on a small range of graphic novels as well. All of their stock is in plastic bags, so be prepared to take a leap of faith now and then. *Does not accept credit or debit cards*.

Open Mon–Sat 12.00–18.00 (Thurs 19.00), Sun 15.00–18.00

Forbidden Planet 5–6 Crampton Quay, Dublin 2, tel 671 0688, web www.forbiddenplanet.com

Your one-stop shop for all things geek, Forbidden Planet is the premier comics retailer in Dublin, selling both single issues and graphic novels, with a decent selection of manga and a number of sidelines in animé DVDs, action figures, card games, and science fiction and fantasy novels.

Open Mon–Tues 10.00–18.00, Wed & Fri 10.00–19.00, Thurs 10.00–20.00, Sat 09.00–8.00, Sun 11.00–16.00

Sub City 2 Exchequer St, Dublin 2, tel 677 1902, web www.myspace.com/subcitycomics

Sub City are to Forbidden Planet as Avis are to Hertz: they're number two, so they try harder. In their small, slightly cramped premises, they can't compete on the sheer breadth of stock, so they make up for it with friendly and knowledgeable customer service and a range of titles that's high on quality even if it's not quite as wide as FP's.

Open Mon–Sat 09.30–18.30 (Thurs 20.00, Fri 19.30), Sun 12.00–18.00

MISCELLANEOUS
Connolly Books 43 East Essex St, Dublin 2, tel 670 8707, web www.communistpartyofireland.ie/cbooks

Specialists in old-school left-wing politics, and we do mean *old* school: if your library is in dire need of a *Complete Works of Lenin*, this is the place to go.

Open Tues–Sat 09.30–18.00

Murder Ink 15 Dawson St, Dublin 2, tel 677 7570

Specialists in crime fiction of all varieties, including imports from the USA.

Open Mon–Sat 10.00–17.30, Sun 12.00–17.00

Daily life

An Siopa Leabhair 6 Harcourt St, Dublin 2, tel 478 3814
  Run by Conradh na Gaeilge, this is the best bookshop in Ireland for
  Irish-language books.
  Open Mon–Fri 09.30–17.30 (closed 12.30–13.30) Sat 10.00–16.00 (closed
  13.30–14.00)

Music

Dublin has a small number of large music outlets, and a much
larger number of small ones—little hole-in-the-wall places with
stocklists an inch wide and a mile deep, record stores with more
atmosphere in a single cubic centimetre than every Virgin Mega-
store in the world combined. Don't be put off by the aggressive
individuality of the people behind the counter: as a rule, they're
friendly, knowledgeable and only too glad to answer your questions and help you find what you want.

BIG AND GENERAL

HMV 65 Grafton St, Dublin 2, tel 679 5334 & 18 Henry St, Dublin 1, tel 872
2095, web www.hmv.com
  General music stores, with DVDs, video games, MP3 players and
  music-related merchandise on offer as well.
  Open Grafton St Mon–Wed 08.30–19.30, Thurs 08.30–21.00, Fri 08.30–
  20.00, Sat 08.30–19.00, Sun 10.30–18.30
  Open Henry St Mon–Sat 09.00–19.00 (Thurs 20.30), Sun 11.30–18.00

Tower Records 6–8 Wicklow St, Dublin 2, tel 671 3250 (also second floor of
Eason's O'Connell St, Dublin 1), web www.towerrecords.ie
  Though originally connected to the defunct US chain, the Irish
  branch was bought out in 2003 and is now wholly Irish-owned. It
  continues to sell the broadest range of popular music you're likely
  to find in a brick-and-mortar music shop, as well as an impressive
  selection of DVDs, and the inevitable vaguely music-relevant
  magazines, T-shirts and books. In general their prices are on the high
  side, but they have frequent sales and special offers that make the
  stock worth a look.
  Open Mon–Sat 09.00–21.00 Sun 11.30–19.30pm

Daily life

SMALL AND SPECIAL

Beat Finder Records 4 Upr Fownes St, Dublin 2, tel 672 9355, web www. beatfinderrecords.com

Upstairs from a clothing store. Vinyl and CDs; specialists in dance music.

Open Mon–Sat 10.00–18.00 (Thurs 19.00)

Borderline Music Temple Bar, Dublin 2, tel 679 9097

Mostly rock and punk; even if you don't actually buy anything, take a look at it after it's closed for the eye-catching mural on the shutter.

Open Mon–Sat 10.00–18.00, Sun 13.00–18.00

Claddagh Records 2 Cecelia St, Dublin 2, tel 677 0262, web www. claddaghrecords.com

Folk and traditional music, attached to the record label of the same name; as well as having a very good selection in their physical shop, they also do mail order via their website.

Open Mon & Fri 11.30–17.30, Tues–Thurs 10.30–17.30, Sat 11.00–18.00

Freebird Records 15A Wicklow St, Dublin 2, tel 707 9955 & 5 Cope St, Temple Bar, Dublin 2, tel 675 9856

The Wicklow St branch is the 'Record' part of the Secret Book and Record Store. Lots of vinyl and a good selection of country, dance, hip-hop, folk, jazz, reggae, and metal.

Open Wicklow St Mon–Sat 11.00–18.00 (Thurs 19.30)

Open Cope St Mon–Sat 10.30–18.30 (Thurs 19.30)

Road Records 16B Fade St, Dublin 2 tel 6717340, web www.roadrecs.com

Small shop focused on indie rock; also sells gig tickets.

Open Mon–Sat 10.00–18.00 (Thurs 19.00) Sun 14.00–18.00

Sentinel Records 4 Upr Fownes St, Dublin 2, tel 635 1589, web www. sentinelrecords.com

Downstairs from the same clothing store that Beat Finder is upstairs from; specialists in metal, attached to the Irish record label of the same name.

Open Mon–Fri 10.00–18.30 (Thurs 19.00), Sat 10.00–18.00

Spindizzy Records Market Arcade, Dublin 2, tel 671 1711, web www. myspace.com/spindizzyrecords

To judge from the labels on the secondhand CDs, this seems to be one of the places where Dublin's DJs offload their free samples. Lots of interesting and unusual stuff to be found here.

Open Mon–Sat 10.00–18.30 (Thurs 20.00), Sun 12.00–18.00

Daily life

Daily life

The body beautiful

Being on a budget doesn't have to mean forgoing the little luxuries in life. Getting your hair cut or coloured, or having a facial or massage or tattoo, is still affordable if you're prepared to be looked after by a student and aren't in too much of a hurry.

BEAUTY

Dublin Institute of Beauty/Aspens Beauty Clinic 83 Lr Camden St, Dublin 2, tel 475 1940/475 1079, web www.dibdublin.com / www. aspensireland.com

Basic treatments (massage, waxing, facial, manicure and pedicure) done by students for 40 per cent less. However, students may not be available at all times of the year so ring ahead for details. Appointments not necessary but there may be a wait. The clinic also has a 10 per cent discount on all treatments for students and seniors on Monday and Tuesday.

Open Mon–Fri 09.00–20.00, Sat 09.00–18.30

Galligan Beauty College 109 Grafton St, Dublin 2, tel 670 3933, web www. galligangroup.com

The Galligan Group have both a student salon and pro salon here, with massive discounts on a full range of treatments in the former. A manicure in the student salon, for example, will set you back €17, whereas in the professional salon you'll pay €45. Appointments necessary. Ring for details.

Open Mon–Fri 09.30–17.00

HAIR You can have your hair cut and blow-dried by a student at the **Peter Mark Academy** or their **Training Centre** for €15. A tint and a cut costs €25. Easi-mèche highlights are €50 for a half head and €60 for a full head. A perm costs €15. The boys can have their cut for €8. There are other good offers too—call for details or an appointment. Not surprisingly, these sessions are extremely popular.

Toni&Guy offer a similar service in their Academy on Sth William St, where it's €27 for a cut and €40–60 for highlights.

Appointments are necessary. All student sessions are fully supervised and the models (that's you!) are fully consulted about the styles used.

Peter Mark Academy Level 3, St Stephen's Green Centre, Dublin 2, tel 475
  1126, web www.petermark.ie
  Wheelchair access.
  Open Mon–Thurs 09.00–18.00
Peter Mark Training Centre 18 Nth Earl St, Dublin 1, tel 874 3495
  Open Mon–Thurs 09.00–20.00
Toni&Guy Academy 26 Sth William St, Dublin 2, tel 670 8749, web www.
  toniandguy.ie
  Open Mon–Fri 09.00–17.30

Aside from the training college route, it is generally cheaper to have haircuts and beauty treatments in the suburbs than in the city centre, so if you live or work outside Dublin 1, 2 or 4, always look locally first for the best deals and you might find an enormous difference in price.

For specialist **African** hair styling, dreadlocks or extensions, the **Charity Hair Studio** in the Moore St Mall, Dublin 1, tel 086 873 8299, has skilled staff and always seems to be busy. There is also a hair accessories store here. Alternatively you could ask for an African styling recommendation in your local salon or at any reputable high street hairdressers.

For sharp new men's looks or a traditionally masculine beauty treat which won't leave you feeling hung out to dry, there is great value to be had in Dublin's many **barber shops**. Some of the best deals in central locations:

Just Cuts 3 Bachelor's Walk, Dublin 1, tel 872 8401, web www.justcuts.ie
  A very reasonably priced establishment with friendly staff. Dry cuts €7
  Monday to Wednesday. A wash and a cut is only €11 and you can have a
  hot towel shave for €20. Wheelchair access.
  Open Mon–Sat 09.00–19.00 (Thurs 19.30), Sun 12.00–18.00

Daily life

—Other branches with the same prices at 2 Cathal Brugha St, Dublin 1, tel 874 0108; 3 Nth Earl St, Dublin 1, tel 874 0108; and 197–199 Rathmines Rd, Dublin 6, tel 496 9600

Regent Barbers 2 Lr Fownes St, Dublin 2, tel 677 8719

Even in Temple Bar, you can get a basic hair cut for an OK price. Regent Barbers also has quite a nice traditional feel to it. €14 for a cut, or €17 including a wash. A hot towel shave and a head massage costs €22. Wheelchair access.

Open Mon–Sat 09.00–18.00

Sam's Barbers 5 Dame Court, Dublin 2, tel 679 5788, web www. samsbarbers.ie

Seniors and students can get an €8 cut Monday to Friday before 12.00 (your hair must not have gel or anything else in it, though). A cut with an optional wash generally costs €15 and you can get a clipper shave for €11. A beard trim is free if it's part of a cut or €4 if you want it on its own. Wheelchair access.

Open Mon–Sat 09.30–18.00 (Thurs 19.30)

Sam's Barbers 28 Lr Ormond Quay, Dublin 1, tel 874 7500 / 086 196 2525 (text for appointments)

More jazzed up than the Dame Court branch, with a full range of manly treatments. A wash, cut, style and Chinese head massage is €25 including free tea/coffee/juice. A traditional 30-minute hot towel shave is €30 (or €15 for an Express Shave), while the 45-minute, €40 'Ormond Hot Towel Steam Shave' incorporates a full upper torso massage. They also do teeth-whitening at €45 a session. Wheelchair access.

Open Mon–Fri 10.00–19.00 (Thurs 20.00), Sat 09.00–18.00

TATTOOS AND PIERCINGS Safe tattoo/piercing work and 'on a shoestring' don't exactly go together. Having said that, it is possible to get a great tattoo or piercing at reasonable value with a little research beforehand. As it happens Dublin does have a number of very good establishments. The typical rate is €50–80 euro for the first hour and €100 for each subsequent hour.

Body Station/Just Jewellery 15–16 Market Arcade, Sth Great George's St, Dublin 2, tel 707 9999

Open Mon–Sun 11.00–18.30 Wheelchair access.

Colour Works Tattoo Studio 4 Upr Fownes St, Temple Bar, Dublin 2, tel 677 9555
Open Mon–Sat 11.00–18.00, Sun 13.00–18.00; late appointments by booking
Inkwell Tattoo 41 Arran Quay, Dublin 7, tel 878 8118, web www. inkwelltattoo.net
Open Mon–Sat 11.00–19.00 (Wed–Thurs 20.30), Sun 12.00–18.00
Wheelchair access.
Getting there Luas Red Line from Connolly Station to Smithfield (the studio is right beside the stop).
Miss Fantasia 25 Sth William St, Dublin 2, tel 671 3734, web www. missfantasia.ie
Open Mon–Sat 10.00–19.00 (Thurs–Fri 20.00), Sun 14.00–19.00
Wheelchair access.
Stigmata-Tau Town Centre Mall, Main St, Swords, Co Dublin, tel 813 7091, web www.stigmata-tau.com
Open Tues–Sat 11.00–18.00 (Thurs–Fri 20.00), Sun 12.00–16.00, closed Mon
Getting there Dublin Bus nos 33, 41, 41B, 41C from Lr Abbey St to Swords

Daily life

Jonathan Swift contrasts his ideal city with the Dublin of the early 18th century

'Here were no gibers, censurers, backbiters, pickpockets, highwaymen, housebreakers, attorneys, bawds, buffoons, gamesters, politicians, wits, spleneticks, tedious talkers, controversialists, ravishers, murderers, robbers, virtuosos; no leaders or followers of party or faction; no encouragers to vice by seduction or example; no dungeons, axes, gibbets, whipping posts or pillories; no cheating shopkeepers or mechanics; no pride, vanity or affectation; no fops, bullies, drunkards, strolling whores or poxes; no ranting, lewd, expensive wives; no stupid, proud pedants; no importunate, overbearing, quarrelsome, noisy, roaring, empty, conceited companions; no scoundrels raised from the dust upon the merit of their vices or nobility thrown into it on account of their vices; no lords, fiddlers, judges or dancing-masters.'

Swift *Gulliver's Travels* 1726 part 4 chapter X

On the town

Dublin is a grand place to be entertained. For a start, the week-end starts on Thursday (some would say Wednesday), which means a whole extra night when the city lets rip. To find out what's on look up www.entertainment.ie for thorough and consistently updated information, or grab a paper—The Irish Times' entertainment supplement, 'The Ticket', comes out on Friday.

To get entertained on a budget you need to be a pioneering punter, thinking outside the box. Want to see a movie? Go suburban. A play? Go experimental. A comedy act? Get in free to Dáil Éireann.

At least, you will need something to get you out of the pub every now and then . . .

How to find a pub in Dublin

Dublin's life can be measured by its pubs. There are some eight hundred in the city and, as James Joyce's Leopold Bloom famously said, it would be a fine puzzle to cross Dublin without passing at least one. So, it's not hard to find a pub in Dublin.

Finding the right pub, however, the one that best fits with your own taste and sensibility, or the mood you're in at any given moment, can be a challenge.

Old, quiet pubs still abound, the old pubs where much that was funny or sad or historic in Dublin life has taken place. The literary pubs, the journalists' pubs and the barristers' bars can still be found. However, discrimination is required: gone are the days when it was possible to pop into pretty much any pub and have a quiet pint.

How to drink

Mostly pubs sell beer—stout, lager and ale—and spirits, though the choice of wines is a lot better now than it was a few years ago (and in some places can actually be quite good). Pints are the usual quantity for beer, and a half pint is referred to as a 'glass'. However, be warned: just because it is half the quantity does not mean it is half the price. Beer is also available in 330ml bottles, but you will often pay more for a bottle than you will for a pint (568ml).

Stout—Guinness, Murphy's, Beamish—is the cheapest drink. It is a much more delicately balanced concoction than your typical lager. The quality and taste of a pint can vary considerably from establishment to establishment, with cognoscenti seeking pubs serving the best smooth, creamy pint. The differences can be due to any number of factors: how far the stout has to travel from keg to tap, how clean the pipes are, how gently the barman pulls . . .

If you order stout, don't worry if it looks like you're being ignored after you've ordered. The recommended way to serve stout is to pour about two-thirds of the glass, then wait two minutes or more to let it settle, before filling up. Take a seat while you wait and keep an eye on the bar for when your pint is ready.

The rounds system

You order drinks at the bar and pay for them when you get them (some pubs, however, particularly suburban ones, have table service). Often a group of people buy drinks in 'rounds', where each person in turn buys the drinks for everyone else. This convivial custom was of course the favourite target for temperance campaigners. If you get caught up in this, you have three choices: either make your excuses and leave after the first drink

On the town

(which is OK); team up with one other person and take turns buying each other's drinks; or be prepared to stump up when your turn comes. Failure to buy a round is a breach of etiquette and is not forgotten. As usual in Ireland delicate exceptions to the rule abound. Sometimes someone will offer to buy you a drink and expect nothing in return, and in fact get annoyed if you become obsessed with returning every pint they've bought you. The key is to know the difference between the situations.

Talking to strangers

A common misconception about pubs in Dublin is that people will automatically talk to you—this is not true, particularly if you're on your own. In the early evening after-work individuals drop in to their favourite watering hole for a quiet wind-down over the paper and a pint. At this time there will be plenty of seating—later in the evening, especially on Friday or Saturday night, there won't be a spare seat in the house. Dubliners are well used to standing quite happily all night long.

If you're with a group, your chances of striking up conversations with strangers are dramatically increased. If you're lucky, you may be invited to a house party, a regular post-pub activity in Dublin. House parties are basically spur-of-the-moment affairs, soberly decided upon in the wee hours by someone who doesn't own the house you're heading to. It's a great way of meeting people in a new city. Make sure you bring 'take out' (cans or bottles from behind the bar), but for safety's sake don't think of going alone—without another member of your group.

For male readers

Do not be surprised, when using the toilet, if your neigbour enters into conversation. he is merely being friendly, and intends no ulterior motive. A favourite story tells of the rock star Bono going to the urinal before a performance. A stranger comes in and expeditiously relieves himself. Having made no previous signs that he recognises Bono, who is still standing there quite unproductively, the stranger cheerfully comments: 'Stage fright, is it?'

Peter Costello *Dublin's Literary Pubs*

On the town

Smoking

Smoking is banned in all indoor workplaces in Ireland—and this includes pubs. If you want to light up, you'll have to go outside. Initially greeted with some grumbling, the smoking ban has become a well-accepted and even enjoyed aspect of Dublin drinking. (The fact that Ireland pioneered this practice and it was taken up across the world allows a quiet proprietorial pride.) Many pubs have spruced up their beer gardens so that they are now quite pleasant places to both drink and have a smoke and a chat. The ban has also given rise to such phenomena as smirting—smoking and flirting: meeting like-minded people of the appropriate sex out the back of the pub while filling your lungs with tobacco.

Lunch

Most pubs will serve at least something at lunchtime, and occasionally something rather good. There is little to beat a simple plate of smoked salmon and brown bread washed down with a pint of Guinness. The popular pubs tend to fill up quickly at lunchtime, so get your orders in before the office rush at one o'clock. Don't expect anything much in the evenings or weekends.

Events

Lots of bars have various events going on throughout the week, from live music of all kinds and stand-up comedy in the more traditional watering holes, to more live music, themed nights and promotions in the younger bars. You'll usually see upcoming entertainment advertised outside if it's not important enough to be mentioned in the various listings magazines/websites. For more on events in pubs see the *Gigs and bands*, *Jazz*, *Traditional music* and *Comedy* sections.

Children

It is a serious offence, punishable by a €4,000 fine to buy alcoholic drink for anyone under 18. Most Dublin pubs, and especially those serving food, will welcome children within their walls until about 19.00. This means that families can happily gather 'to watch the match', and this is a common sight especially in the country. Some, however, such as The Long Hall on George's St, do not allow kids in at all. By law whippersnappers (i.e. under 14 years old) must be accompanied and must definitely be out of the pub by 21.00.

Prices

The price of a pint of Guinness varies from pub to pub and is a great indicator of the general level of prices there. The law obliges the publican to list prices in a visible place, so when you see that the Mint, for instance, charges €5.80 for a pint of Guinness you can bet that they are not giving anything away free. Elsewhere in the city centre you will generally pay €4.40–€5 for a pint. Posher districts will always be more expensive than less prosperous areas, but you can expect the prices in any one area to be more or less the same.

Some late bars raise their prices after 23.00 (or even before), particularly at the weekend—we've indicated below where this happens.

Opening (and more crucially, closing) hours

Most Dublin pubs serve drink Mon–Thurs 10.30–23.30, Fri–Sat 10.30–00.30, Sun 12.00–23.00. On the eve of public holidays opening is extended to 00.30. These times don't include half an hour's 'drinking up time' at the end of the night. 'Last orders' is usually marked by frantic multiple pint buying, as drinkers scramble to neck that last slew of booze before heading out into the street.

Many pubs now operate late licences—serving till up to 02.30 around the weekend, 01.00 Sundays and nightclubs are currently bound by the same law, so will close at roughly the same time. Precise closing times remain a contentious issue at the time of publishing, so don't be surprised to find your establishment operating ever so slightly outside the bounds of the law around closing time. Just remember to thank them.

Pubs can't sell you cans or bottles for 'take out' after 22.00, so if you are planning on bringing booze home or to a party, remember to get it early. This applies to supermarket alcohol sales also.

On the town

Wheelchair access

The best advice is to phone ahead and check accessibility with the individual establishment. Most pubs in the city have level access, but at peak times it may be impossible for anyone larger than a leprechaun to get inside, never mind a wheelchair user. Newer pubs and upgraded places should be decently accessible and have accessible toilets; older places not so much, particularly when it comes to toilet facilities.

Traditional pubs

The Brazen Head 20 Lr Bridge St, Dublin 8, tel 677 9549, web www. brazenhead.com

pint of Guinness €4.80

Tucked away west along the quays, this pub claims to be the oldest in Ireland. Bridge St is so called because for hundreds of years it led to the only bridge over the Liffey. The owners assert, and nobody seems interested in challenging them, that there has been an inn or a pub here since before the Norman invasion of 1171. Obviously none of that survives, but a part of the building does look extremely old indeed: low ceilings, dark small bar room; take out the TV and you could be in a medieval world. Well, not really, actually: where others have survived, the Brazen Heads who run the pub have not been as assiduous in keeping out the marches of modernisation. This isn't always without interest, though—one area is covered floor to ceiling in dollar bills signed by visiting celebrities and passers-through.

Open Sun–Thurs 10.30–00.00, Fri–Sat 10.30–02.30

Doheny & Nesbitt's 5 Lr Baggot St, Dublin 2, tel 676 2945

pint of Guinness €4.80

From the northeast corner of St Stephen's Green runs Baggot St, and at this end of the street you will find a handful of highly traditional pubs, the finest of which is Doheny & Nesbitt's. It is a favourite with politicians, journalists and civil servants from the nearby Department of Finance. The narrow bar and the back room are decked out in traditional wooden furnishings, and even early in the week you'll have to weave your way through the pint-bearing masses. The rivalry between here and nearby **O'Donoghue's** is long-standing, with O'Donoghue's the place to go for a great session (see page 161)

(see page 161)

On the town

and D&N's the spot for 'serious drinkers' (hence the politicians and journalists). In look, style and atmosphere this is a true Dublin classic, complete with the traditional hide-away side rooms originally for women drinkers.

Open Mon–Thurs 10.30–23.30, Fri–Sat 10.30–00.30, Sun 10.30–23.00

Kavanagh's ('The Gravediggers') Prospect Square, Glasnevin, Dublin 9, tel 830 7978

pint of Guinness €4.25

Tucked away in a residential close behind Glasnevin Cemetery, Kavanagh's is a real hideaway. Walk into the dark of the bar, through a set of swinging cowboy-style doors, and you enter the perfect place to put everything on hold for a pint of contemplation. The interior is decorated in plain, unassuming wooden slats and the furniture is bare and functional. This is very much a local pub, filled with people from the surrounding area, lending it a friendly, familiar atmosphere.

The pub's nickname, The Gravediggers, comes from the fact that this was where the gravediggers at Glasnevin Cemetery would refresh themselves—poking the blade of a spade through the window to have it returned laden with pints of stout.

The bar, for the moment at least, remains 'original and unspoilt', the ideal place for a tasty pint or a game of rings if you're up for it. While Kavanagh's is a little out of the way, it is the perfect spot if you are on a trip to the nearby Botanic Gardens or Glasnevin Cemetery (see *Green and Silent*, page 184), or if you need to soothe a hoarse throat after an afternoon of Gaelic games at Croke Park, which is relatively nearby.

Open Mon–Thurs 10.30–23.30, Fri–Sat 10.30–00.00, Sun 10.30–23.00

Kehoe's 9 Sth Anne St, Dublin 2, tel 677 8312

pint of Guinness €4.70

Kehoe's doesn't quite know what to think of itself. The front main bar is a traditional old pub, with a bar, a corridor, a snug and not much else. At the back is what the generous would call a lounge, but which is little more than a fat corridor with tables. Upstairs was renovated some years ago to become the most spacious part of the pub, but the decorators did not change the front room much, so that it still resembles granny's sitting room.

With all its confusing personalities, Kehoe's remains a favourite with students and young professionals tired of sleek modern bars in the heart of the shopping district.

Open Mon–Thurs 10.30–23.30, Fri–Sat 10.30–00.30, Sun 10.30–23.00

On the town

The Long Hall 51 Sth Great George's St, Dublin 2, tel 475 1590
  pint of Guinness €4.50
  The Long Hall, just on the curve of George's St whose shape was
  originally dictated by the course of the now undergrounded Poddle
  River, is a grandly opulent pub. The mahogany interior, the rich red
  walls, the real chandeliers, the colonial portraits and old copper jugs
  and pots . . . This is a classic straight from Victorian times, and a Dublin
  institution.
  Open Mon–Wed 16.00–23.30, Thurs 13.00–23.30, Fri–Sat 13.00–00.30, Sun
  15.00–23.00

McNeill's 140 Capel St, Dublin 1, tel 874 7679
  pint of Guinness €4.60
  McNeill's recently reopened as a pub, though the music shop upstairs
  has been around a long time. The traditional instruments in the
  window and the warm green exterior seem to invite you in, and you'll
  be very glad if you accept. 'New' though it may be, McNeill's is far from
  new in style: this is a classically traditional pub, a back-to-basics gem.
  And with its musical pedigree, you'll find real trad sessions too.
  Open Mon–Thurs 10.30–23.30, Fri–Sat 10.30–00.30, Sun 12.30–23.00

Mulligan's 8 Poolbeg St, Dublin 2, tel 677 5582
  pint of Guinness €4.60
  Mulligan's serves the best pint of Guinness in the city. This is, of
  course, a totally subjective judgement and a hotly debated point, but
  the Guinness at Mulligan's is our winner: the white, white head; the
  ultra-sharp line between white and black; the cool, crisp taste; the full
  flavour . . . A pint at Mulligan's is Guinness as it should be, served in
  congenial surroundings.
      However, Mulligan's has other charms—the bar is a delightful
  low-ceilinged den of old-style authenticity, with a famous back room
  for private plotting.
  Open Mon–Thurs 10.30–23.30, Fri–Sat 10.30–00.30, Sun 12.30–23.00

The Palace Bar 21 Fleet St, Dublin 2, tel 671 7388
  pint of Guinness €4.60
  Empty it is tatty and a little bedraggled looking, but like Dublin's best
  pubs the Palace comes to life when it fills up with the chattering,
  nattering punters that cram into this small city centre bar at night.
  With mini-booths along the bar to allow little groups to gather there,
  making it impossible to order a drink, and a little parlour room at the
  back for the more sedate groups, the Palace is charm itself, a good

traditional pub for a good traditional pint of black. If Shane McGowan is in town, you might see him here.

Open Mon–Wed 10.30–23.30, Thurs–Sat 10.30–00.30, Sun 12.30–23.00

Sackville Lounge 16 Sackville Place, Dublin 1

pint of Guinness €4.40

The Sackville is a great place to end up, though as it's small, cosy and often busy you may not get a seat. There is one long, wine leather couch with knee-height tables placed along it, and a TV at either end of the pub for watching the racing. If there's horse racing on it'll be on here—and with a bookies next door you're set up for the afternoon.

Open Mon–Thurs 10.30–23.30, Fri–Sat 10.30–00.30, Sun 12.30–23.00

The Stag's Head 1 Dame Court, Dublin 2, tel 679 3687

pint of Guinness €4.70

On a quiet Tuesday afternoon go to The Stag's Head with one friend, order two pints and sit in the plush, red leather seating in the heavily mirrored, oak-clad back room. Say nothing for a couple of minutes, take a long, careful first draw on your pint, and breathe. Nobody following these instructions could find a single fault with the world or their situation in it. The Stag's Head is such an institution in Dublin that if you walk up Dame St you will find a mosaic embedded right into the pavement pointing you in its direction. The back room is one of the loveliest rooms in the city, while the bar is a long, narrow, more functional space, though its ceiling is particularly notable.

The food here is fantastic: plain pub grub impeccably well done. Students and young business people come back time and again to join older regulars and line their stomachs for the night ahead.

Open Mon–Thurs 10.30–23.30, Fri–Sat 10.30–00.30, Sun 12.30–23.00

Literary pubs

Davy Byrne's 21 Duke St, Dublin 2, tel 677 5217, web www.davybyrnes.com

pint of Guinness €4.80

A self-consciously Literary Pub. However, in its efforts to attract sophisticated literary types it ruins the original atmosphere described most famously in Joyce's *Ulysses*, though it no doubt still lives up to its moniker there as a 'moral pub' (whatever that means).

It is an art deco creation of 1941 inside, and the menu is full and adventurous by pub standards.

Open Mon–Thurs 11.00–23.30, Fri–Sat 11.00–00.30, Sun 11.00–23.00

On the town

Grogan's (The Castle Lounge) 15 Sth William St, Dublin 2, tel 677 9320
pint of Guinness €4.60

Grogan's is not as formally a Literary Pub as Davy Byrne's or McDaid's,
though the likes of Patrick Kavanagh did hang out here and it still
attracts a literary set. You will find all sorts in Grogan's—from plasterers
and carpenters discussing Greek tragedy outside at the silver tables,
to foreign students curled up with books in the snug booths, to
politicians huddled with advisers at the bar. This is Everybody's Local;
yet, for all its openness to whoever, it seems to ward off the sort of
obnoxious drinkers you will inevitably find from time to time at other
Best Bars.

There is no music here, unless you count the clink of glasses and
the sound of conversation. Most pleasantly, there is no TV—and it
is rare to find a Dublin pub about which that can be said. The walls
are covered in art for sale, from simple sketches to attempts at
impressionism.

Open Mon–Thurs 10.30–23.30, Fri–Sat 10.30–00.30, Sun 12.30–23.00

McDaid's 3 Harry St, Dublin 2, tel 679 4395
pint of Guinness €4.80

McDaid's is a wonderful pub, a high-ceilinged dark bar whose
slightly eerie atmosphere is at least partially explained by its original
function as the city morgue. Early in the 20th century it was a centre
for republican anarchist activity but, in the 1940s and 1950s, it moved
seamlessly away from this to attract the more dissolute, and perhaps
less productive, end of the literary scene. It would be possible to blame
McDaid's for actually depriving us of literature: if Kavanagh, Behan,
Cronin, et al had paid more attention to pen and less to pub, perhaps
we would have more to read. Then again, it probably wouldn't be half
as good. A wild place in the middle of the last century, McDaid's has
settled easily into the city centre respectability of a thriving business.

Open Mon–Thurs 10.30–23.30, Fri–Sat 10.30–00.30, Sun 12.30–23.00

Neary's (The Chatham Lounge) 1 Chatham St, Dublin 2, tel 677 8596
pint of Guinness €5

Neary's, in its proximity to the Gaiety Theatre, has been a resting place
for actors as well as literary types, a den of bohemia mid-20th century
which, like McDaid's, has quietened into a fairly regular city centre pub.

The racing fraternity has also had a history here, adding to its
decadent past. This was the hostelry where Kavanagh could keep away

from Behan. A bizarre Neary's fact is that the publican after whom it is named doubled up as the Honorary Consul to the Republic of Guatemala.

The Victorian design is still evident, lending the place a certain elegance, and it's gorgeous, bright and very comfortable inside, with the always welcome extra of a big sofa.

Open Mon–Thurs 10.30–23.30, Fri–Sat 10.30–00.30, Sun 12.30–23.00

New horizons

The Bank 20–22 College Green, Dublin 2, tel 677 0677, web www.bankoncollegegreen.com

pint of Guinness €4.80

The Bank used to be a bank. Now it is not. It is a pub. The building was designed by William Henry Lynn, one of the British Empire's foremost architects, and the interior is richly ornate, in that way only the Victorians knew how: mosaic floors, stained glass ceiling, marble pillars, hand-carved plasterwork. The men's toilets are located in the old vaults. The Bank is undoubtedly a novelty and undeniably beautiful, so deserves your patronage for at least a drink or two. They serve breakfast too.

Open Mon–Thurs 09.30–00.00, Fri–Sat 09.30–01.30, Sun 10.00–00.00

The Church Junction of Mary St & Jervis St, Dublin 1, tel 828 0102, web www.thechurch.ie

pint of Guinness €4.95, €5.50 after 23.00 Fri-Sat

The icons of modern Ireland—a bank and a church. Another converted historical building, this time resulting in a cross between a church, a bar, and a Star Trek set. Arthur Guinness was married here in what was St Mary's Protestant Church. On four levels there is a café, three bars, a restaurant and a club, all on the doorstep of the northside's busiest shopping district. Come here to party and you will literally find yourself dancing on the graves of Mary Mercer, founder of Mercer's Hospital, and Lord Norbury, the man who ordered Robert Emmet's execution. The Renatus Harris organ is a sight to behold, as is the glorious stained glass window, contrasting with the cool lighting and bizarre futuristic 'tower' out front. The outdoor terrace is the biggest in Dublin.

Open Mon–Wed 11.00–23.30, Thurs 11.00–00.00, Fri–Sat 11.00–02.30, Sun 11.00–23.00

On the town

Hogan's 35 Sth Great George's St, Dublin 2, tel 677 5904
pint of Guinness €4.60, €4.85 after 23.30
Hogan's is the old new pub, one of the first to cater for a young, hip clientèle and the father and mother of the pub trends that swept the city during the boom years. In keeping with that fine pedigree, it is a little more stately and more refined than the brash upstarts listed here. Always dark and always filled with a relaxed rather than frantic crowd, it's the perfect place for the Sunday afternoon wind down. Hogan's is the original and, arguably, best of the new lot.
Open Mon–Wed 14.00–23.30, Thurs 14.00–01.00, Fri–Sat 14.00–02.30, Sun 14.00–23.00

Market Bar Fade St, Dublin 2, tel 613 9094, web www.marketbar.ie
pint of Guinness €4.60
Pleasant for its ever so slightly Irish take on Tapas early in the evening, this large, appealing space gets steadily more crowded later in the week. Even with plenty of standing room it tends to end up very full on a Friday evening, with a varied crowd.
    The bar was once a sausage factory, and just to confuse you further, you enter through what could be the front of a gothic church, with a beer garden/courtyard on your way in. The place has a real warehouse feel, and its plain redbrick walls (apart from the one covered in shoes) and sheer airiness make it a delightful change from the usual.
Open Mon–Thurs 12.00–23.30, Fri–Sat 12.00–00.30, Sun 15.00–23.00

Ocean Charlotte Quay Dock, Ringsend, Dublin 4, tel 668 8862, web www.oceanbar.ie
pint of Guinness €5.25
Ocean is an outpost of urban cool in the regenerated area of Ringsend, taking up the bottom floor of an exclusive high-rise apartment complex beside the old canal dock. In summer it affords a delicious view of the docks and is the perfect spot for spacious summer pints outside on the cobblestones at the water's edge.
Open Mon–Thurs 12.00–23.30, Fri–Sat 12.00–00.30, Sun 12.00–23.00

Odeon Bar 57 Harcourt St, Dublin 2, tel 478 2088, web www.odeon.ie
pint of Guinness €4.60, €5 after 00.00
The Odeon is a classic. Housed in a converted railway station, its high ceilings, long main room and slightly separated bar area make it stand out. It is airy, yet not cavernous. The Odeon has survived novelty to become a welcome fixture in a relatively 'dry' part of town.
Open Mon–Thurs 12.00–23.30, Fri–Sat 12.00–02.30, Sun 12.00–01.00

Pravda Lr Liffey St, Dublin 1, tel 874 0090, web www.pravda.ie
pint of Guinness €4.80, €5.20 after 23.30
A Russian-themed bar that serves dozens of different vodkas from around the globe, Pravda is another pub that was once the new thing but has moved on to carve its own niche. It is very popular with Dublin's Polish community, and it tries hard to stay hip—with themed nights Monday to Saturday and DJs, dancers and other live acts to beat the band.
Open Sun–Thurs 16.00–23.30, Fri–Sat 12.00–02.30 (occasional late bar Wed–Thurs)

Sin É 14–15 Ormond Quay, Dublin 1, tel 878 7078
pint of Guinness €4.20, €4.40 after 21.00 Fri–Sat
For all its vague likeness to a Connemara stalwart in the centre of Dublin, **Sin** É is in fact a hip spot for wayward youthy types, an old bar revamped for a trendier set. The cottage/barn feel clashes with the red lights illuminating the upturned glasses behind the bar. This place has pretensions towards being an Irish-speaking bar, but only in so far as that's trendy and 'now'. It is always home to some randomly themed night or other, and there's always great music playing (either live or through the speakers). All told, this is a fantastic spot
Open Mon–Wed 12.00–23.30, Thurs 12.00–02.00, Fri–Sat 12.00–02.30, Sun 12.00–23.00

Best . . .

. . . first pint

The Flowing Tide 9 Lr Abbey St, Dublin 1, tel 874 4108
pint of Guinness €4.30
For that very first pint of Dublin Guinness to count, you need to take the cheaper Dublin Bus no 41 from the airport, rather than the Airlink, and get off at the last stop in town, on Abbey St. Cross the road and enter The Flowing Tide. Inside you will discover a cosmopolitan old pub where theatre types vie with the TV for attention, while hard, bitter old men mutter in the corner. Straight off the bus, and serving a fine pint of stout, this pub has everything you need to prime you for that most crucial of cultural experiments: the pub life of Dublin.
Open Mon–Thurs 10.30–23.30, Fri–Sat 10.30–00.30, Sun 12.00–23.00

On the town

...hotel bar

Library Bar Central Hotel, Exchequer St, Dublin 2, tel 679 7302 (hotel), web www.centralhoteldublin.com

pint of Guinness €4.60

On the first floor of the Central Hotel, this little hideaway is beautifully comfy, oozing sophistication and class without seeming prohibitive. Wander in here on your own or with one friend some slow afternoon. Just as nice for a coffee as for a pint, this is the perfect place for contemplation or a quiet chat, for that bit of work you need to get done or that book you want to finish reading.

Open Mon–Thurs 10.00–23.30, Fri–Sat 10.00–00.30, Sun 12.00–23.30

...sports bar

The Wool Shed Sports Baa and Grill Unit 4, Parnell Centre, Parnell St, Dublin 1, tel 872 4325, web www.woolshedbaa.com

pint of Guinness €4.20, €4.50 after 00.30

From the big blue Fosters awning out front and its very name, The Wool Shed Sports Baa and Grill, this place does exactly what it says on the tin. It's a rugby bar, a shrine to New Zealand, Australia and South Africa. Fantastic place if any of those teams are playing. However, for any sport, if you can't be there this is the place to be. There are two giant screens perfectly placed so that you've a great view of the match whether you're upstairs or down.

Good pub food—nothing too fancy, just tasty chicken wings, burgers and such like. Lots of events throughout the week too—comedy, karaoke and live music. Oh—and there's a pool table.

Open Sun–Tues 12.00–23.30, Wed–Sat 12.00–01.30

...rock bar

Bruxelles 7–8 Harry St, Dublin 2, tel 677 4038

pint of Guinness €4.90, €5.10 after 23.30

The musical pedigree of this bar off Grafton St should be obvious, with Phil Lynott standing proudly in bronze out front. Bruxelles comes with split personalities. On a sunny afternoon, it's lovely to sit outside and take your time over a pint while the shoppers pass by and classic tunes play in the background. At night head downstairs for rowdy hard-rock madness. There's an indie bar downstairs too.

Open Mon–Sat 10.30–02.30, Sun 12.00–01.00

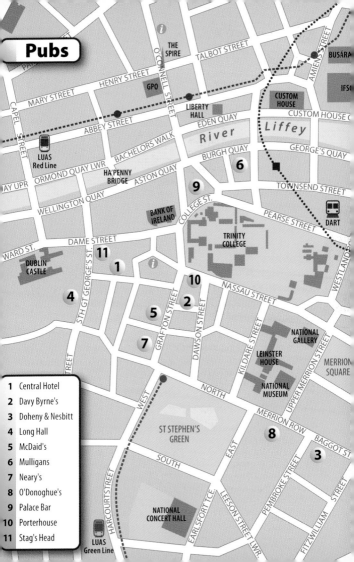

Pubs

1 Central Hotel
2 Davy Byrne's
3 Doheny & Nesbitt
4 Long Hall
5 McDaid's
6 Mulligans
7 Neary's
8 O'Donoghue's
9 Palace Bar
10 Porterhouse
11 Stag's Head

. . . Czech bar

The Czech Inn Lr East Gate, Temple Bar, Dublin 2, tel 671 1561, web www. czech-inn.org

Pilsner Urquell €5

If you are not Czech or Slovak you may get a few odd glances as you walk through the door, but that's just because you're a novelty. There's no point coming here for Guinness: have what the locals are having; there's an impressive selection of beers and Czech spirits, and the grub isn't half bad either. The place can get pretty wild at night—you better know how to party. Drinking here you'll also get a sense of what it was like for the Irish in London and New York decades ago: finding their feet in foreign lands, where the bars were the centre of community activity. True to the tradition of the best Dublin pubs, The Czech Inn is something real.

Open Mon–Sat 12.00–03.00, Sun 12.00–01.00

. . . beer bar

When it comes to the best beer bar, you have three options— **The Porterhouse**, The Porterhouse or The Porterhouse. There are three around the city, and they specialise in beers, be they draught, bottled or their very own brews. Banana beer from Ghana? Strawberry beer? Or something a little more masculine, like Wrasslers, the stout that Michael Collins used to drink? For the beer aficionado this really is the only show in town. Each of the pubs has a warm, inviting feel to it. They do good pub grub as well, and the Temple Bar branch has live music every night. There's also a Porterhouse, the original, in Bray, Co Wicklow.

The Porterhouse Central 45–47 Nassau St, Dublin 2, tel 677 4180, web www.porterhousebrewco.com

Pint of Plain porter—don't ask for Guinness, they don't like it—€4.40, €4.90 after 23.00 Thurs–Sat

Open Mon–Tues 11.00–00.00, Wed 11.00–01.00, Thurs 11.00–01.30, Fri–Sat 11.00–02.30, Sun 12.00–00.00

The Porterhouse Temple Bar 16–18 Parliament St, Dublin 2, tel 679 8847
  pint of Plain €4.40, €4.90 after 23.00 Thurs-Sat
  Open Sun–Wed 11.30–23.30, Thurs–Sat 11.30–02.00
Porterhouse North Cross Guns Bridge, Glasnevin, Dublin 9, tel 830 9884
  pint of Plain €4.20, €4.70 after 23.30
  Open Mon–Thurs 12.00–23.30, Fri–Sat 12.00–02.30, Sun 12.30–23.00

... cocktail

The Octagon Bar The Clarence Hotel, 6–8 Wellington Quay, Dublin 2, tel
  407 0800 (hotel), web www.theclarence.ie/octagonbar-dublin
  Cosmopolitan €9
  Tucked away in The Clarence Hotel, owned by Bono and The Edge, is
  The Octagon Bar. You'll pay for them all night, but the cocktails here
  are lip-smackingly, sense-numbingly gorgeous, full-bodied with booze
  and made with skilled care. There's no way you can be said to be
  ripped off (by Dublin standards), even at around €10–15 a pop. The bar
  itself doesn't always guarantee surroundings befitting the price of the
  drinks, but it is generally quiet and pleasant.
  Open Tues–Thurs 17.00–23.30, Fri–Sat 17.00–00.30

... view of Dublin

Messrs Maguire 1–2 Burgh Quay, Dublin 2, tel 670 5777, web www.
  messrsmaguire.ie
  pint of Guinness €4.60, €5.10 after 23.00 Thurs–Sat
  If there's a problem getting a seat in many Dublin pubs, the opposite
  can be said for Messrs. There are four huge floors filled with them, the
  best of which being the very top floor, where you can have a great
  view of Dublin from one of the window seats. They also have a more
  comprehensive selection of beers than most Dublin bars, with their
  own microbrewery attached. The door staff are strict, particularly at
  weekends, so try not to show up in trainers. If you're part of a large
  group of males, split up!
  Open Mon–Tues 10.30–23.30, Wed 10.30–01.30, Thurs 10.30–02.00,
  Fri–Sat, 10.30–02.30, Sun 12.30–23.30

On the town

. . . early bars ('early houses')

Hughes's 19–20 Chancery St, Dublin 7, tel 872 6540
pint of Guinness €4.50
Open Mon–Thurs 07.00–23.30, Fri–Sat 07.00–00.30, Sun 19.00–23.00

Ned's 44 Townsend St, Dublin 2, tel 677 9507
pint of Guinness €4.00
Open Mon–Thurs 07.00–23.30, Fri–Sat 07.00–00.30, Sun 12.20–23.00

The Wind-Jammer 111 Townsend St, Dublin 2, tel 677 2576
pint of Guinness €4.10
Open Mon–Thurs 07.30–23.30, Fri–Sat 07.30–00.30, Sun 12.30–23.00

. . . beer garden

McCoy's Bar North Star Hotel, Amiens St, Dublin 1, tel 836 3136 (hotel), web
www.northstarhotel.ie/dublin-restaurant
pint of Guinness €4.40
Just opposite Connolly Station, in the North Star Hotel, lies McCoy's
Bar, and with it the best beer garden in the city centre. The pub uses
this as one of its selling points, so it's not exactly an undiscovered
treasure, but it is nevertheless a very attractive beer garden. The pub
itself is bright and often quiet, with excellent service; the garden is
comparatively spacious and perfectly sheltered from the rain, lying
under a wide arch. There's the odd small tree dotted here and there as
well as big, glowing, old-style lamps. The spot is supremely well heated
with comfy, cushioned dark-wood furniture. A little haven in which to
have your pint or your smoke.
Open Mon–Thurs 10.30–23.30, Fri–Sat 10.30–00.30, Sun 12.30–23.00

And also . . .

. . . smallest pub in Dublin

The Dawson Lounge 25 Dawson St, Dublin 2, tel 677 5909
pint of Guinness €4.90
At the Stephen's Green end of Dawson St, across from the Mansion
House, is Dublin's smallest pub, and they make sure you know it. Its
front consists of a narrow doorway with steps leading down to the bar,
so you could be forgiven for missing the entrance except for the big
Carlsberg-sponsored sign announcing it as 'Probably the smallest pub
in the world'.

A group of ten people here constitutes a crowd, and it attracts a mixed but primarily jovial suit-and-tie clientèle. Seating and stools are few, so be prepared to stand, particularly at weekends. Worth a visit for a pint or two, if only for novelty value.

Open Mon–Thurs 12.30–23.30, Fri–Sat 12.30–00.30, Sun 15.00–23.00

. . . hardest pub to find in Dublin
The Hideout House
pint of Guinness €3.90

The clues: it's on the northside, near Mountjoy Square, down an alley that isn't named on maps, and on the edge of a housing estate (never say the Irish aren't pioneers when it comes to pub-building!). The Hideout is popular with punters from northern counties Fermanagh and Cavan as well as Dubliners—as the old road signs in the lounge might suggest. Most interesting feature: there's a guillotine in the bar. So—be on your best behaviour. The Hideout is worth searching for, as you'll feel like you've achieved something, the drink is comparatively cheap, and it's usually peaceful and uncrowded, except when there's a match on.

Open Mon–Wed 12.00–23.30, Thurs 11.00–23.30, Fri–Sat 12.00–00.30, Sun 12.00–23.30

. . . cheapest pint in Dublin (that we could find)
Caulfield's 18–19 Lr Dorset St, Dublin 1, tel 878 1550 (hotel)
pint of Guinness €3.30

A walk up O'Connell St, past Parnell Square and onto Dorset St will bring you to Caulfield's Hotel, with a bar selling probably the cheapest pints around the city centre. It's a little out of the way and a little rough around the edges but inflation has passed Caulfield's by, with all prices the same as they were a few years ago. It's decidedly local in terms of its clientèle but the staff are friendly, and in our humble opinions €3.30 Guinness is every man and woman's birthright.

Open Mon–Thurs 10.30–23.30, Fri–Sat 10.30–00.20, Sun 12.30–23.00

The most expensive pint in Dublin (that we came across) was at The Mint Bar, downstairs in The Westin Hotel on Westmoreland St, Dublin 2—€5.80 for a *pint of Guinness*!

On the town

Eating out

Dublin is a great place to eat out, whatever your budget. At the top end there's the likes of the double-Michelin-starred Patrick Guilbaud's, where a three-course dinner with wine will set you back upwards of €150 per head; at the bottom end, there are fast-food franchises much like in any other city, where you can fill up on burgers and fries for €1.50. The restaurants listed here are closer to the bottom than the top, but only in price. At any one of the restaurants in this section, you can get a two-course meal for €20 or less (not including drinks). Many of them are cheaper than that. All of them are reliably good quality; some are more than merely 'good'.

Café chains

Dublin's been known for its cafés since the 19th century and the foundation of Bewley's; Bewley's itself went into a slow decline in the 1990s that led to its being sold and its flagship Grafton St branch being turned into a shell for another café chain (although its handsome façade remains); it ultimately failed because it had a lot of competitors who were doing a better job of providing quality coffee and a comfortable place to drink it. Since then, Dublin's been colonised by Starbucks, with 23 branches open at the time of writing. The Starbucks in Dublin are much the same as the Starbucks everywhere else in the world, although some coffee fanatics have reported that the quality of the coffee is inferior to their US branches. Such connoisseurs prefer the home-grown coffee chains. There are three worth mentioning: the **Insomnia Coffee Company**, with 19 branches, **Café Sol**, with 13 branches, and **Butler's Chocolate Café**, with 11 branches. Insomnia and Café Sol are broadly similar, offering a full range of hot and cold coffee drinks, tea, pre-made sandwiches, soft drinks and snacks; as of this writing, Insomnia has an offer available that lets you get a sandwich and a hot drink for a mere €5. Butler's Chocolate Café is something different: owned and operated by Butler's, the makers of quality chocolates, they sell coffee drinks, chocolates, and the best hot chocolate in Dublin, but nothing more substantial. But the hot chocolate is really something special.

Lunch/grazing

Avoca Foodhall, Suffolk St, Dublin 2 tel 777 4215
Open Mon–Wed 10.00–18.00, Thurs 10.00–20.00, Fri 10.00–18.00, Sat 10.00–18.30, Sun 11.00–18.00

In the basement of Avoca Handweavers is a food hall that's a true gourmet's delight. As well as stocking a mouth-watering array of food you can take home with you, there's also a small seating area where you can enjoy your salad, scone, or sausage roll in peace before you head upstairs to buy your floral-patterned wellies.

Café Irie 11 Fownes St, Temple Bar, Dublin 2, tel 672 5090
Open Mon–Sat 09.00 20.00, Sun 12.00–17.30

Upstairs from an alternative clothing shop and downstairs from a tattoo parlour is one of Dublin's hidden treasures: a modestly charming café that serves the best sandwiches in the city. Small and unassuming, with a permanent soundtrack of reggae music, Café Irie is the perfect place to go to get away from the crowds on the ground; even when it's busy, it's up so high that you can't help but feel detached from the crush and noise of the street.

Café Léon
Pastry Café, 17 Wicklow St, Dublin 2 tel 671 7331
Pastry Café, 14–15 Trinity St, Dublin 2 tel 677 1060
Bistro, 33 Exchequer St, Dublin 2, tel 670 7238
Open Mon–Fri 07.30–19.00 (Thurs 20.00), Sat, Sun 09.00–19.00

Café Léon's three branches exemplify the best of the traditional French café: exquisite patisserie, excellent coffee, filling and delicious sandwiches, prompt and polite service, all in elegant and comfortable surroundings. The cakes and pastries look like works of art and taste like slices of heaven; they may not seem cheap, but considering the quality of what you get, they're excellent value, and the hot filled croissants make an excellent breakfast. The Bistro branch on Exchequer St offers more substantial food as well, which is up to the high standards set by the two Pastry Cafés.

The Cake Café The Daintree Building, 65 Pleasant's Place, Dublin 8, tel 478 9394, web www.thecakecafe.ie

Open Mon 08.30–18.00, Tues–Fri 08.30–20.00, Sat 09.00–17.30

The cakes here are delicious, of course, but so is everything else. On our latest trip we had a scrumptious caramelised onion tart with sundried tomatoes, green salad and chutney, divine lemon tart and a coffee, all for €13. There's a range of specialist teas and a small but tasty wine list. The café itself is charming with its black and white tiled floor and old-fashioned china teasets. On fine days you can sit outside in the sheltered courtyard and enjoy the peace and lack of traffic noise. Pleasant's Place is parallel with Camden St but the café can also be accessed through the Daintree Paper Shop on 61 Camden St—worth a visit in itself for its fabulous handmade papers and trimmings.

Cornucopia 19 Wicklow St, Dublin 2, tel 677 7583 web www.cornucopia.ie

Open Mon–Fri 08.30–21.00, Sat 08.30–20.00, Sun/Bank Holidays 12.00–19.00

The kind of restaurant that makes you feel like a better person just by walking in the door: the food is healthy and vegetarian (with notes on the menu marking dishes suitable for vegans and people with allergies to nuts, wheat or dairy), the atmosphere is down-to-earth and friendly, there's art by local artists on the walls, and before you even go in the door you'll pass posters advertising classes in yoga and meditation. Cornucopia is cosy and often crowded at peak times, with good reason: the food is as delicious as it is healthy. Main courses cost around €12–15, but they're extremely filling (especially considering each main course comes with two salads), and probably the only way to fit in one of their delicious desserts is to share one plate between two; two portions of their scrumptious salads will set you back under €5.

The Epicurean Food Hall Middle Abbey St/Liffey St, Dublin 1

A godsend for shoppers (see *Shopping*, page 86), the food hall is also the perfect place for a mid-shop snack.

It collects the world's cuisine under one roof in stalls and small shops. A mix of café and food shops, you can often take home at least the ingredients of your lunch if you enjoyed it. The Mexican, Indian and Turkish outlets are particularly fine, but a couple of Italian café and an excellent fish restaurant complete a tasty picture.

Prices vary enormously, but are in the café rather than the restaurant range; expect to pay between €5 and €20 for a complete meal.

Itsa Bagel Arnotts Department Store, Abbey St, Dublin 1, tel 804 4555
Open Mon–Wed 10.00–18.30, Thurs 10.00–20.00, Fri & Sat 10.00–18.30pm, Sun 12.00–18.00

Formerly located in the Epicurean Food Hall, Itsa Bagel serves the freshest and best bagels in the city from its new location in the ground floor of Arnotts. You can have your bagel (be it plain, poppy-seed, pumpernickel, high-fibre . . .) stuffed with traditional New York deli-style fillings—pastrami, smoked salmon, cream cheese—or make up your own concoction from the range available. Chase it with rich and delicious brownies (available in a flour-free version, if that's what tickles your tastebuds) and wash it down with organic lemonade. Or coffee, if you're feeling conventional.

The Joy of Coffee 25 East Essex St, Temple Bar, Dublin 2, tel 679 3393
Open Mon–Sun 08.30–23.00 (Sat 00.00)

There's many an art gallery with a café attached, but The Joy of Coffee is the reverse: a café that's also an art gallery. It would be worth visiting just to see the small but fascinating exhibitions of art by contemporary Irish artists, but add to that the best cappuccino in Dublin and scrambled eggs so perfect they melt in your mouth, and what you have in sum is the perfect place to while away an idle hour.

Lemon 66 Sth William St, Dublin 2, tel 672 9044; 60 Dawson St, Dublin 2, tel 672 8898
Open Mon–Wed 09.00–19.30, Thurs 08.00–21.00, Fri 08.00–19.30, Sat 09.00–19.30, Sun 10.00–18.30

Possibly the only restaurant in Dublin that needs a special ordering system on Shrove Tuesday; Lemon's speciality is pancakes, and like many restaurants with a very narrow specialisation, it does them superbly. You can have your pancakes with spinach, ham, cheese, mushrooms, roast beef, maple syrup, ice-cream, Bailey's, sliced bananas, or, if you're feeling unimaginative, sugar and lemon juice. All pancakes are available as galettes, which are made with buckwheat flour rather than ordinary flour; they also do sandwiches, waffles, excellent coffee and Italian beer, and all their food and drinks are available to eat in or take away.

The Sth William St branch is a trifle cramped, and the Dawson St branch uses benches rather than chairs, no doubt to discourage

On the town

customers from staying too long, especially at busy times (and most times are busy times for Lemon). This does mean that eating in Lemon can be a bit of an economy-class experience—but only with regard to the furnishings; the food is first class, all the way.

Queen of Tarts 4 Cork Hill, Upr Dame St (opposite Dublin Castle), tel 670 7499; Cow's Lane, Dublin 2, tel 633 4672

Open (both branches) Mon–Fri 07.30–19.00, Sat, Sun 09.00–19.00

They serve the best pastry ever. It's that simple. They serve it in savouries, in sausage rolls and in baked savoury tarts with smoked fish or chicken or any number of simply delicious things, all at wonderfully reasonable prices. They also serve the most exquisite cakes and buns, along with divine scones, all home baked. The café is comfortable, but very small, making access for wheelchairs difficult, but it is on the ground floor at least. Delicious sandwiches are €7.95, while the gorgeous cakes are around €5.50. And if you're really hungry, don't miss the savoury tarts at €9.95 (with focaccia bread and salad)—small but powerful tasty treats.

Silk Road Café, The Chester Beatty Library, Dublin Castle, Dublin 2 tel 407 0770

Open Mon–Fri 10.00–17.00 (1 Oct–30 April closed on Mon) Sat 11.00–17.00, Sun 12.00–17.00

Attached to the Chester Beatty Library but worthy of a visit for its own sake, the Silk Road Café serves the most delicious and the most reasonably-priced Middle Eastern cuisine in Dublin. It's self-service and often rather crowded when there's a popular exhibition on in the Library, but give it a go at off-peak hours and you'll find yourself not minding the fact that you have to carry your own tray. The aubergine stuffed with minced lamb is a particular *Shoestring* favourite.

Smock Alley Café 3–4 Smock Alley Court, West Essex St, Temple Bar, Dublin 2

Open Tues–Sat 08.00–18.00

Tucked away at the extreme west end of Temple Bar is this unassuming little place, its frontage so modest it almost vanishes from sight, its name chalked up on a blackboard; venture in, and you'll find a quietly comfortable (and fully wheelchair-accessible) café serving organic coffee and food. Everything is utterly simple, from the furnishings to the ham sandwiches, and in this simplicity a kind of perfection is born.

Steps of Rome Chatham St, Dublin 2, tel 670 5630

Open Mon–Fri 12.00–23.00, Sat 12.00–23.30, Sun 13.00–20.00

On any day you will be lucky to hear any language but Italian spoken by staff or customers here, and often the tiny space will be crammed with people standing around slugging the best espressos this side of Paris. Funnily enough, it is pretty much impossible to predict when this diminutive delight will be busy or quiet: it opens till about 20.00, and all day it kind of ticks over, never empty, rarely full.

The espresso here is simply amazing, a real chewy treat that will have you buzzing all day. Their pizza (which you can take out if you wish) comes in slices cut from rectangular trays on the counter and heated in a pizza oven: with its delicious light crispy base it bears very little resemblance to the doughy round things we are used to this side of Europe, so you may be surprised. Everything here is utterly authentic but don't expect to be stuffed, they are not the biggest portions in the world.

For a quick, delicious snack, it is ridiculously cheap—the divine pizza slices cost €4.20 (€3.20 take-out). Main courses (some only available in the evening) range from €11 to €12.95.

Restaurants

Chez Max 1 Palace St, Dublin 2 tel 633 7215 web www.chezmax.ie

Open Mon–Fri 08.00–00.00, Sat–Sun 11.00–00.00

Tucked away beside Dublin Castle is a little French bistro so traditional and so authentic you could swear you'd stepped through a teleport door and wound up in Lyon. Cosy and welcoming, Chez Max serves hearty, filling French food, utterly unpretentious but no less delicious for that. Located as it is just across the road from the Olympia Theatre, the pre- and post-theatre menus are excellent value and very convenient. Not surprisingly it's very popular so it's wise to book in the evenings.

Green 19 19 Camden St Dublin 2 , tel 478 9626, web www.green19.ie

Open Mon–Sat 10.00–23.00, Sun 12.00–18.00

The chic surroundings and contemporary art on the walls might lead you to expect something nouvelle cuisine-y and hideously overpriced, but no fear: Green 19 serves traditional Irish food like Mammy used to make at shockingly low prices. Main courses all go for €10, desserts (including the best apple crumble you are ever likely to taste) for €5, and you can wash down your pot roasted chicken or your club sandwich and chips with a variety of wines, beers, and cocktails. Eating corned beef and cabbage and drinking a vanilla daiquiri: now that's the best of Dublin in a nutshell.

Gruel 68A Dame St, Dublin 2, tel 670 7119, web www.gruel.ie

Open Mon–Fri 07.00–23.00, Sun 09.00–22.00

A superior café, serving fairly simple, hearty food made to delicious perfection. Not far from Trinity College, it's very popular with students. Best and best-value during the day, though they also do evening meals. After a night on the town try the Taxi Driver's Giant Bacon Sandwich (€6.95), available on the breakfast menu from 07.00 to 11.00. For lunch the sweet, meaty Roast in a Roll is the business. A half soup and half Roast in a Roll (€6.40) is a nicely filling lunch if you don't feel like all that beef in the middle of the day. Some good veggie options too on a menu full of variety. The soups are thick and scrumptious; the breads are excellent, as are the sweets and treats (especially the brownies). Be prepared to wait at peak times.

Jo'Burger 137 Rathmines Road, Dublin 6, tel 491 3731

Open 12.00 till 'late' 7 days a week

Easily reached on the Luas Green line (a minute's walk from Charlemont station), Jo'Burger is worth a detour. Its intensely stylish décor manages to be utterly cool and warmly welcoming at the same time—no mean feat. As the name implies, the menu offers burgers, burgers, and more burgers—but *what* burgers! Tender organic beef, cooked to perfection and to exactly the degree you specify, garnished with the freshest and most flavoursome of toppings (in many different variations), and served inside a soft Breton bun. If you have the space in your stomach, you can accompany your burger with sweet potato fries and chase it down with organic ice-cream. The burgers are available in beef, lamb, chicken, fish, and two different vegetarian versions, and the restaurant's owners have thoughtfully provided an array of board-games you can play while waiting for your food. The humble hamburger has never been so well-served.

Juice 73–83 Sth Great Georges St, Dublin 2, tel 475 7856

Open Mon–Sun, 11.00–23.00

If the cosy friendliness of Cornucopia (see page 136) doesn't satisfy you, and you'd rather have vegetarian food that's a touch more sophisticated, look no further than Juice, whose immaculately stylish surroundings are matched by equally stylish food. Fruit juices, beers and organic wines can accompany your stir-fry, curry, or salad, and although the food has a cordon bleu sheen, it's very reasonably priced—main courses are around €15, with starters ranging from €5 to just under €10.

Madina 60 Mary St, Dublin 1, tel 872 6007, web www.madina.ie

Open Mon–Sun 12.00–23.00

A very reasonably priced, small Indian restaurant along one of the northside's top shopping streets. Relatively undiscovered too, except within the Indian and Pakistani communities themselves, which should tell you all you need to know about quality and authenticity. Try the dosa—there's nowhere else in Dublin that does it, apparently. The menu has a great range including excellent vegetarian choices. Vegetable biryani will set you back €7.95, though it is very spicy so you may want to order some raita with it. For those who like their curries and kebabs there are plenty of options, all for under a tenner. The portions are huge—a side of rice at €2.95 looks like it could feed your whole family. Be warned: there is no alcohol here, though the non-alcoholic fruit beers are actually quite tasty.

Milano web www.milano.ie

38 Dawson St, Dublin 2, tel 670 7744

19 East Essex St, Temple Bar, Dublin 2, tel 670 3384

Excise Walk, Clarion Quay, Dublin 1, tel 611 9012

Unit 1, Hanover Quay, Grand Canal Harbour, Dublin 2, tel 679 9579

Open hours vary by branch; usually open at least from 12.00 to 22.00 but check website for individual branch details

Branches of the chain called Pizza Express in the UK. Milano's menus are perhaps a little staid and predictable, but predictability can be good when it's married to good quality. Milano's pizzas and pasta dishes are dependably tasty and well-priced for what you get, and the service is reliably prompt and friendly.

Salamanca 1 St Andrew's St, Dublin 2, tel 677 4799, web www.salamanca.ie

Open Mon–Thurs 12.00–23.00 last order 22.45, Fri–Sat 12.00–00.00 last order 23.45, Sun 13.00–22.00 last order 21.45

Authentic tapas and other Spanish food, exquisitely cooked and served in elegant and comfortable surroundings. Salamanca is a good place to push the boat out, if you have a little extra money, since its tapas dishes vary quite widely in price, and if you're dining in a group it can be fun to share several dishes between everyone at the table— each diner is given a separate clean plate, and the individual tapas

On the town

dishes are left in the centre for you to serve yourselves. At lunchtime, you can enjoy a really good steak with potatoes for just under €10.

Shebeen Chic 4 Sth Great George's St, tel 679 6007, web www. shebeenchic.ie

Open Mon–Fri 17.30–22.00/23.00, Sat 12.00–23.00, Sun 13.00–22.00. Bar open till about 1 hour later. Wheelchair access and accessible toilet.

Is it a restaurant? Is it a bar? In fact, it's a restaurant and two bars—one upstairs, one down—and a swap shop, **Swap Idol**, which is held here on Saturday from 12.00 to 16.00. The Shebeen (we refuse to add the word chic) seems tailor-made for these times: decent value (depending on what you order), environmentally friendly, and serving back-to-basics, not-too-much-nonsense food. It's decorated with recycled materials: bric-a-brac, clothes lines and paintings hung at odd angles—plenty to keep you entertained while you wait for your food. And you may have to wait a while: service can be slow.

Boxty, a traditional Irish crispy potato cake, is a big thing here—a plain salt'n'pepper one will cost you €6.50. With various fillings (cheese and tomato, leek and blood, smoked mackerel and seaweed) you'll pay €8.50, getting a nice portion of salad too. Elsewhere on the menu you'll find other traditional favourites—Irish stew; bacon, cabbage and potatoes—for €16.

Wagamama, Sth King St, Dublin 2, tel 478 2152 web www.wagamama.ie

Open Mon–Wed 12.00–22.00, Thurs–Sat 12.00–23.00, Sun 12.00–21.30. No disabled access.

A branch of the international chain. Don't let the low prices, the kitchen noise or the cafeteria-style bench seating fool you: Wagamama is a classy place to eat, slick and professional and very high-quality. Along with their trademark huge bowls of ramen noodles, Wagamama do a range of mouthwatering curries, side dishes and desserts, with main courses ranging from around €10 to €18. The speed of service makes Wagamama an excellent place to nip into for a quick lunch, although you may need to queue at peak hours; despite the large number of seats, demand often outstrips supply.

Yamamori Noodles 71–72 Sth Gt George's St, Dublin 2, tel 475 5001

Yamamori Sushi 38–39 Lr Ormond Quay, Dublin 1, tel 872 0003

Open Sun–Wed 12.15–23.00, Thurs–Sat 12.15–23.30

Noodles, sushi, and miscellaneous Japanese food. Like Wagamama, Yamamori Noodles has bench seating and specialises in big bowls of ramen soup (while Yamamori Sushi specialises in . . . well, sushi), but Yamamori has a wider range of dishes and a rather more upscale décor and theme, with paintings by Graham Knuttell on the walls and waitresses wearing kimonos. The food is delicious, and exceptionally good value: the tofu steak, at just under €11, could feed two very hungry vegetarians (if they wanted to leave a little room for dessert). To complete the authentically Japanese experience, you can have sake or plum wine with your meal.

Zaytoon 14–15 Parliament St, Dublin 2, tel 677 3595; 44–45 Lr Camden St, Dublin 2, tel 400 5006

Open Mon–Sun 12.00–04.00

The best kebabs in Dublin—simple as that. A sort of slightly upscale fast food restaurant, but serving authentic Persian cuisine. You can get a meal for €10–11 which will leave you disgusted at the very thought of food for the rest of the day. This is substantial stuff, not your usual fast food rubbish, and they do kids' meals too.

Entertainment

Cinema

Dublin's first cinema, the Volta, was run by James Joyce. Today's cinemas are more likely to be run by multinational corporations than literary geniuses, but the films are more interesting than they were in 1909, so it all evens out.

There are fifteen dedicated cinemas in Dublin, and some venues that are strictly speaking not cinemas still have regular or occasional film showings. For example, during July and August there are showings in **Meeting House Square** in Temple Bar. **Rathmines Library** hosts the 'First Friday Film Club' which shows both classic international arthouse movies and Irish documentaries and shorts. Both the Meeting House Square showings and the First Friday Film Club are free, though the Meeting House Square events are ticketed; tickets can be collected in advance from the Temple Bar Cultural Information Centre at 12 Essex St, Dublin 2. (Since Meeting House Square is exposed to the elements, it's a good idea to bring a raincoat and/

On the town

or umbrella—it takes very heavy, persistent rain for the organisers to cancel these events.)

If you want to save money while still enjoying the best new films on release, it helps to go to the cinema in the afternoon, if possible—since most cinemagoers are restricted to evening shows, it's the evening shows that have the most expensive tickets. You'll spend about a third less, on average, if you go before 18.00. For real movie buffs who go three or more times a month, **Cineworld** (page 146) has a special subscription service: you pay €19.99 a month for an Unlimited card which allows you to attend as many screenings at Cineworld as you like.

Major movies often have longer runs in suburban cinemas than in the city centre, while city centre cinemas have a more eclectic selection of films; there's no such thing as a cinema that suits everyone.

*If you want to see **arthouse and foreign films in the city centre**, there are three main venues.*

- The **IFI (Irish Film Institute)** is distinguished, comfortable, stylish, centrally located, has its own bookshop and café/bar, and shows a range of films from the almost-mainstream to the mind-bogglingly obscure. It has two cinemas: Cinema One is medium-sized with slightly raked seating so that everyone gets a good view of the screen, while Cinema Two (upstairs, so not wheelchair-accessible) is small and cosy, with a smaller screen and a distinctly intimate atmosphere most cinemas can't aspire to. All of this in the elegant surroundings of what was once a Quaker meeting house, with its spacious and airy courtyard glassed-over to form a bright and, importantly, warm and dry place for patrons to gather before or after they go to see a film.

  Due to its status as a club, the IFI is allowed to show films that have not passed through the Censor's office and been given an age-rating certificate; since obtaining a certificate can be expensive, the IFI's ability to sidestep the process gives it a much wider range of films to choose from for its programme. This also means that for many of the films on show, you will be required to join the IFI, which is a simple process—just sign a sheet and add €1 to the ticket price as a 'daily member's fee'. If you go to the IFI often, you'll probably find it worth your while to buy yourself an annual membership; costing €20 (€15 for students, seniors and the unemployed), this entitles you to a 10 per cent discount on IFI tickets, food at the IFI café and books at the IFI bookshop.

One final note: the IFI is relatively small, and it's popular among Dublin's cinephiles, so it's quite common for screenings to sell out, especially festival screenings and evening screenings of well-publicised films. Turn up early, or you may be disappointed.

- For a less rarefied selection of films, there's the **Screen** cinema on D'Olier St (tel 0818 300 301), with its delightful little statue of a uniformed usher outside, complete with torch, and the sign in the foyer politely asking patrons not to put their tickets in their mouths 'for reasons of hygiene'. The Screen, unlike the IFI, is a commercial cinema, so its offerings tend to be a little more mainstream, but they're still the arthouse end of mainstream—no big-budget blockbusters here.

- The recently-opened **Lighthouse** cinema in Smithfield is a little less central (although it's easily reached on the Red line of the Luas, and located in a very pleasant new square with several decent restaurants a stone's throw away). What it lacks in accessibility it makes up for in style—the décor of its new building is breathtakingly gorgeous. And, although it may not be accessible in the sense of being as easy to get to from

On the town

the centre of town as the IFI or the Screen, the Lighthouse is, unlike either of those cinemas, fully wheelchair-accessible. It has four screens seating 600 people, and an attached café/bar every bit as stylish as the rest of the building. Its programming covers very similar ground to the Screen (and often the same films can be seen in both cinemas), but the sheer stylishness of the surroundings makes it worth seeking out.

IFI (Irish Film Institute) 6 Eustace St, Temple Bar, Dublin 2, tel 679 5744, box office 679 3477, web www.ifi.ie
Ticket prices €7.75 Mon–Fri, 14.00–18.00 (concession price €6.00); €9.20 Mon–Fri, 18.00–21.00 (concession price €7.75). €7.75 Sat–Sun 14.00–16.00 (concession price €6.00); €9.20 Sat–Sun, 16.00–21.00 (concession price €7.75). IFI members receive a 10 per cent discount.
Lighthouse Cinema Market Square, Smithfield, Dublin 7, tel 879 6701, web www.lighthousecinema.ie
Ticket prices €7.50 Mon–Fri until 18.00 (concession price €6.00); €9.00 Mon–Fri after 18.00 (concession price €7.50). €7.50 Sat–Sun and public holidays before 16.00 (concession price €6.00); €9.00 Sat–Sun and public holidays after 16.00 (concession price €7.50)
Screen Cinema D'Olier St, Dublin 2, tel 0818 300 301, web www.omniplex.ie/cinema/screencinema/screendublin.htm
Ticket prices Adult €9, off peak (Mon–Fri before 18.00) €7; senior, student (Mon–Thurs all day, not hols) €6.50: child (not hols) €6

*On the other hand, maybe you want to see **a blockbuster in the city centre**.*

In this case, you have two choices: the **Savoy** on O'Connell St, with its famously huge screen, ideal for wide-scale movies with lots of explosions and fights and swooping crane shots of gorgeous landscapes, and **Cineworld** on Parnell St, with its many, many screens, some bigger than others.

The Savoy is relatively low on frills; it has comfortable seats, one very big screen and five other screens of varying sizes, along with a pretty basic snack counter. The major attraction is Savoy

One, the biggest cinema screen in Ireland.

Cineworld has over 20 screens in a multi-level cineplex, and the refreshments available are just as impressive. The building is big enough that you'd be well-advised to go early, both to beat the queues and to make sure you make it to the relevant cinema on time, without getting lost or spending hours entertaining yourself in the self-service popcorn shop. Cineworld also has the Unlimited card, as mentioned above: for a mere €19.99 a month, you can see as many films as you like.

Cineworld Parnell St, Dublin 1, tel 1520 880 444, web www.cineworld.ie
Ticket prices adult (after 18.00 Mon–Fri, all day Sat–Sun and bank hols) €9.70; adult (before 18.00 Mon–Fri) €7.70; child (14 & under) €5.70; senior (60+)/NUS €6.70; family (after 18.00 Mon–Fri, all day Sat–Sun & bank hols) €26.60; family (before 18.00 Mon–Fri) €22.00; Early Bird (before 12.00) €5.40

Savoy 17 Upr O'Connell St, Dublin 1, tel 0818 776 776, web www.savoy.ie
Ticket prices Adult €9, off peak (Mon–Fri before 18.00) €7; senior, student (Mon–Thurs all day, not hols) €6.50; child (not hols) €6

On the town

Of course, there are cinemas in the **suburbs** of Dublin as well—a great number of them. Being run by chains, they're all pretty much the same: lots of screens showing mostly mainstream films with the occasional surprisingly obscure title slipping in as well; concession stands selling overpriced popcorn and oversized drinks; comfortable seats and lots of them. We're not going to list every single suburban cinema here—for a more complete guide, try **www.entertainment.ie**—but there are a few worth picking out from the crowd: **Movies @ Dundrum, VUE Liffey Valley, IMC Dún Laoghaire** and **UCI Tallaght** are conveniently located in or near large shopping centres, easily accessed by the Luas, bus or Dart, which makes them ideal if you want to enjoy a movie after an afternoon's shopping.

IMC Dún Laoghaire Lr Georges St, Dún Laoghaire, Co Dublin, tel 230 1399, web www.imccinemas.ie
  Ticket prices adult (after 18.00) €9.30, adult (before 18.00) €7.30, child €6.00, senior €6.00, student €6.00

Movies @ Dundrum Dundrum Town Centre, Dundrum, Dublin 16, tel 1520 880 333, web www.movies-at.ie
  Ticket prices All tickets €5.50 before 13.00, adult (13.00–17.00) €7.00, adult (17.00–19.00) €8.00, adult (after 19.00) €9.90, student (13.00–17.00) €6.50, student (17.00–19.00) €7.00, student (after 19.00) €7.90, senior (before 19.00) €6.50, senior (after 19.00) €7.50

UCI Tallaght Level 3, The Square, Old Blessington Road, Tallaght, Dublin 24 tel 1520 88 00 00, web www.uci.ie
  Ticket prices adult (after 17.00 Mon–Fri, all day Sat, Sun & bank holidays) €9.80, adult off-peak (all other times) €7.80, under 15 €6.70, senior €6.50, student (Mon–Fri) €6.50, student (Sat, Sun & bank holidays) €7.00

VUE Liffey Valley Shopping Centre, Fonthill Road, Clondalkin, Dublin 22, tel 1520 501 0000, www.vue.ie
  Ticket prices adult off-peak (Mon–Fri before 17.00) €8.20, adult peak (all other times) €10.40, child €7.10, student €7.10, senior €7.10

Clubs

The Dublin club scene has exploded in the last few years, as the Irish propensity to party was duly noted and abused. With so much choice it is essential to have a fair idea where you are going, why you are going there and what to expect.

Of course, it all depends on what you are looking for in a night—keep an eye on listings to find a place that suits you. If you're on a budget then it's down to night by night, so this is a run-through of our ideal clubbing week.

Mondays to Wednesdays the best move would be to go to **21 Club & Lounge**, which does €3 drinks during the early week and has a €1 cover charge on Monday. **Tripod** on Harcourt St is also recommended for its two amazing floors (big one downstairs, small one upstairs) and its eclectic music mix, particularly midweek. **Crawdaddy** next door also offers a great cheap midweek indie/electro night with two rooms playing guaranteed indie/electro floor-fillers.

Come Thursdays and Fridays, things heat up in the city, but to be honest most venues are too crowded and too drunken to be much fun. Thursday sees almost every alcohol vender doing some deal. Two of the best are the **Button Factory** (formerly Temple Bar Music Centre) and **Fibber Magees**, despite Fibbers recently developing a huge overcrowding problem after 23.30. Both venues offer the best of what they do—electronica/oddities and rock/metal respectively. Both clubs also offer €3 drinks, with a €6–8 entry fee for the BF and €5 for Fibbers. The Button Factory has some interesting guest DJs and Fibbers has some interesting corsets, to put it simply. On Friday try **The Academy** on Middle Abbey St (formerly Spirit).

Come the weekend, the **Gaiety Theatre** is highly recommended on Saturday for its three floors of friend-losing madness. The Gaiety's doppelganger, **The Sunday Club** at D Two, is recommended for the following night, with its late-night party spirit, three floors and frequent good promotions.

It is worth remembering that the club scene is much safer and quieter early in the week. Key tips: travel with a group, don't accept candy from strangers, and keep as level a head as possible and you should be fine.

The opening times below are for club nights only, and while closing times may seem shockingly early, the boundaries of the law are thankfully often pushed. Cover charges are generally €5–12, but can be double that if there are guest DJs playing or any other excuse to hike up the price.

The Academy 57 Middle Abbey St, Dublin 1, tel 877 9999, web www.theacademydublin.com
Open Fri–Sat 22.30/23.00–02.30

Button Factory Curved St, Temple Bar, Dublin 2, tel 670 9202, web www.
buttonfactory.ie
Open Thurs–Sat 23.00–02.30, Sun 23.00–01.00

Crawdaddy Old Harcourt St Station, Harcourt St, Dublin 2, tel 476 3374,
web www.pod.ie
Open Wed, Fri, Sat 23.00–02.30

D Two Harcourt Hotel, 60 Harcourt St, Dublin 2, tel 476 4603, web www.
dtwonightclub.com
Open Wed–Sat 22.00–02.30, Sun 22.00–01.00

Fibber Magees 80 Parnell St, Dublin 1, tel 872 2575, web www.
fibbermagees.ie
Open (bar and club) Mon–Sat 12.00–02.30, Sun 12.00–01.00

Gaiety Theatre Sth King St, Dublin 2, tel 677 1717, web www.gaietytheatre.
com
Open Fri–Sat 23.30–02.30

Tripod Old Harcourt St Station, Harcourt St, Dublin 2, tel 476 3374, web
www.pod.ie
Open Wed, Fri, Sat 23.00–02.30

XXI Twentyone Club & Lounge 21 D'Olier St, Dublin 2, tel 671 2089, web
www.21.ie
Open Mon–Sat 23.00–02.30

Comedy

Ireland has produced some of the funniest comics there have
ever been, from Jonathan Swift and Myles na Gopaleen/
Flann O'Brien/Brian O'Nolan's literary comedy right up to the
vulgar pleasures of Tommy Tiernan. Dublin's comedy scene is
well established and packed with talent. TV has helped many
young Dublin careers and now there is a large comedy industry
operating in the city, proving itself week after week, with both
established names and a regiment of promising unknown talent
working the circuit.

A handful of pubs have given themselves over as venues
for comedy a couple of nights a week, with much success. **The
International Bar** and the **Ha'penny Bridge Inn** are the old

hands in this regard. The International has comedy seven nights a week—improvisation, amateur stand-up and established acts—as well as singer-songwriters and traditional music sessions. The **International Comedy Club** with established talent is on Thursday to Sunday, web www.theinternationalcomedyclub.com, with new acts and material showcased on a Sunday. On Tuesdays and Thursdays at the Ha'penny Bridge Inn, **Battle of the Axe**, web www.battleoftheaxe.com, offers a 'whatever you're having yourself' programme of stand-up, improv, sketches, singer-songwriters, poetry and more (check out the website and you may be able to print out coupons that cut a couple of euro off the entry price). This is fine if you're after something a little more experimental, but for plain old belly laughs the Ha'penny also hosts the **Capital Comedy Club**, web www.capitalcomedyclub.com, on Wednesdays and Sundays.

The **Comedy Shed**, Mondays at **The Wool Shed Baa and Grill**, is a relative newcomer sporting a good few established acts. Also worth your attention are the **Craic Pack's** improv show, web www.improvatbankers.com, inspired by Channel 4's *Whose Line Is It Anyway?*, at **The Bankers** bar Thursdays and Fridays; and the **Belvedere Comedy Club**, with improv and stand-up, Sundays at **The Belvedere** pub attached to The Belvedere Hotel.

The **Laughter Lounge** is a dedicated comedy venue on the north side of the quays, just off O'Connell St. The 320-seat venue does shows every Thursday, Friday and Saturday and has a full bar and a nightclub too. The trick is to check the billing carefully—the young Dublin comics can be seen at the above pubs for €10 or less. The Laughter Lounge really comes into its own when it brings international talent to play, so save your cash for those nights when you will get three Irish comics plus a major international talent—and entry to the nightclub—for a well-worth-it €25. It's half price for students on Thursday, and if you arrive on any night between 19.00 and 19.30 you can have a free cocktail of your choice.

In the end, personal taste will probably determine whether or not a gig is worth forking over your hard-won cash, but in our authoritative opinions the following always put on a good show: David O'Doherty, Dermot Whelan, Neil Delamere, Jarlath Regan, Andrew Stanley, Des Bishop, Ross Noble and Damien Clark. Also look out for the one- and two-man shows of Simon Toal.

The Bankers 16 Trinity St, Dublin 2, tel 679 3697
  The Craic Pack improv show, Thurs–Fri 21.30 (doors 21.00); stand-up on Sat; admission €10, students €8.
The Belvedere Great Denmark St, Dublin 1, tel 872 9199
  Belvedere Comedy Club, Sun, doors 20.30, admission €8, concessions/hotel residents €6. Wheelchair access by arrangement at hotel reception.
Ha'penny Bridge Inn Wellington Quay, Dublin 2, tel 677 0616
  Battle of the Axe, Tues & Thurs 21.30 (doors 20.30), admission €8, students €6. Capital Comedy Club, Wed & Sun 21.30 (doors 20.30), admission €7, students €5.
The International Bar 23 Wicklow St, Dublin 2, tel 677 9250, web www.international-bar.com
  Shows Mon-Fri 21.00 (doors 20.30); Sat 20.00 (doors 19.30), 22.30 (doors 22.15); Sun 20.45 (doors 20.15). Admission €10, students €8; Tues & Sun €5.
Laughter Lounge Basement 4–8 Eden Quay, O'Connell Bridge, Dublin 1, tel 878 3003, web www.laughterlounge.com
  Shows Thurs–Sat 20.30 (doors 19.00), admission €25 including entry to the After Lounge nightclub. Wheelchair access and accessible toilet.
The Wool Shed Baa & Grill Unit 4, Parnell Centre, Parnell St, Dublin 1, tel 872 4325, web www.woolshedbaa.com
  Comedy Shed, Mon 21.00, admission €5

On the town

Free entertainment

There's a lot of free entertainment in Dublin and the best of it can be found just by walking around with your eyes and ears open.

There are **buskers** every day and night, without fail, on and around Grafton St; naturally some of them are godawful, but there are some fantastic student, amateur, part-time and semi-pro musicians who make a few extra bob this way. Glen Hansard, Damien Rice, and the Hothouse Flowers started here. Performers vary wildly—from earnest young men with guitars singing 'Falling Slowly' to string quartets to limbo dancers to six-person trad groups.

Many pubs have **free music**, especially (but not only) trad music; some of the best are listed in the *Traditional music* section (see page 161).

Look out for events going on in the **public libraries**: film showings, exhibitions, conversation exchanges, readers' groups, and many other events; look for leaflets and posters in your local library or check the Dublin City Council website (www.dublincity.ie) for details.

Almost all **art galleries** in Dublin are free; see page 195, but there are many other, smaller galleries tucked away in side streets. Many of them are essentially showcases for living artists and are mostly intended for potential buyers, but you'll still be welcome even if all you want to do is look.

If you're into **classical music**, there are intermittent seasons of free lunchtime concerts at the Bank of Ireland and the National Concert Hall—check the NCH website (www.nch.ie) for details, or look for flyers in the foyer.

In fact, that's good advice in general: look at flyers and posters in cafés, bars, gig venues, libraries; a lot of free and cheap entertainment is provided on an ad hoc, once-off basis, and the best way to keep informed is to keep your eyes open.

Finally, if you fancy a look at the dark and seedy side of Dublin life, why not pop into the **Four Courts** on Inns Quay and take in a murder trial? Unless the courtroom door has an 'In Camera' sign on it, all trials are open to the public, with no charge (although there's limited space, and you will be expected to behave yourself; if your phone goes off at a crucial moment, expect to be thrown out).

On the town

Other venues for comedy, along with much else:

Bewley's Café Theatre—for comedic lunchtime shows as well as evening comedy (see page 170)

Mill Theatre, Dundrum—of all the suburban theatres, the best for comedy (see page 171)

The O₂—for big names, big events and big prices (see page 159)

Olympia Theatre (see page 172)

The Sugar Club—prices really depend on what's on, but for comedy usually €20–30 (see page 161)

Vicar Street—more intimate than other big venues but still pricey: stand-up €23–28 (see page 159)

Music

CHURCH MUSIC

Christ Church Cathedral, web www.cccdub.ie, holds Choral Evensong on Wednesdays and Thursdays at 18.00 (all year), and Saturdays at 17.00 (not July/Aug), Sung Eucharist Sundays at 11.00 and Choral Evensong Sunday 15.30. Frequent ticketed concerts held in the evenings and afternoons; see website for details. Wheelchair access if informed in advance.

St Mary's Pro-Cathedral Marlborough St, Dublin 1 tel 874 5441. Sung Mass by the world-renowned Palestrina Boys choir every Sunday at 11.00 except July/August.

St Patrick's Cathedral Patrick St, Dublin 2, web www.stpatrickscathedral. ie, Sung Eucharist or Matins 11.15 Sundays, Sung Matins 09.40 Mon–Fri (except July/Aug), Choral Evensong Mon–Fri 17.45, Sundays 15.15. Occasional lunchtime concerts by visiting choirs. There are no sung services Sat and Wed July/August. Wheelchair access through the side door. No toilets.

Trinity College Chapel Dublin 2, Choral Evensong every Thurs at 17.15 and Choral Eucharist Sun 10.45 during term time. There are often small receptions afterwards to which the congregation is invited. Not wheelchair accessible. The **traditional carol service** is held in the chapel in early December, with the best-loved carols in which everyone can join and more esoteric works sung by the Chapel Choir. Admission is free, but get there early as it is always *very* full.

CLASSICAL MUSIC For classical music lovers on a budget, there is a lot happening in Dublin.

The **National Concert Hall** at Earlsfort Terrace is Ireland's main classical music venue. It houses the national broadcaster's orchestra, the **RTÉ National Symphony Orchestra**, which plays most Friday evenings. You can also hear these concerts on RTÉ's Lyric FM, either live or at a later stage; if you miss the broadcast, you can listen again within a week from the RTÉ website at www.rte.ie. Adjoining the main concert hall is the **John Field Room** (otherwise used as the bar area) which hosts a variety of jazz, country music, traditional Irish music, folk, and world music concerts as well as smaller classical lunchtime recitals. Details of the concerts can be found in a monthly brochure available in the NCH itself and in some libraries; also listed in *The Irish Times* and at the NCH website at www.nch.ie.

Ticket prices vary widely, depending on who's playing—you can expect to pay €60 or more for the big names, but for less well-known performers decent tickets will be available for less than €10. For most concerts, the cheapest seats are in the choir balcony behind the stage; when the balcony's not being occupied by an actual choir, there are unreserved seats available for purchase on the day of the performance at prices at least €5 lower than the lowest standard seating price. Full time students with ID can take a chance on standby tickets; for a mere €5, one ticket per person can be bought an hour before the performance—subject to availability, of course. If you're a regular concert-goer, check the NCH website for special offers; there are often ticket bundles available for seasons of related concerts that can be a lot cheaper than buying each ticket individually.

The National Concert Hall, Earlsfort Tce, Dublin 2, tel 417 0000 (box office) 417 0077 (admin), web www.nch.ie
Wheelchair accessible. Loop system.

On the town

Free **Music in the Park** sponsored by Dublin City Council takes place in various Dublin parks on Sunday afternoons during the summer, with brass and reed bands, brass quintets, youth bands and jazz. Check upcoming concerts at the notice boards near the gates in St Stephen's Green.

Check the listings in Friday's 'The Ticket' supplement to *The Irish Times* and on www.entertainment.ie for information on **occasional concerts**. The following are some of the more regular venues.

The Bank of Ireland Arts Centre Foster Place, Temple Bar, Dublin 2, tel 671 2261. Wheelchair users ring beforehand.
The Goethe-Institut Library 37 Merrion Sq, Dublin 2, tel 661 1155
The Hugh Lane Gallery (also known as the Municipal Gallery) Charlemont House, Parnell Sq Nth, Dublin 1, tel 222 5550
    Free Sunday concerts at noon; both classical and contemporary music. Wheelchair accessible and toilets.
Instituto Cervantes Lincoln House, Lincoln Place, Dublin 2, tel 631 1500
National Gallery of Ireland Merrion Sq, Dublin 2, tel 661 5133, web www. nationalgallery.ie
    Hosts classical concerts, including performances of the National Chamber Choir, in the Shaw Room. Some events are free while others require a ticket which can be bought on the door; prices vary. See website or in-gallery brochures for details. Wheelchair accessible and toilets.

GIGS AND BANDS The city is on all the major European touring circuits, so most of the leading international acts will stop off for a gig or two at some point. What's more, the calibre and sheer number of gig venues in the city has increased wildly in the last few years, much to the delight of the music lovers of Dublin.

Amongst the big hitters is the spectacular, amphitheatre-style **The O$_2$ arena**, which is the go-to guy for all the big international acts.

Outdoor sporting arenas in the city, such as **Croke Park** and the **RDS** (Royal Dublin Society), often host major gigs, as do **Marlay Park** and the **Phoenix Park**. The downside to these venues is that ticket prices can be extortionate depending on the act playing, with some heading up towards the €90 mark.

The number of smaller, more intimate venues popping up throughout the city has made it far easier to check out up-and-coming bands and artists, Irish or otherwise, who may be stopping by. In fact, the Dublin live scene has never been better in this regard, with fantastic little venues like **Crawdaddy**, **The Academy**, **Tripod**, **The Village**, **Thinktank**, **Whelan's** and the **Button Factory** playing host to such acts on a weekly basis. Best of all, ticket prices for most gigs are usually only between €15 and €30 depending on the band (and can be as low as €8–10 in places like Whelan's for local acts).

If you're up for a bit of talent scouting, you can try the numerous pubs and bars around the city which put on live music on a regular basis. Of course, there is no guarantee that any of the bands will be worth your while, but if all you're looking for is some cheap live music in friendly surroundings, then you could do worse than trawl the pubs the city has to offer (see also *Jazz*, page 160 and *Traditional music*, page 161). With these more intimate music sessions in mind, you really can't beat the dingy yet welcoming surroundings of **Eamonn Doran's** in Temple Bar, a particular favourite for bands from around the local area. It generally has a lively, chatty atmosphere, and gigs cost only €5–10. The price is at the discretion of the band, who get to keep all the money—ED's charge nothing themselves. Keep an eye on your stuff, though, as pick-pocketing has been known to happen.

The middling-sized venues—**Vicar Street, The Ambassador** and the **Olympia**—often play host to more well-known, quality bands, with the Olympia also branching out into musical theatre, comedy and its notorious Midnight at the Olympia sessions.

These days the midnight sessions cater almost exclusively for tribute acts, but can still offer a rewarding night out given the right crowd, and a decent band in their element. Ticket prices for these venues again depend on the act playing but usually hover between €25 and €40—though Vicar Street can head up towards €60.

Tickets for almost every venue in Dublin are available from **Ticketmaster**, which has booking outlets in the Jervis Centre, Dublin 1 and the St Stephen's Green Centre, Dublin 2, as well as elsewhere throughout the city. Bookings can also be made online at www.ticketmaster.ie. If it's a small gig you're looking into and you can't seem to find it listed on Ticketmaster, it usually means that you'll just have to pay at the door. Best to check in advance though.

As for other costs, generally pubs will have normal drinks prices (€4.40–4.80 for a pint of Guiness) but the bigger venues will charge more. The O_2 will sting you €6 for a pint and €3 for a bottle of water.

www.entertainment.ie should be your bible when it comes to what's on; it covers all gigs and events in the city. See also **www.eventguide.ie**. and if you must you could also check out **www.indublin.ie**.

The Irish Times' Friday supplement **'The Ticket'** provides a good source of entertainment options as well as interesting features and reviews. ***Hot Press*** combines music views and interviews with political pieces and is usually worth a read; pop into a public library and take a look if you don't feel like paying. The website **www.hotpress.com** has some free content but to access it all you need to subscribe. The Dublin zine scene has been hampered by the internet and the affluence of recent years, but you might still find some fanzines and freesheets, offering a fuller and less orthodox view of music in Dublin—in the smaller record shops. *Analogue* deserves attention at **www. analoguemagazine.com**.

The Academy 57 Middle Abbey St, Dublin 1, tel 877 9999, web www. theacademydublin.com
  Wheelchair access and accessible toilet.
The Ambassador O'Connell St, Dublin 1, tel 0818 333 773, web www.mcd.ie
Button Factory Curved St, Temple Bar, Dublin 2, tel 670 9202, web www. buttonfactory.ie
  Wheelchair access and accessible toilet.
Crawdaddy Old Harcourt St Station, Harcourt St, Dublin 2, tel 476 3374, web www.pod.ie
  Wheelchair access and accessible toilet.
Croke Park Jones's Rd, Dublin 3, tel 819 2300, web www.crokepark.ie
  Wheelchair access and accessible toilet.
  Getting there Dublin Bus nos 3, 11, 11A, 16, 16A, 41.
Eamonn Doran's 3A Crown Alley, Temple Bar, Dublin 2, tel 679 9114, web www.myspace.com/eamonndorans
Marlay Park Rathfarnham, Dublin 14
  Getting there Dublin Bus nos 16, 48N.
The O$_2$ North Wall Quay, Dublin 1, tel 819 8888, web www.theo2.ie
  Wheelchair access and accessible toilet.
Olympia Theatre 72 Dame St, Dublin 2, tel 679 3323, web www.mcd.ie/ olympia
  Wheelchair access and accessible toilet.
Phoenix Park Dublin 8
  Getting there Luas Red line to the Museum stop; Dublin Bus nos 25, 25A, 25N, 26, 66, 66N, 67, 67A, 68, 69, 69X.
RDS Ballsbridge, Dublin 4, tel 668 0866, web www.rds.ie
  Wheelchair access and accessible toilet.
  Getting there DART to Sandymount; Dublin Bus nos 7, 7A, 45.
ThinkTank 23–24 Eustace St, Temple Bar, Dublin 2, tel 670 7655
Tripod Old Harcourt St Station, Harcourt St, Dublin 2, tel 476 3374, web www.pod.ie
  Wheelchair access and accessible toilet.
Vicar Street 58–59 Thomas St, Dublin 1, tel 454 5533, web www. aikenpromotions.com
  Wheelchair access and accessible toilet.

The Village 26 Wexford St, Dublin 2, tel 475 8555 (venue)/1890 200 078 (tickets), web www.thevillagevenue.com
Wheelchair access and accessible toilet.

Whelan's 25 Wexford St, Dublin 2, tel 478 0766 (bar)/1890 200 078 (tickets), web www.whelanslive.com
Wheelchair access and accessible toilet.

JAZZ (AND MORE) The jazz scene in Dublin has definitely become more glamorous over the last few years. There are still very few casual, free pub jazz gigs but a handful can be found around the city, usually on a Sunday afternoon.

The most prominent venue for jazz in Dublin has to be **JJ Smyth's**, which has live blues and jazz music five or six nights a week. This is where many musicians got their start and where top names continue to play. The place also attracts a friendlier, more dedicated crowd than most and great gigs are guaranteed almost every week. Gigs usually cost €8–10, with the doors opening at 21.00.

The pricey new **Le Cirk Culture Café** and Bar on Dame St, nevertheless has good things going on jazz-wise in their tapas bar downstairs. In low season you can catch jazz here Thursday to Sunday, and in high season there are gigs seven nights a week.

The Boom Boom Room, below Murray's Bar on O'Connell St, fashions itself as Dublin's alternative music venue. All styles are welcome and it's particularly good for world and electronica as well as the experimental. Check www.entertainment.ie or other listings to see what's on.

The Sugar Club, on the Stephen's Green end of Leeson St, features live bands (usually of the Latin and swing variety) as well as DJs. Their regular Saturday club with live bands and DJs starts at 23.00 and if you arrive between then and midnight you can get two-for-one entry at €15. Gig tickets range from €10 to €25. Tables can be reserved here for wheelchair users and there is complete wheelchair access.

The Pier House bar in Howth has a free jazz session on Sundays from 16.00 to 20.00, and the **Cobblestone** in Smith-field—on the Luas Red line—hosts gigs of all kinds so it's worth checking out the bill there too.

The Boom Boom Room 34 Upr O'Connell St, Dublin 1, tel 087 669 2489, web www.theboomboomroom.tv

The Cobblestone 77 Nth King St, Smithfield, Dublin 7, tel 872 1799, web www.myspace.com/thecobblestone
Wheelchair access but no accessible toilet.
Getting there Luas Red line to Smithfield

JJ Smyth's 12 Aungier St, Dublin 2, tel 475 2565, web www.jjsmyths.com

The Pier House 4 East Pier, Howth, Co Dublin, tel 832 4510
Wheelchair access but no accessible toilet.
Getting there DART to Howth; Dublin Bus nos 31, 31B to Howth.

The Sugar Club 8 Lr Leeson St, Dublin 2, tel 678 7188, web www.thesugarclub.com
Wheelchair access and accessible toilet.

Le Cirk Culture Café and Bar 32 Dame St, Dublin 2, tel 635 0056/635 0058, web www.lecirk.ie

TRADITIONAL MUSIC Pubs all over Dublin regularly offer Irish traditional music. This can range from obscure *sean-nós* singers to the generic yet lively dance tunes of a session. Trad sessions can sustain themselves without the need for sheet music and last for many hours, which makes them the ideal form of pub entertainment.

O'Donoghue's bar, one of Dublin's most famous, is only two minutes from Stephen's Green and provides live music seven days a week, kicking off at 21.00 Monday to Saturday and all day Sunday. The establishment was once notable for its long-running association with the Dubliners and Christy Moore, who spent many a night entertaining the crowds here in years gone by. Today, O'Donoghue's has lost some of its flair but it is still one of the premier session venues in the city.

A newcomer in the city centre is also something of an old-timer: **McNeill's** on Capel St recently reopened as a pub and hosts a well-known traditional music shop upstairs. With such a pedigree, you'd expect the sessions here to be the real thing—and they are, held from 21.30 till late Tuesday, Thursday, Friday and Saturday, and from 15.00–19.00 on Sunday. There's a bluegrass session every Wednesday from 21.30.

The Temple Bar area is home to a handful of decent traditional music pubs, such as **The Temple Bar**, which provides Irish music every day with no cover charge. Also worth a visit is **The Oliver St John Gogarty**, with its live music bar on the first floor hosting trad sessions from 15.00 till late every day of the week. It is also the starting point of an famous musical pub crawl.

The Pier House bar in Howth provides great free sessions every Friday and Saturday from 22.00 and on Sunday from 13.00 to 16.00. The Guinness out here is cheaper than you'll usually get in the city centre too.

The Cobblestone pub at the top of Smithfield Square in the north inner city has recently become quite popular amongst the late 20s and early 30s demographic, and you can find many a young thing mingling with the inner city clientèle. The back room hosts nicely priced pay-in gigs of various kinds, and there are free traditional sessions in the bar each night, with musicians from all over Ireland. The Sunday session starts at 14.00. There's also a free old-time guitar/bluegrass session on Saturday from 16.00 to 19.00. The Cobblestone is within walking distance of the centre or you can get the Luas Red line to Smithfield. The bar itself is very pleasant, like a country pub in the heart of the city.

Across the river, **O'Shea's The Merchant** is worth a look—a bar that over the years has hosted a good few famous trad musicians. Live trad is held here every night from 22.00.

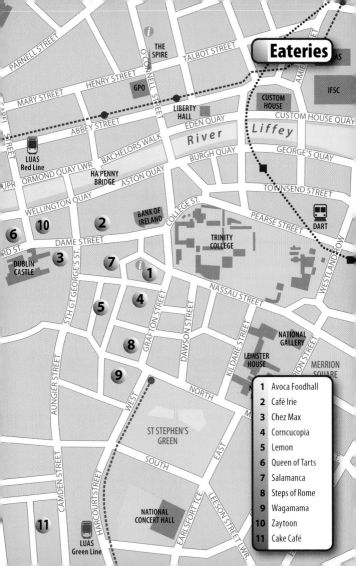

Eateries

1	Avoca Foodhall
2	Café Irie
3	Chez Max
4	Corncucopia
5	Lemon
6	Queen of Tarts
7	Salamanca
8	Steps of Rome
9	Wagamama
10	Zaytoon
11	Cake Café

PARNELL STREET

THE SPIRE

TALBOT STREET

HENRY STREET

O'CONNELL STREET

MARY STREET

GPO

ABBEY STREET

LIBERTY HALL

EDEN QUAY

CUSTOM HOUSE

IFSC

CUSTOM HOUSE QUAY

GEORGE'S QUAY

River Liffey

BURGH QUAY

LUAS Red Line

ORMOND QUAY LWR

BACHELORS WALK

HA'PENNY BRIDGE

ASTON QUAY

TOWNSEND STREET

WELLINGTON QUAY

BANK OF IRELAND

COLLEGE ST.

PEARSE STREET

DART

DAME STREET

TRINITY COLLEGE

DUBLIN CASTLE

STH GT GEORGE'S ST.

NASSAU STREET

GRAFTON STREET

DAWSON STREET

KILDARE STREET

NATIONAL GALLERY

LEINSTER HOUSE

MERRION SQUARE

AUNGIER STREET

NORTH

WEST

ST STEPHEN'S GREEN

EAST

SOUTH

CAMDEN STREET

HARCOURT ST.

NATIONAL CONCERT HALL

EARLSFORT TCE.

LEESON STREET LWR

LUAS Green Line

WESTLAND ROW

AMIENS STREET

Just beyond The Merchant, **The Brazen Head**—also known as the oldest pub in Ireland (and they make sure you know it)—holds a popular Sunday afternoon session between 14.00 and 17.00 during which customers (that means YOU) have the opportunity to sing their hearts out with accompaniment from the band. There's live Irish music Monday to Friday too and a bit of variety on Saturday with blues and other things. Van Morrison, the Hothouse Flowers and the Dubliners have played here, and the pub was once featured in a Garth Brooks video.

These are only a handful of the sessions going on throughout the city, but they are all free and they represent probably the best balance between authentic traditional fare and the exciting, vibrant nature of this most accessible form of folk music.

On the town

The Brazen Head 20 Lr Bridge St, Dublin 8, tel 677 9549, web www. brazenhead.com
   Wheelchair access and toilets are accessible though not specially adapted.
The Cobblestone 77 Nth King St, Smithfield, Dublin 7, tel 872 1799, web www.myspace.com/thecobblestone
   Wheelchair access but no accessible toilets.
   Getting there Luas Red line to Smithfield
McNeill's 140 Capel St, Dublin 1, tel 874 7679
O'Donoghue's 15 Merrion Row, Dublin 2, tel 660 7194, web www. odonoghues.ie
   Wheelchair access but no accessible toilet.
The Oliver St John Gogarty 58–59 Fleet St, Temple Bar, Dublin 2, tel 671 1822, web www.gogartys.ie/pub
The Pier House 4 East Pier, Howth, Co Dublin, tel 832 4510
   Wheelchair access but no accessible toilet.
   Getting there DART to Howth; Dublin Bus nos 31, 31B to Howth.
O'Shea's The Merchant 12 Lr Bridge St, Dublin 8, tel 679 3797, web www. osheahotel.com
The Temple Bar 47–48 Temple Bar, Dublin 2, tel 672 5286/672 5287, web www.thetemplebarpubdublin.com

Theatre

Ireland's biggest export may well be words—ironically, English words—and Irish theatre has steadfastly clung to wordy drama, while other countries experimented with ways to create theatre without a script. Why change a winning formula? Irish playwrights have a long tradition of success and quality on the world stage, from J. M. Synge to Brian Friel to Marina Carr. And theatre has been thriving in Dublin—at least as far as infrastructure is concerned, with a raft of 'necklace' theatres built in the suburbs in recent years, and stalwarts like the Gate and the Gaiety undergoing upgrades. The city has two major theatre festivals—the **Dublin Theatre Festival** and the **Dublin Fringe Festival**, both held around September/October every year, and both featuring performances at venues and locations all across town. The former is the more stuffy and often attracts world-famous stars to the Dublin stage; the latter offers wacky acts from all corners of the globe, and is perhaps the best opportunity to see experimental theatre in the city, or theatre which is not happening in theatre buildings. A third, burgeoning festival is the **International Dublin Gay Theatre Festival**, showcasing work by gay theatre artists (writers or otherwise), as well as works with gay themes or relevance. Begun in 2004 to celebrate the 150th anniversary of Oscar Wilde's birth, it's now held annually in May.

Much of the pride surrounding theatre in Dublin rests with the Abbey and the Gate. Founded by W. B. Yeats and Lady Augusta Gregory, the **Abbey** is, of course, Ireland's National Theatre, the first state-subsidised theatre in the English-speaking world. It opened in 1904, and is perhaps as famous for its controversies as for the plays that were first put on there. The row sparked by Synge's *Playboy of the Western World,* which the Nationalists furiously denounced as a slander on the purity of Irish womanhood, is a good example. In recent times, the Abbey has struggled to define its role in this post-nationalist, largely post-theatre, and very commercial modern Ireland. However, you will still find some of the best new Irish playwriting here—though, given its remit, it tends to favour plays about the 'Irish experience' rather than plays that just happen to be written by Irish people. You'll also find a healthy serving of Irish and Western classics, done usually safely but well.

The Abbey has a baby sister called the **Peacock**, which concentrates on the contemporary and unusual. Whereas new writing on the Abbey main stage tends to be from established playwrights, the Peacock is where up-and-comers get to strut their stuff. 'Contemporary classics' are also regular fare. The Peacock is altogether much less formal than the Abbey proper, though both venues together constitute the National Theatre. At the moment the two theatres are still in Abbey St but there is a plan to move to a larger venue at George's Dock by 2012.

The **Gate** was originally founded in 1928 to present within Ireland what the Abbey wasn't presenting: European and American drama, both classic and new. Nowadays, however, there are strong overlaps in the kinds of theatre covered by each. The guy in the tux telling you to turn off your mobile phones before every show always makes you feel you're in a bastion of privilege.

The **Gaiety**, on the other hand, for the most part makes no pretensions to Serious Theatre. It is Dublin's oldest surviving commercial theatre (opening in 1871) and it behaves as such, shamelessly putting on middlebrow and populist shows which often do better (financially) than their highbrow counterparts. Fans of raw tack—keep an eye out. After all, this is where the first Eurovision Song Contest to be hosted in Ireland was held.

Another reason to keep an eye out for the Gaiety is that it is a venue for hire—and this is when it can get serious. Touring companies of international repute sometimes perform there and completely outshine domestic theatre. On these occasions, the Gaiety can be the best place in the city to see quality theatre. On Fridays and Saturdays, the Gaiety is also a nightclub.

If it is pure entertainment you're after, then the **Olympia**, even more than the Gaiety, specialises not so much in plays as in a broader spectrum of performative delights. It hosts gigs of all kinds, from tribute bands to visiting and local originals, as well as musicals, revue, pantomime, variety and comedy, and more. Another venue offering a range of music, comedy, and light (on the mind) theatre is the **Tivoli**.

For more artistically 'important' work, often from young Irish theatre artists, check out the **Project Arts Centre** or **The New Theatre**, beside each other in Temple Bar. The Project in particular markets itself as modern and cool, for trendy youthful arty types. Its origins date back to a three-week festival at the Gate in 1966, and it boasts a central place in the early careers of U2, Neil Jordan and Jim Sheridan. The centre's two theatres are called the Cube and the Space Upstairs, and it also holds visual arts exhibitions which are all free. If avant-garde work is happening in Dublin, it's more likely to be found here than at the Abbey.

The **Focus Theatre**, where Gabriel Byrne cut his theatrical teeth, could also fit into the group of small venues that host much new work by Irish writers, directors and designers, but it is closed for renovations until at least 2010. The theatre's creative team, however, is still producing shows at other locations (such as Bewley's and the Mill). **Smock Alley Theatre**, Dublin's first legal playhouse, was given a Royal Patent or licence to show plays in 1662, and it's now being restored to its former glory. Smock Alley is currently managed by the Gaiety School of Acting, where Colin Farrell trained; the theatre at the moment is a black box venue for hire, but the Gaiety School hopes to complete the restoration in 2011.

On the town

At **Bewley's Café Theatre**, you can get soup, bread and a 50-minute lunchtime show for €15. If nothing else it's a novelty to be able to eat while watching a performance. The Café Theatre specialises in comedy, new writing and lesser-known pieces by well-known authors. In the evenings, it does cabaret, music and comedy from both established and emerging talent.

If you're around Dublin at the end of August/beginning of September, it's worth seeing if **Public Shakespeare** is giving any of its signature performances in St Stephen's Green. The group grafts its own exuberant style onto the Bard's words, playing in the open air and for free.

For children, there is the **Lambert Puppet Theatre**, near Dún Laoghaire, which puts on versions of fairy tales and well-known children's adventures every Saturday and Sunday. It's also worth checking out **The Ark**, a cultural centre for children in Temple Bar, which puts on all sorts of cool events, including theatre. Even the Project occasionally stages children's plays, so do keep an eye out. The Gaiety and the Olympia offer competing Christmas pantomimes every year, and often play host to kids' musicals, but these are expensive.

The 'necklace' theatres (so called because they circle the city by being in the suburbs)—such as the **Civic** in Tallaght, the **Pavilion** in Dún Laoghaire, **Draíocht** in Blanchardstown and the **Mill** in Dundrum—provide a mix of community/amateur work and more challenging pieces. Music, comedy and special arts events—poetry festivals, dance festivals—are also common.

If your main interest is simply in seeing a play in Dublin, then your best shoestring bet is to check out the drama societies of Trinity College and UCD, **Players** and **Dramsoc** respectively. Being university societies, they are amateur, but the standard is always tolerable and can be surprisingly high. The mix of plays runs from traditional Shakespeare to medieval drama to the most avant-garde and unique types of theatre imaginable. You're bound to find eager students struggling to put their own stamp on things, which can result in utter flops, but can also lead to something quite inspiring. What's more, the average performance will set you back just €5 or less, so if it's no good you can't complain too much. And while UCD is a little far out, Players Theatre is one of the most central in the city.

Also in Trinity is the **Samuel Beckett Theatre**, the venue which Mr Beckett once described as the worst place in the world to stage his plays (because there is no possibility of silence, apparently). Happily, then, you won't find much Beckett at the Samuel Beckett Theatre, but they do put on relatively cheap shows starring Department of Drama students at various points throughout the year. At other times, the SBT presents work by touring companies.

Most evening performances start at 20.00 and Saturday matinées at 14.00, 14.30 or 15.00, but always check. Long plays sometimes begin at 19.30 or earlier.

Concession tickets are generally available to students, under-18s, the unemployed, senior citizens, people with disabilities and members of Equity. Discounts may also be available for groups (usually of ten or more).

If you aren't eligible for a concession (or even if you are), another way to see a show for less than the standard price is to go to a **preview**. These are treated like dress rehearsals by the cast and crew—though this rarely affects the quality, and in some cases can in fact make the performance fresher. Watch the event listings for this worthwhile and economic option.

Most theatres have **wheelchair access** and wheelchair spaces in the auditoria, but book in advance and inform the theatre of your needs. Some venues are wheelchair accessible but don't have dedicated toilet facilities. We have indicated below which theatres

On the town

have **loop systems** for the hearing impaired; other venues may acquire them from time to time, so don't hesitate to ask.

Abbey Theatre Lr Abbey St, Dublin 1, tel 878 7222, web www.abbeytheatre.ie
Tickets €22–35, concessions €15–25, matinées and previews €18–22. Wheelchair access and accessible toilet. Loop system for the hearing impaired. Audio-described performances for the visually impaired, sign language-interpreted performances, and captioned performances (similar to TV subtitling) are available on certain dates—see the website or contact the theatre for more details.

The Ark 11A Eustace St, Temple Bar, Dublin 2, tel 670 7788, web www.ark.ie
Prices vary depending on the event. Shows are aimed at children aged 3–14. Wheelchair access and accessible toilet. Loop system for the hearing impaired.

Bewley's Café Theatre Second Floor, 78 Grafton St, Dublin 2, tel 086 878 4001, web www.bewleyscafetheatre.com
Lunchtime shows €15 including soup and bread. Performances begin at 13.10 (doors 12.50), duration 50 mins. For evening cabaret, prices and times vary. Wheelchair access and accessible toilet.

Civic Theatre Tallaght, Dublin 24, tel 462 7477, web www.civictheatre.ie
Standard ticket price €20, concessions €16, but varies depending on the production. Wheelchair access and accessible toilet. Loop system for the hearing impaired.
Getting there Luas Red line from Connolly Station to Tallaght; Dublin Bus nos 49, 49A, 50, 54A, 56A, 65, 65B, 77, 77A to The Square, Tallaght.

Draíocht Arts Centre The Blanchardstown Centre, Blanchardstown, Dublin 15, tel 885 2622, web www.draiocht.ie
Prices vary depending on the event, but for a play expect to pay around €12–20, concessions €10–18. Wheelchair access and accessible toilet. Loop system for the hearing impaired.
Getting there Dublin Bus nos 39, 70 to Blanchardstown Shopping Centre.

Dramsoc Theatre Lr Ground Floor, Newman (Arts) Building, UCD, Belfield, Dublin 4, tel 716 8545, web www.ucddramsoc.com
For members tickets €3, student non-members €4, non-students €5. Performances at 13.00 and 19.00 throughout college term time. Wheelchair access and accessible toilet.
Getting there over two dozen Dublin Bus routes serve UCD, including nos 46A, 145 and no 10, which goes inside the campus.

Dublin Fringe Festival
> Runs for around two weeks in September annually. For information tel 817 1677 or visit www.fringefest.com.

Dublin Theatre Festival
> Runs for two and a half weeks in September–October annually. For information tel 677 8439 or visit www.dublintheatrefestival.com.

International Dublin Gay Theatre Festival
> Runs for two weeks in May annually. For information visit www.gaytheatre.ie.

Focus Theatre 6 Pembroke Place, off Pembroke St, Dublin 2
> Closed for renovations until at least 2010, but producing shows at other venues such as Bewley's and the Mill. For more information tel 671 2417.

Gaiety Theatre Sth King St, Dublin 2, tel 677 1717, web www.gaietytheatre.com
> Prices vary depending on the production. Wheelchair access and accessible toilet. Loop system for the hearing impaired.

Gate Theatre Cavendish Row, Parnell Sq, Dublin 1, tel 874 4045/874 6042, web www.gate-theatre.ie
> Tickets €30–34; matinées, Mondays and previews €25; concessions (not always available) €15. Wheelchair access and accessible toilet.

Lambert Puppet Theatre Clifton Lane, Monkstown, Co Dublin, tel 280 0974, web www.lambertpuppettheatre.com
> Adults €13, children and concessions €11. Performances at 15.30 Saturday and Sunday. Wheelchair access and accessible toilet.
> *Getting there* DART to Salthill & Monkstown; Dublin Bus nos 7, 7A to Monkstown.

Mill Theatre Dundrum Town Centre, Dundrum, Dublin 14, tel 296 9340, web www.milltheatre.com
> For plays tickets generally range from €12 to €25 depending on the production. Other events (music, etc) may be more expensive. Concessions available. Wheelchair access and accessible toilet.
> *Getting there* Luas Green line from St Stephen's Green to Dundrum or Balally; Dublin Bus nos 14, 14a, 44, 44C, 48A to Dundrum Town Centre.

On the town

On the town

The New Theatre 43 East Essex St, Temple Bar, Dublin 2, tel 670 3361, web www.thenewtheatre.com

Standard ticket price €20, concessions €15–18, but varies depending on the production. Wheelchair access (but a small step at the entrance) and accessible toilet.

Olympia Theatre 72 Dame St, Dublin 2, tel 679 3323, web www.mcd.ie/olympia

Prices vary depending on the production. Wheelchair access and accessible toilet. Can arrange facilities for the hearing impaired on request.

Pavilion Theatre Marine Rd, Dún Laoghaire, Co Dublin, tel 231 2929, web www.paviliontheatre.ie

Standard ticket price €20, concessions €15, but varies depending on the production. Wheelchair access and accessible toilet. Loop system for the hearing impaired.

Getting there DART to Dún Laoghaire; Dublin Bus nos 7, 7A, 8, 45, 46A, 746 to Dún Laoghaire.

Peacock Theatre Lr Abbey St, Dublin 1, tel 878 7222, web www.abbeytheatre.ie

Tickets €22, matinées €18, concessions and previews €15. There is no wheelchair access to the Peacock as it is a basement theatre located down three flights of steps, with no lift. The Abbey loop system is not currently available in the Peacock. Occasional performances, however, are sign language-interpreted.

Players Theatre Trinity College, Dublin 2, tel 896 2242, web www.duplayers.com

Performances at 13.00 and 18.00/20.00 throughout college term time. Tickets for 13.00/18.00 shows generally €2 for members, €3.50 for non-members; 20.00 shows €3.50 for members, €5 for non-members. Wheelchair access and accessible toilet.

Project Arts Centre 39 East Essex St, Temple Bar, Dublin 2, tel 881 9613/881 9614, web www.project.ie

Tickets for plays €5–25, concessions available. Visual arts exhibitions free. Wheelchair access and accessible toilet. Loop system for the hearing impaired.

Public Shakespeare

Admission free. Performances at the Yeats Memorial in St Stephen's Green. Two performances per day, usually starting in the last week of August, for two weeks. Keep an eye on entertainment papers and websites and look out for people handing out flyers nearby.

Samuel Beckett Theatre Trinity College, Dublin 2, tel 896 2461, web www.tcd.ie/drama

Prices vary depending on the company presenting. Department of Drama productions around €8–12, concessions €3–5. Wheelchair access and accessible toilet.

Smock Alley Theatre Lr Exchange St, Temple Bar, Dublin 2

For more information contact the Gaiety School of Acting, tel 679 9277, web www.gaietyschool.com/smock_alley_theatre

Tivoli Theatre 135 Francis St, Dublin 8, tel 454 4472, web www.tivoli.ie

Prices vary depending on the event. Wheelchair access but no accessible toilet.

Festivals

The Irish will leap at any excuse for a party. Sport, arts, religion, being young, being old—you name it, there's a festival for it, either ongoing or being planned.

The following is a month-by-month selection of the annual big-hitters in the city and its surrounds, but there are countless other festivals from the obscure to the mainstream. To keep up-to-date with exact dates and details see **www.visitdublin.com/events**.

NOVEMBER—EARLY JANUARY

Dublin on Ice Smithfield, Dublin 7 web www.dublinonice.ie

Smithfield Plaza is transformed into a 1,000 square-metre ice rink, with Santa and Belgian hot chocolate thrown in as well! Great for families or couples in particular.

JANUARY

Temple Bar TradFest web www.templebartrad.com

One of the best trad music festivals of the year. A four-day celebration of traditional Irish music and culture, with live performances from some of Ireland's best musicians, as well as children's events, exhibitions, workshops, a music trail, Irish dancing and storytelling.

On the town

FEBRUARY

Jameson Dublin International Film Festival web www.dubliniff.com
One of the most high-profile events in Ireland, screening diverse film premieres and hosting many popular forums throughout 10 days in February.

MARCH

St Patrick's Festival web www.stpatricksday.ie
Five days of music, street theatre, family carnivals, comedy, street performances, dance, and night spectacles… culminating on March 17th with the Paddy's Day Parade to celebrate the day when the whole world wants to be Irish.

DLR Poetry Now Festival Dún Laoghaire, web www.poetrynow.ie
The biggest and most prestigious poetry festival in Ireland, bringing together poets of different styles and nationalities.

APRIL

Dublin: One City, One Book web www.dublinonecityonebook.ie
A project designed to encourage everyone in the city to read the same book during the month of April.

Dublin Handel Festival
A yearly commemoration of the first performance of Handel's Messiah in 1742 on Fishamble St, Temple Bar. Free talks, music, concerts and tours.

MAY

Bealtaine Festival web www.olderinireland.ie
A nationwide arts festival throughout May celebrating creativity in older age.

Heineken Green Energy web www.heinekenmusic.ie
Annual festival in Dublin Castle over the May bank holiday weekend that opens the music festival season; includes street carnival, music seminars and the notorious 'Band Challenge'.

The International Dublin Gay Theatre Festival web www.gaytheatre.ie
Runs for two weeks in May annually.

JUNE

Docklands Maritime Festival web www.dublindocklands.ie
Very popular event over the June bank holiday weekend that features spectacular tall ships that the public can board and walk around on. Also includes street theatre, music and various family activities.

Flora Women's Mini Marathon web www.womensminimarathon.ie
The world's largest all-women sports event takes place along the streets of south Dublin as women walk, trot, jog or skip the 10km mini-marathon for charity. Some would say it's sexist, but they'd be male chauvinist pigs.

Dublin Writers' Festival web www.dublinwritersfestival.com
If you're Irish you have a statistically higher chance of winning a Nobel Prize for Literature than if you were from any other country. It's no surprise, then, that we should be celebrating our literary heritage

Bloomsday Festival James Joyce Centre 35 Nth Great George's St, Dublin 1, web www.jamesjoyce.ie
Joyceans from all over the world congregate in Dublin to celebrate the life and work of their favourite author—with readings, performances, breakfasts, walks, conferences and visits to the pub. The first Bloomsday was on 16 June 1904 when James Joyce went on his first date with Nora Barnacle. Years later, Joyce chose to set *Ulysses* on the same day.

Dublin LGBTQ Pride Festival web www.dublinpride.org
With its explosion of colour transforming the streets of Dublin, the festival lasts about a week, culminating in the Pride Parade commemorating the Stonewall riots in New York in 1969.

JULY

Oxegen Festival Punchestown, Co Kildare, web www.oxegen.ie
One of the biggest events on the Irish music calendar. Formerly known as Witnness, this three-day rock festival presents the very best acts on the international music scene.

AUGUST

Fáilte Ireland Dublin Horse Show RDS, Ballsbridge, Dublin 4, web www.dublinhorseshow.com
A Dublin institution. A celebration of our country's affinity with the horse, from the best show horses to the best international show jumpers. One of Ireland's largest events, a highlight of the summer each year, with close to 80,000 visitors from all over the world.

Dún Laoghaire Festival of World Cultures web www.festivalofworldcultures.com
An annual international arts festival, celebrating artistic traditions from around the world through a programme of concerts, club nights, theatre, dance performances, circus, markets and exhibitions.

On the town

SEPTEMBER

Bulmer's Comedy Festival web www.bulmerscomedy.ie

Attracts top international acts and takes place in various venues in the city for around three weeks.

Dublin Fringe Festival (theatre)

Runs for around two weeks in September annually. For information tel 817 1677 or visit www.fringefest.com.

Dublin Theatre Festival

Runs for two and a half weeks in September–October annually. For information tel 677 8439 or visit www.dublintheatrefestival.com.

Electric Picnic web www.electricpicnic.ie

Held in Stradbally, Co Laois, this rival for Oxegen is considerably cooler and more grown-up. The music choice is more eclectic and alternative and they work hard with lots of diverse events: silent disco, cinema, comedy, plus far better food and sleeping arrangements than you'll usually find at such affairs. This is the highlight of the year for many twenty- and thirty-something Irish.

International Puppet Festival Ireland Lambert Puppet Theatre, Clifton Lane, Monkstown, Co Dublin, web www.puppetfest.ie

Ireland's only festival dedicated to the art of puppetry features up to 10 of the world's best puppet theatre companies in mid-September each year. Something for all ages and tastes is generally on offer.

OCTOBER

Lifestyle Sports Adidas Dublin Marathon web www.adidasdublinmarathon.ie

Internationally known as the 'friendly marathon' (whatever that means), the Dublin Marathon attracts participants from all over the world to run through the historic Georgian streets.

DECEMBER

12 Days of Christmas at Docklands web www.dublindocklands.ie

A charming event in a waterside village setting, with over 80 market traders selling a range of festive goodies, gifts, seasonal food and stocking fillers.

Quiet moments

Religious groups and services

Ireland is, famously, a religious country. Few streets are out of
sight of a church tower, or the sound of bells summoning the
faithful to Sunday services. However, for some congregations,
notably the Church of Ireland and the Jewish, the number of
faithful has diminished considerably in recent years. This has led
to quite a problem of handling sensitively now disused former
places of worship, such as the handsome synagogue in Adelaide
Road, victim of the shrinking of Ireland's Jewish community,
or St Mary's Church of Ireland in Mary St, where many historic
figures were baptised and buried, which has now been turned
into a pub.

Dublin, like the rest of the Republic, is predominantly
Roman Catholic, at least in spirit. Although regular churchgoers
tend to be concentrated in the older section of the Catholic
population, a good section of any age group will regularly attend
Mass, for all sorts of spiritual and social reasons. Jokes about
religion are therefore socially risky unless you definitely know
your audience. No matter where in the city you are, there will be
a Catholic parish church nearby, with the times of Masses posted
for the public.

Catholic Ireland, **www.catholicireland.net**, is a portal site
for Irish Catholic organisations and activity, with many interesting articles on spirituality and Church issues. Dublin Churches,
www.dublinchurches.com, lists what seems to be every church
(of any Christian denomination) in the Dublin area, along with
contact information, in an easy-to-search format. Some of the
details on individual churches, such as service times, may be out
of date, but it is still a useful site. There's also a link to a Christian

event guide/calendar at **www.irishchristians.ie**. The Saturday edition of *The Irish Times* lists some religious services.

The **Jewish** community in Dublin, which once numbered about 5,000, was initially based around the Sth Circular Rd. It later expanded into Terenure as it became more established and successful. Sadly, however, the Dublin Jewish population has greatly reduced and now numbers just over a thousand, with some 2,000 in the whole country. The principal orthodox synagogue is at 32A Rathfarnham Rd, Terenure, Dublin 6. For further information on all services contact the office of the Chief Rabbi, tel 492 3751. For more on the community in Ireland see www. jewishireland.org.

The **Muslim** community, in contrast to the Jewish population, has expanded greatly in recent years and continues to grow, going from some 4,000 in the whole of Ireland in the 1990s to over 32,500 in the country today, with over 17,000 living in Dublin. Muslims now represent the third largest religious group in the State. The large, confident, yellow-brick (Sunni) Islamic Cultural Centre of Ireland, tel 208 0000, web www.islamireland. ie, opened in 1996 at 19 Roebuck Rd, Clonskeagh, Dublin 14, near the back entrance of UCD. The centre includes a mosque, a primary school and a library; a great-value restaurant and a shop selling a wide selection of food, including halal meat, are open to visitors. There is another mosque (the original in the city) at 163 Sth Circular Rd, Dublin 8, tel 453 3242/473 8276, which serves as the headquarters of the Islamic Foundation of Ireland, web www.islaminireland.com.

The **Hindu** population in Ireland is also growing at a rapid rate. The International Society for Krishna Consciousness, Dublin Hare Krishna Temple is at 83 Middle Abbey St, Dublin 1, web www.krishna.ie. The Ireland Vinayaka Temple does not yet have a permanent location of its own but details of pooja events are posted online at www.ivt.ie, or phone 086 888 1905 for information. The Hindu Cultural Centre Ireland can be reached at tel 085 721 8803, web www.hindu.ie.

Other Christian groups

The Grace Bible Fellowship is a **Baptist** church at 28A Pearse St, Dublin 2, tel 832 7993, web www.grace.ie. The Swords Baptist Church, tel 890 2857, web www.swordsbaptistchurch.com, meets Sundays at 10.45 in St Finian's Community College, Jugback Lane, Swords, Co Dublin. There is also a Baptist Church at Grosvenor Rd, Rathmines, Dublin 6, tel 497 4798, web www.grosvenorbaptist.org. The website of the Irish Association of Baptist Churches is at www.baptistireland.org.

The (**Evangelical**) Destiny Church meets Sundays at 11.30 for relatively informal services with a contemporary Gospel band at 64 Great Strand St, Dublin 1, tel 874 7691, web www.destinychurch.ie. The address for the Dún Laoghaire Evangelical Church is Lr Glenageary Rd, Dún Laoghaire, Co Dublin, tel 284 1016, web www.dec.ie.

Immanuel Church, tel 873 0829, web www.immanuelchurch-dublin.org, is an Evangelical Anglican (Church of Ireland) denomination meeting at Irish Church Missions, 28 Bachelor's Walk, Sundays at 11.00 and 18.45. The later service is more informal, with an opportunity to chat to the preacher about the sermon afterwards. Both attract a range of nationalities.

The **Greek Orthodox** Church (which also caters for other orthodox communities in the city) is at 46 Arbour Hill, Dublin 7, tel 677 9020.

The **Lutheran** Church in Ireland (which has regular services in both German and English) is at 24 Adelaide Rd, Dublin 2, tel 676 6548.

The Abbey St **Methodist** Church and the base of the Dublin

Quiet moments

Central Mission is at 9c Lr Abbey St, Dublin 1, tel 874 4668, web www.dcmiss.ie, and there are Methodist churches at various locations around the city as well as the suburbs.

The **Mormon** community in Dublin can be contacted at The Willows, Finglas Rd, Glasnevin, Dublin 9, where they have a chapel, tel 830 6684. On the southside of the city there is an LDS chapel at 48 Bushy Park Rd, Terenure, Dublin 6, tel 490 5657.

Lively **Pentecostal** services take place at St Mark's Church, 42A Pearse St, Dublin 2, tel 671 4276, web www.stmarks.ie, every Sunday at 10.00, 12.00 and 18.00 (the 12.00 service is Irish Sign Language-interpreted). The Metropolitan Church Dublin is relatively new Pentecostal church, located at 57 Irishtown Rd, Dublin 4, tel 087 958 8513, web www.mcd4.cc. Hope and Glory Christian Ministries is a Pentecostal church with a primarily African congregation, though anyone is welcome to attend. Their address is First Floor, City House, Newmarket Square, off Cork St, Dublin 8, tel 473 4249/087 680 6390, web www.hope-andglorychurch.com. Meetings are held on Sunday at 11.00 and Wednesday and Friday at 18.30.

The **Religious Society of Friends (Quakers)** have their headquarters at Quaker House, Stocking Lane, Rathfarnham, Dublin 16, tel 495 6888, web www.quakers-in-ireland.ie. Sunday meeting places include Temple Bar; Churchtown, Dublin 14; and Monkstown.

The Dublin **Unitarian** Church is at 112 St Stephen's Green West, tel 478 0638, web www.unitarianchurchdublin.org.

And also

The National **Baha'i** Centre is at 24 Burlington Rd, Dublin 4, tel 668 3150, Freephone 1800 441 919, web www.bahai.ie.

The Dublin **Buddhist** Centre is at Liberty Corner, 5 James Joyce St (sometimes called Corporation St), Dublin 1, tel 817

8933, web www.dublinbuddhistcentre.org. The centre's meditation and yoga classes are open to everyone.

The **Humanist** Association of Ireland, tel 841 3116, web www.humanism.ie has a mostly Dublin-centred membership. It holds a meeting in the city on the first Sunday of every month, usually in Buswells Hotel on Molesworth St, Dublin 2 from 16.00 to 18.00. Anyone with an interest is welcome to attend. They also publish a magazine in conjunction with the Humanist Association of Northern Ireland and provide humanist ceremonies, such as a non-religious baby-naming ceremony in place of a traditional christening. For ceremonies contact Brian Whiteside, tel 086 384 8940.

The Irish **Sikh** Council can be reached at PO Box 9828, Dublin 2, tel 087 652 1060/086 345 6154, web www.irishsikh-council.com.

Green and silent

A good park can make a big difference to your day. Somewhere to sit down for a couple of hours, look at your maps, guidebooks, the newspaper, write a diary, watch the natives at play or even have a quick snooze. As somewhere to relax, a park can't be beaten. And crucially they are, of course, free. You can sit around in the parks all day long without anyone bothering you.

There is one seriously really big park in the city, the Phoenix Park. It lies on the northern outskirts of the city and is massive (the biggest city park in Europe). But there are many smaller parks and gardens dotted all around the city.

Phoenix Park, St Stephen's Green and the National Botanic Gardens are covered here as the main parks. But you will also find some of Dublin's best, most central and most secret parks so that you can get it together in peace. And don't forget Trinity

College: a green haven from city traffic where you can sit and watch the heartier students playing rugby or cricket, or just peacefully enjoy the passing crowd.

Most parks are open from 10.00 to dusk.

Ashtown Castle/Visitor Centre Phoenix Park Dublin 1, tel 677 7129
Ashtown Castle is a real 17th-century tower house. There are daily tours of the castle and a Victorian walled garden which is being restored. Café, restaurant, toilets.
Open Nov–mid-March Wed–Sun 09.30–17.30 (closed Mon, Tues, and Dec 25–29, 1 Jan) mid-March–Oct 10.00–18.00 *Admission* free

Blessington St Basin Blessington St, Dublin 7
In complete contrast to the big green spaces of Iveagh Gardens is a park with no green at all: Blessington St Basin. This park is truly a secret and if you like water and birds, this is the one for you. It consists of a large pond surrounded by a concrete path and a fence. There is no grass, but there are many bushes, and the basin backs on to a filled-in part of the canal, a straight stretch of green.

The pond, once a reservoir and the source of water for the famous Jameson and Powers whiskeys, is home to rudd, a fish which makes up for its inedibility with its talent for swimming near the surface of water, making it the perfect spectator fish. Loads of ducks and seagulls and a delightful island in the middle of the pond combine with the seclusion provided by the surrounding houses and the lovely view including an impressive big church in the background to make this a marvellously contemplative spot well worth the trot up O'Connell St and into Blessington St.

Dubh Linn Garden Dublin 2
Hidden behind Dublin's busiest building, Dublin Castle, and not far from the must-see Chester Beatty museum, is an extraordinary find: a whole street that nobody knows about and a garden to match. It looks like any town street, and is quiet most of the time, and just off the street is a beautiful, refined, minimalist garden, the perfect oasis from bustle and noise, a place of true tranquility.

The garden is called Dubh Linn Garden. It is a smallish circle of grass with many benches round the perimeter. The grass is interwoven with snakes made out of paving stones in a celtic pattern which, when viewed from above, is amazing. The gate you enter through (not the

Quiet moments

one with the name of the gardens written on it: walk another twenty yards and turn left) takes you onto a raised walkway so that you get a super view of the pattern.

Farmleigh Phoenix Park Dublin 1, tel 815 5900

Guided tours of an old Guinness house, now used by the Government for visiting dignitaries. The extensive pleasure grounds include a lake, walled and sunken gardens and fine planting. Various events are held in the estate during the year. There is also a working farm. Café, restaurant, toilets.

Open mid-March–Dec Thurs–Sun, and bank hols 10.00–18.00.
Admission free.

Glasnevin Cemetery Finglas Rd, Dublin 11, tel 830 1133

Graveyards are fascinating places to stroll, look at the graves and decipher the worn headstones. Glasnevin is really crowded and tightly packed, filled with the ordinary Dubliners who have been buried there for a century and a half. There is also a very high celebrity grave count: many of the big names in Irish political history are here. Charles Stewart Parnell, James Stephens, Eamon de Valera, Michael Collins and Daniel O'Connell all rest here. Not to mention Maud Gonne (Yeats' love), Brendan Behan and Gerard Manley Hopkins. Nobody could miss O'Connell: a grotesquely huge tower stands just inside the main gate, a monument to 19th-century overblown pomp, and quite amusing, despite, of course, being in a graveyard. (For cemetery freaks, Vivien Igoe's *A Literary Guide to Dublin* gives 'who's buried where' maps of Glasnevin and Mount Jerome cemeteries.)

And after all that fresh air, you can retire to the highlight of any trip up Glasnevin way: a fine pint of stout at the next door pub, the Gravedigger's, as Kavanagh's is known

Getting there Dublin Bus nos 40, 40A, 40B
Open 08.30–17.00 *Admission* free

Iveagh Gardens Clonmel St, off Harcourt St, Dublin 2

The lovely Iveagh Gardens are the thinking person's Stephen's Green. The entrance is about forty seconds' walk from the south-west corner of the Green, in a left turn as you go down Harcourt St. Enter a garden as central and convenient as Stephen's Green, but far less well known. This walled garden was restored in the 1990s and its high walls and buildings on all four sides not only give it a secretive, secluded aura, but bring much needed silence as well. It was presented to the state in 1939 by Lord Iveagh (what would Dublin be like without the money earned from Guinness?), then gifted to University College Dublin in 1941.

As you walk in two things strike you: the two beautiful tree-lined avenues and the massive lawns seemingly taking up most of the garden. It feels as if there is far more space than in other parks due to these large open lawns, and the park is given a majestic feel by the two fountains perched rather oddly in the middle of one of the lawns. But take the time to wander round the back of the park, and relish the opportunity to find its little idiosyncrasies. Around the wall at the east end of the park there is a great hidden muddy path which takes you to a rose garden and a tiny maze, surely the easiest maze in the world—thanks to the short hedges. There is also a bizarre fountain made out of big huge lumps of stone mixed in with two or three large Greek statues and even the trunk of a tree thrown in for good measure. Iveagh Gardens is in many ways the most eccentric of the parks of the city, so take the time to seek out its secrets hidden in its corners.

On a more practical note, there is not nearly so much shelter from the rain here as in Stephen's Green, and there are far fewer seats.

Merrion Square Dublin 2

Merrion Square is by no means a secret, but is the best kept garden in the city. The flowers, the winding walkways, the smells, the statues all make for a full sensory treat, parked right in the middle of the city, surrounded by the calm self-confidence of Georgian domestic architecture. There are lots of hideaways and secluded spots to rest in and absorb the real stars of this garden: the fantastic flowers and trees. Imagine what it would have been like with an enormous cathedral in the middle, probably in the execrable clerical architectural taste of the day—this was the Catholic Church's plan from 1920 until they finally gave up the idea in 1974. In the houses round the square once lived W. B. Yeats, Daniel O'Connell, and Oscar Wilde who is commemorated by a multi-coloured statue at one of the entrances to the square.

National Botanic Gardens Botanic Rd, Glasnevin, Dublin 9, tel 857 0909, web www.botanicgardens.ie

The Botanic Gardens lie on the north of the city in Glasnevin. It is a curious place to spend time, and wonderfully entertaining. Botanic gardens are places of science as well as recreation, a haven for obsessive amateurs to mingle with professional scientists. The ones in Glasnevin have all the usual paraphernalia of botanic gardens, funny shaped greenhouses and all.

The sight of rare plants in greenhouses just sitting on a window ledge in plant pots is wonderful, as is a walk round the various specialised plant houses. And don't forget to coo admiringly at the magnificent 19th-century curvilinear glasshouses designed by Richard Turner.

But still the gardens are of interest to botanists: the 19 ha gardens, dating from 1795, boast an impressive 20,000 species of plants as well as a large number of truly beautiful trees. A 400-year old fern, cacti, a giant Amazon water lily, and a rose raised from a cutting of the one that inspired Thomas Moore to write that 19th-century favourite *The Last Rose of Summer* are all among the peculiarities of these gardens.

The most exciting aspect, however, is the smells: as soon as you pass the gate from the busy smelly traffic, a clash of pungent plant perfumes hits you and follows you all round the gardens.

Getting there Dublin Bus nos 13, 19, 19A

Open summer (mid-Feb–mid-Nov) daily 09.00–18.00 winter (mid-Nov–mid-Feb) daily 09.00–16.30. Greenhouses closed 12.45–14.00. *Admission* free.

Phoenix Park Dublin 1

Out on the north of the city, this is the place you have to go if you want wide open spaces and lots of grass. This is where Mary Makebelieve met her tall policeman in James Stephens' classic Dublin tale *The Charwoman's Daughter*. Watch out for real polo (May to September) not to mention numerous other sports. Basically the park is just a massive expanse of space, stuffed full of plants and wildlife (separate booklets available at the Visitor Centre tell you what to look out for). But over the years privileged citizens have found themselves houses in it. The Park houses the President's residence Árus an Uachtaráin (open on Saturdays) and that of the US Ambassador as well as Dublin Zoo. See also Ashtown Castle and Farmleigh.

Getting there Dublin Bus nos 37, 38, 39

St Audeon's Park High St, Dublin 2

Just down the hill from the old St Audeon's church, this is one of the hidden pleasures of Dublin. High St was the main thoroughfare of medieval Dublin, and St Audeon's is the city's oldest church. The park incorporates part of the very oldest wall, built about 1100 AD (just before they started building Chartres Cathedral in France). The wall is made of limestone, with buttresses. The park is well tended, though buddleia and ivy grow in the walls. The real thrill is to imagine

Quiet moments

the scruffy, smelly, bustling inhabitants of the old town long ago clattering up and down the stairs and through St Audeon's Arch about their business. By the way don't take the arch too seriously—it was imaginatively restored in the 1880s, and the Victorians loved a bit of castellation!

St Stephen's Green Dublin 2

This is the most popular, most central and most famous of Dublin's parks and gardens. It lies at the top of Grafton St at the hub of Dublin's business and retail centre on the southside. Its grounds contain a pond, landscaped gardens, a playground for children, a bandstand, large patches of grass to lounge around on and wooden shelters looking on to the landscaped gardens so that even in the rain you can sit and take in your lovely surroundings.

There are few greater and simpler summer joys than feeding the mallard ducks in the pond, lying in a soporific stupor on the grass or popping over to see some of the summer bands or Shakespeare in the little amphitheatre. For the botanist there are over two hundred varieties of tree to spot, housing a large number of common and rare birds to be seen and heard. And the historian can envisage the lads in 1916 carefully digging trenches across the Green—that is until they realised that all the British soldiers had to do was to climb to the roofs of the surrounding buildings and shoot down.

In the winter, wrap up and take advantage of a slightly less busy Green, sit watching the rain and the fountain and enjoy the fact that you can see the grass, for once not obscured by people.

The key to enjoying the Green is recognising how big it is: don't just head for the central landscaped gardens, look all around the edges for the little spots of seclusion, or for the many super spots around the pond where the ducks and the water drown out the nearby traffic.

War Memorial Gardens Islandbridge, Dublin 8 (entrance from Con Colbert Rd and Sth Circular Rd)

A few minutes walk from the Irish Museum of Modern Art in Kilmainham, these gardens were designed by the architect Sir Edwin Lutyens to commemorate the Irish soldiers who died in the First World War. For years they were meanly neglected by successive national governments who thought the soldiers would have been better off fighting against Ireland's ancient enemy, not doing her dirty work in the trenches. All forgotten and forgiven now, more or less. On a mild day, a stroll around these unexpectedly large, formal gardens provides

a pleasant break between visits to IMMA and Kilmainham Gaol (see pages 200–201). You might even be lucky enough to enjoy the sight of rowing teams killing themselves in the heat on the river.
Getting there Dublin Bus nos. 51, 68,69 from Aston Quay

Wildlife

Dublin, like other cities, was built for people, but somehow Nature creeps in. Wherever you look there are trees, shrubs and plants. The *Flora of Inner Dublin* by P. Wyese Jackson and M. Sheehy Skeffington identified some 345 separate plants, including 38 grasses. Most of these are the normal hardy city plants, but a visit to Bull Island gives you a reasonable chance of orchid hunting. A campaign of tree planting in recent years has seen Dublin City Council experimenting with over two hundred tree types.

If you are very lucky indeed you might spot fragrant, common spotted or pyramidal orchids near Cross Guns Bridge, Glasnevin, Dublin 9—and if you don't find any, hopefully the trills of the greenfinch which nest around there will console you.

Birds are everywhere, For Dubliners the harsh cry of the herring gull as it swoops through the city is as evocative of their native city as the coo of the wood pigeon to the country dweller (and you can hear wood pigeons in Dublin too).

In his marvellous *Exploring Dublin Wildlife, Parks, Waterways*, Christopher Moriarty lists 87 species of birds to be seen in the city, from the ubiquitous pigeons and house sparrows to kestrels. siskins and skylarks. The best place to bird watch in the inner city is Trinity College Park.

Mammals are fewer. In the very early morning foxes can often be spotted, perhaps in Merrion Square. No doubt there are bats, probably in the parks that close at dusk. Otters and grey seals occasionally make an appearance in the Liffey, while rats and mice are as usual universal (though for some reason Christopher Moriarty does not mention them).

For something more exotic, you will have to go to **Dublin Zoo** in the Phoenix Park. *Open* 09.30–18.00 in the summer, admission €15. How to get there: 15 mins walk from Heuston Station on the Luas Red line or buses 10, 25, 26, 67, 68, 69.

Quiet moments

Other highlights and quirks

And other green spaces to look out for: **Broadstone Park** (beside the Blessington St Basin) is just a 1km long stretch of straight grass, because it is a filled in canal, entertaining in an odd kind of way; **Croppies' Acre** beside the Liffey beyond the Four Courts, is an area of untended grass left uncultivated because it is the grave of many of the United Irishmen killed in the late 18th century (they were called Croppies because many of them cut their hair short in imitation of the revolutionary French); **Sandymount Strand** (take the DART to Sandymount) is not green, but at low tide an area of sand as big as a small airport is revealed (and in the 1920s they seriously considered siting Dublin's first airport here); in the middle of the strand is a decayed old sea-bath. There used to be a wooden walkway going out to it. **King's Inns Fields,** beside the Four Courts on the north side of the river, has a fascinating tree which has grown around a park bench over the years, so it looks like the tree is hugging the bench. And the world's best cure for a hangover—take the DART to **Howth**, and walk all round Howth Hill (taking care to walk *into* the wind), the spectacular seascapes will set you up for the evening!

Libraries

Public libraries are a godsend for the weary and cash-strapped. On a rainy day, with time to kill, you can wander in, find a good book, a newspaper, a magazine, a comfortable chair—and it's all completely free!

If there's anything you need to know about your local area, or about life in Dublin in general, the library should be your first port of call: it's in the library that you can most easily find telephone directories, the voting register, local directories, reference books of all kinds, books in languages other than English, and helpful, knowledgeable people who can answer your questions.

Even if you're just a visitor to the city, the libraries contain a wealth of information you can access for free, and are often venues for cultural events and classes. If you can provide proof of residence in Dublin, you can join the public library system and gain the right to borrow books, CDs and DVDs, as well as free sessions on the libraries' internet terminals (though in most cases you'll have to book in advance).

Find the library nearest you at **www.dublincitypubliclibrar-ies.ie.**

Two key Dublin City public reference libraries:

Central Library, Ilac Centre, Henry St, Dublin 1, tel 873 4333
Anything you want to find out about Dublin business life is here. Large reference library of current business and trade journals; trade reference books; overseas telephone books; multiple filing cabinets of press cuttings of Irish business and news topics; computer access and lessons; music library. You need to be a member of the library to use the computers, but there is WiFi access. Current newspapers. It's a great place, but tends to get crowded.
Getting there Luas Red line, Jervis station
Open Mon–Thurs 10.00–20.00 Fri–Sat 10.00–17.00

The Gilbert Library 138–141 Pearse St, Dublin 2 tel 674 4448
This library, which is part of the Pearse St Library, holds hard copies of Irish newspapers, from a few months old right back to the 19th century, microfilms of the more fragile ones and a large collection of books and maps about Dublin. It has a marvellous new reading room poised above the hurly-burly of Pearse St.
Open Mon–Fri 10.00–20.00, Fri–Sat 10.00–17.00

Other state libraries include:

The National Library Kildare St, Dublin 2, tel 603 0200, web www.nli.ie
Over half a million books; also manuscripts, prints and Irish newspapers.
Enjoy the great domed reading room that has been home to
generations of Irish students, from James Joyce on. You will need a
reader's ticket, which can be got (free) on the premises during normal
office hours.
Open Mon–Wed 09.30–21.00, Thurs–Fri 09.30–17.00, Sat 09.30–13.00

And finally, two favourites:

Central Catholic Library 74 Merrion Sq, Dublin 2, tel 676 1264
OK, the older stock is bit single-minded, being almost exclusively of
Catholic theological interest, though there is an increasing breadth
to the buying policy, but the reference library upstairs is quiet—one
previous librarian was heard to complain bitterly when the third visitor
in an hour appeared: 'It's like Piccadilly Circus in here!', and there is a
calming view over the trees of Merrion Sq. with the gas fire popping
quietly in the background. New members welcome.
Open Mon–Fri 11.00–18.00, Sat 11.00–17.30

Marsh's Library St Patrick's Close, Dublin 8, tel 454 3511
This library is the only one here that charges an entrance fee. It is
fascinating not only because it was the first public library in Ireland
and has a valuable collection of early books and manuscripts, but also
because you can see the wire cages where they used to lock readers
when reading rare books—who said learning was easy? These, of
course, are not in use today.
Open Mon–Fri (closed Tues) 09.30–13.00, 14.00–17.00; Sat 10.00–13.00
Admission €2.50, concessions €1.50

Churches to visit

Quite apart from their religious and historical associations,
churches are great places to escape into, away from the crowds,
where you can sit in peace and contemplate or pray for a while.

If you are really into churches, find a copy of Peter Costello's
illustrated guidebook *Dublin Churches* (Gill & Macmillan, 1989),

which contains details and descriptions of over 150 Christian places of worship.

Christ Church Cathedral Christchurch Place, Dublin 8, tel 677 8099, web www.cccdub.ie

Whereas St Patrick's is the national (Protestant) Cathedral, Christ Church is the diocesan cathedral of Dublin and Glendalough. The original Christ Church was founded by Sitric, the Norse King of Dublin, in 1038. Like St Patrick's, it fell into decay and was substantially rebuilt in the 19th century. (The rebuilding of St Patrick's was financed by a brewer, Benjamin Guinness, and that of Christ Church by a whiskey distiller, Henry Roe—is there some message here?) The medieval crypts are worth a visit.

Open every day June–Aug 09.00–18.00, Sept–May 09.45–17.00/18.00
Admission €6, concessions €4, unless attending a service or for private prayer. Most of the cathedral is wheelchair accessible.

Chance your arm

In 1492 Black James, nephew of the Earl of Ormond, fleeing from FitzGerald's soldiers, took sanctuary in the Chapter House of Christ Church Cathedral in Dublin. Though he had the upper hand, with his soldiers surrounding Black James and his men, FitzGerald, Ireland's premier earl, wished to end the bloody feud between the families. He pleaded with Black James through the Chapter House's oak door to negotiate a peace. Black James refused all requests. So FitzGerald ordered his soldiers to cut a hole in the centre of the door. Then, having explained how he wished to see peace between the families, he thrust his arm through the hole to shake hands with Black James. It was a madly risky venture; any of Black James's heavily armed men could have hacked the Earl's arm off, which in the state of medicine at the day was an almost certain death warrant. Astonishingly, James took the truce offer and peace was restored, leading to an expression (in English, a language neither spoke) 'chance your arm'. The door of the Chapter House is on display in St Patrick's Cathedral, where it is now known as the *Door of Reconciliation*.

Quiet moments

St Patrick's Cathedral St Patrick's Close, Dublin 8, tel 453 9472, web www.
stpatrickscathedral.ie
     Ireland's largest church, it was built dangerously outside the safe
circuit of the city walls on the traditional site of St Patrick's Well, where
he baptised converts to the new religion. Not only that but it was
built near the now submerged river Poddle that made it vulnerable
to flooding. The church was made a cathedral around 1220, but
over later centuries it fell into decay. By the 19th century it was so
derelict that plans were on foot to knock it down. Then Benjamin Lee
Guinness offered to rebuild it to what we see today. Over the years the
surrounding land has risen 2 metres, so this ancient structure seems
almost to be sinking into the earth. The great figure associated with St
Patrick's is the writer Jonathan Swift, who was dean of the cathedral
from 1713 to 1745—his famous monument, to a man who has gone to
a place 'where savage indignation can lacerate his heart no more', is
worth contemplating. Look out also for the door through which Earl
FitzGerald famously 'chanced his arm' (see box). Marsh's Library (page
190) is just next door to St Patrick's.
Open 09.00–17.30 daily (last admission 17.00), except Nov–Feb Sat–Sun
(Sat 09.00–17.00, Sun 09.00–15.00)
Admission €5.50, concessions €4.50, family (2 adults, 2 children under
16) €15 unless attending a service. Wheelchair access by arrangement.

St Mary's Pro-Cathedral 83 Marlborough St, Dublin 1, tel 874 5441, web
www.procathedral.ie
     The Catholic Church still considers Christ Church the official
cathedral of Dublin—hence the ongoing temporary status of St Mary's.
Erected 1814–25, before Catholic emancipation, it is discreetly located
on a side street to avoid offending the sensibilities of the Protestant
Ascendancy. Its inspiration is primarily Greek rather than the Gothic
which would have been insisted on a few decades later. The church
has been the focus of many famous national occasions, notably the
enormous funerals of Daniel O'Connell and Michael Collins. In the
20th century Catholics longed for a grander cathedral, and for years
there were plans to build one on Merrion Square. Thankfully (given the
generally dire taste of 20th-century Irish church-builders) these were
abandoned and the land given to the city by Archbishop Dermot Ryan
in 1974.

Open Mon–Fri 07.30–18.45, Sat 07.30–19.15, Sun 09.00–13.45 and 17.30–19.45. Regular Masses throughout the day. Taizé-style Mass Sat 20.00 in St Kevin's Oratory except in August. Spanish Mass first Sunday of every month 19.00 in St Kevin's Oratory. The exquisite singing of the Palestrina Boys' Choir can be heard at 17.15 Mass on Wednesday and Friday and at the 11.00 Latin Mass on Sunday, except during July and August. Wheelchair access.

Other Catholic churches of note in the city centre:

St Teresa's Church Clarendon St, Dublin 2, tel 671 8466, web www. clarendonstreet.net, where St Teresa's Choir sing at the 11.30 Mass on Sundays.
Open Mon–Fri 06.45–18.15, Sat 06.45–19.15, Sun 07.45–19.15. Wheelchair access and accessible toilet.
Whitefriar St Carmelite Church 56 Aungier St, Dublin 2, tel 475 8821, which houses the remains of St Valentine which were given to the church by Pope Gregory XVI in 1837.
Open Mon–Fri 07.30–18.00, Sat 07.30–19.00, Sun 08.00–19.45 Wheelchair access and accessible toilet.

Some other historically interesting Church of Ireland places of worship still in use today:

St Ann's Church Dawson St, tel 676 7727, web www.stannschurch.ie Handsome 18th-century interior and an impressive Romanesque facade. This is where many of the great and the good of Protestant Dublin were baptised. Revolutionary Wolfe Tone and *Dracula* author Bram Stoker were married here.
Open Mon–Fri 10.00–16.00 daily, Sun for services at 10.45 & 18.30. Wheelchair access.
St Audoen's Cornmarket, High St, Dublin 8, tel 677 0088, is Dublin's only remaining medieval church.
Exhibition open May–Oct 09.30–17.30 daily (last admission 16.45). Most of the exhibition and the church are wheelchair accessible and there is an accessible toilet.

Quiet moments

Mary Mediatrix of All Graces 12 Upr O'Connell St, Dublin 1, tel 878 1085, web www.mariamediatrix.com

In the area of strange marriages, few compete with this conservative Catholic shop which also happens to be a bureau de change. The shop is small but always seems to have a customer or two, with sombre music filling your ears as you enter. You can pick up a copy of *Catholic Home Schooling*, and meanwhile get your euro changed into dollars.

Open Mon–Sat 09.30–18.00

St Michan's Church Church St, Dublin 7, tel 872 4154, web www.cccgroup.dublin.anglican.org

The crypt contains a number of naturally mummified corpses, including that of a nun and a supposed soldier from the Crusades (whose body was cut in half to fit in the coffin), as well as the leaders of the 1798 Rebellion. It's thought that Handel played the organ here as he composed *The Messiah*.

Getting there St Michan's is very near to both the Four Courts Luas stop and the Smithfield stop (Red line), and the open-topped tour buses have a stop at Arran Quay/Smithfield, 100m from the church.

Open Sat all year round 10.00–12.45; Mar–Oct Mon–Fri 10.00–12.45 & 14.00–16.45; Nov–Feb Mon–Fri 12.30–15.30. Services in the church on the second and fourth Sunday of every month at 10.00.

Admission The church and grounds are free to enter; guided tours of the crypt (the only way you can access the crypt) €4, concessions €3.50, children €3, family (2 adults and 2–4 children) €12. The church is wheelchair accessible but not the crypt.

St Stephen's Church Mount St Crescent, Dublin 2, tel 275 1720, web www.peppercanister.ie

Nicknamed the 'pepper canister' for the shape of its cupola, this was the last Georgian church built by the Church of Ireland. It contains a memorial to parishioners who died in the two world wars.

Open to visitors July–Aug and Christmas week & Easter week Mon–Fri 12.00–14.00; for services 11.00 on Sunday. Wheelchair access.

Black churches

Certain Dublin churches are built in the middle of the road, such as
St Mary's just off Dorset St and the Holy Trinity Church in Church Ave,
Rathmines. Tradition had it that if you ran round such a church three times
after dark, you would meet the Devil on the third time round.

Museums and galleries

Culturally, Ireland punches above its weight. We produce a
disproportionate number of painters, sculptors, musicians,
novelists, poets, and such-like creative types, and though we
have a tendency to export some of our best artists and works,
there's still a lot to be seen in Dublin. And that's just the native
art. Dublin is also the home of some remarkable collections of
art from outside Ireland. The Chester Beatty Library is probably
the most distinguished of these, having won multiple awards,
but the unique and fascinating Science Gallery has been the site
of some truly remarkable exhibitions on the edges where art
bleeds into science and vice versa.

Chester Beatty Library Dublin Castle, Dublin 2, tel 407 0750, web www.
cbl.ie

If you only visit one museum in Dublin, this should be the one. This
world-class collection of chiefly Asian and Arab art was bequeathed to
the Irish nation in 1956 by Sir Alfred Chester Beatty, a mining engineer
whose uncanny sense of geology earned him several fortunes.

The collection comprises a unique selection of manuscripts,
rare books and paintings from the Far and Middle East. Included
in the exhibits are over 270 copies of the Koran; Mogul and Persian
manuscripts and illuminations; Syrian, Armenian, Ethiopian and Coptic
Biblical texts as well as papyri dating from the second and fourth
centuries, Chinese furniture, Japanese prints, and early printed books
with engravings by Dürer, Bartolozzi and Piranesi; in addition to the

Quiet moments

permanent collection, there are frequent visiting exhibitions, including at one point a display of the notebooks of Leonardo da Vinci. The surroundings are gorgeous, the bookshop is impressive, and the Silk Road Café is good enough that we've listed it separately in the *Eating Out* section (page 138). Unmissable.

Open May–Sept Tue–Fri 10.00–17.00, Sat 11.00–17.00, Sun 13.00–17.00 (Oct–Apr closed on Mon) *Admission* free

City Hall Dame St, Dublin 2, tel 222 2204, email cityhall@dublincity.ie
Next door to Dublin Castle, the City Hall building is an outstanding example of Georgian neo-classical architecture that houses a multimedia exhibition telling the story of the governance of Dublin through the ages. Drop in to learn some history and admire the beautifully proportioned and exquisitely decorated space, as well as the view from the front doors down to the Liffey and beyond to Capel St.

Open Mon–Sat 10.00–17.15 Sun and bank holidays 14.00–17.00; last admission one hour before closing *Admission* adult €4, senior citizens/students/unwaged €2 children, €1.50; family (two adults and up to four children) €10; group tickets available with advance booking

Douglas Hyde Gallery Trinity College, Dublin 2, tel 896 1116, web www.douglashydegallery.com
Part of Trinity College, this stark concrete-walled gallery provides a temporary home to rotating exhibitions of work by living artists, both Irish and not. It doesn't look welcoming, but the blankness gives the art room to breathe, and the high walls allow for the exhibition of artworks built on an enormous scale. It's fashionable nowadays to refer to a gallery as a 'space', but in the case of the DHG, this is not just up to date terminology; it's the only word that's adequate. No matter what's on display, there is always space between each piece, space for the spectators to step back, breathe, reflect.

Open Mon–Wed 11.00–18.00, Thurs 11.00–19.00, Fri 11.00–18.00, Sat 11.00–16.45 *Admission* free

Dublin Writers' Museum 18 Parnell Sq Nth, Dublin 1, tel 872 2077
Dublin is almost pathologically proud of its literary tradition, and many of the sacred artefacts of the cult of literary Dublin can be found in the Dublin Writers' Museum. There are first editions of books and memorabilia relating to such famous literary names as Swift, Joyce, Kavanagh and Beckett. On the second floor, the main room is hung

In the calm of a sunlit morning the Liffey, the Ha'penny Bridge and, in the distance, Liberty Hall.

with portraits of Irish writers, and the adjoining Gorham Library is noteworthy for its ceiling which is decorated with plasterwork. And if this isn't enough cultural tourism, a trip to the Writers' Museum can be combined with a visit to the James Joyce Centre in Nth Great George's St for a reduced ticket price.

Open Mon–Sat 10.00–17.00, Sun and public hols 11.00–17.00

Admission adults €7.50, concession €6.30, child €4.70, family €20; group rates available for groups of 20+; combined tickets available with the James Joyce Museum, the Shaw Birthplace, and Malahide Castle

GAA Museum Croke Park, St Joseph's Avenue, Dublin 3, web museum. gaa.ie

Gaelic games are not just sport. They are bound up with the anti-colonial struggle as GAA (Gaelic Athletic Association) hurling and football teams became seedbeds of future freedom fighters. Particularly in the country, allegiance to your GAA teams are part of what you are. The museum chronicles and commemorates the history of Gaelic games in Ireland, from the founding of the GAA in the 19th century to the present day.

Open Sept–June Mon–Sat 09.30–17.00, Jul–Aug Mon–Sat 09.30–18.00; Sun 12.00–17.00 (on match days, the museum opens at the same time as the turnstiles and is accessible to Cusack Stand ticket holders only; the museum stays open until one hour after the end of the main match) *Admission* Museum only: adult €5.50, student/senior €4, child under 12 €3.50, child under 5 free, family (2 adults and 2 children) €15; Museum and tour of Croke Park Stadium: adult €10.50, student €8, senior €7.50, child under 12 €7.00, child under 5 free family, (2 adults and 2 children) €28. No unaccompanied under-18s

Gallery of Photography Meeting House Sq, Temple Bar, Dublin 2, tel 671 4654, web www. galleryofphotography.ie

This is the only gallery in Ireland devoted exclusively to the exhibition of contemporary photography; it's the place to go for groundbreaking, hard-hitting, controversial, highbrow art. Its sleek award winning architecture and prime place in Meeting House Square are testaments to its own (often justified) sense of importance. There are seminars and workshops relating to current exhibitions; the gallery runs a selection of courses in photography and there are also darkroom facilities available for use by members. Wheelchair access.

Open Tues–Sat 11.00–18.00, Sun 13.00–18.00 *Admission* free

Guinness Storehouse St James's Gate, Dublin 8, tel 408 4800 web www. guinness-storehouse.com

If you're mad about Guinness, the Guinness Storehouse is the place for you. Located at the brewery where the black stuff is made, it's an exceptionally interesting stone building, divided into seven levels. Once you purchase your ticket downstairs you can either join a guided tour or do your own thing. Everything to do with the brewing process is explained interactively through video, displays and sound. This includes a 'waterfall' of water used to make Guinness, barrels where it's stored (where you can watch a video inside each individual one), and an exhibition of Guinness merchandise from the earliest through to the modern day.

After all this, you can relax with a complimentary pint in the Gravity Bar on the top level, with a spectacular 360 degree view of the city. Though not exactly cheap, a must for Guinness lovers.

Open 7 days 09.30–17.00 except Christmas Eve, Christmas Day, St Stephen's Day and Good Friday. Late opening July–Aug 09.30–19.00
Admission adult €15.00 (10 per cent discount for online booking), student over 18 €11, student under 18 €9, senior €11, child 6–12 €5, family (2 adults, 4 children) €34

Heraldic Museum 2 Kildare St, Dublin 2, tel 603 0311, e-mail herald@nli.ie

Part of the Genealogy Office of the National Library, the Heraldic Museum caters for the legions of people from all over the globe who come here looking to dig up some Irish roots. It exhibits a collection of artefacts relating to genealogies and armorial bearings from Europe and Ireland. The large-scale Ruskin-style building is imposing and is similar to the Museum Building in nearby Trinity College. (It used to be a club for nobs—look out for the satirical billiard-playing monkeys on the outside wall.) The Alliance Française occupies one half of the building and the café there serves delicious quiches and filled baguettes—perfect for lunch after your visit to the museum.

Open Mon–Wed 10.00–20.30, Thurs–Fri 10.00–16.30, Sat 10.00–12.30
Admission free

Hugh Lane Gallery Charlemont House, Parnell Sq Nth, Dublin 1, tel 874 1903, web www.hughlane.ie.

Also known as the Municipal Gallery, this gallery grew initially from a private donation by Hugh Lane, who died in the sinking of the *Lusitania* in 1916, and the current content still retains the slightly esoteric feel of the original. Situated in a late-18th-century townhouse

that was designed by William Chambers, the exhibits include 19th-century sculpture and painting by Irish and international artists as well as more recent work. The gallery's permanent collection includes a reconstruction of the studio of Irish-born artist Francis Bacon, painstakingly put together from the contents of the original in London, where he spent his last 30 years living and working; the studio was listed by the *Guardian* newspaper as one of the '100 Artworks To See Before You Die'. (In fact, so was 'The Eve of Saint Agnes' by Harry Clarke, also on display in this gallery.) The gallery also hosts free lectures and concerts on Sunday afternoons. Very friendly and helpful staff.
Open Tues–Thurs 10.00–18.00, Fri–Sat 10.00–17.00, Sun 11.00–17.00
Admission free. Wheelchair access.

Irish Jewish Museum 3–4 Walworth Rd, (off Victoria St), Sth Circular Rd, Dublin 8, tel 490 1857/475 8388, web www.jewishireland.org/museum. html

A fascinating if eccentric memorial to a fast vanishing part of Dublin life. Although there have been Jews in Ireland for centuries, the big influx came after the Russian pogroms in the late 19th century. At its peak in the 1940s the community numbered over 5,000. Now there are fewer than 2,000. The Museum, housed in two adjoining terraced houses, which were converted into a synagogue, is in the heart of what was once Dublin's Little Jerusalem. Well worth the hunt.
Getting there Ten minutes' walk from Charlemont or Harcourt Green line Luas stations. Dublin Bus nos 14, 15, 16, 19, 65, 83, 122.
Open May–Sept Sun, Tues, Thurs, 11.00–15.30; Oct–April Sun 10.30–14.30
Admission free but donations gratefully accepted

Irish Museum of Modern Art (IMMA) Royal Hospital, Military Road, Kilmainham, Dublin 8, tel 612 9900 web www.imma.ie.

The superb 17th-century building that houses this museum was originally built as a home for 300 retired soldiers and was styled on the design of Les Invalides in Paris. High over the Liffey the building has an enduring grandeur that is worth experiencing by itself. (The stucco work on the chapel ceiling is a wonder.) The Royal Hospital, as it is known, now provides a bright and airy backdrop to a range of Irish and international art from the 20th and 21st centuries. Temporary exhibitions are on show throughout the year and there is also a permanent collection of work by top contemporary Irish artists. On a raised site, the building is surrounded by an extensive and splendid garden area which is a lovely place to walk in summer. If you are in the mood for a further wander, then try a stroll to the nearby War Memorial Gardens (see page 186).

Getting there 5 minutes walk from Heuston Station via Military Road, or from James St via steps to Bow Lane on to Irwin St and Military Rd

Open Tues 10.00–17.30, Wed 10.30–17.30, Thurs–Sat 10.00–17.30, Sun and bank holidays 12.00–17.30. Last admission at 17.15. *Admission* free. Wheelchair access.

James Joyce Centre 35 Nth Great George's St, Dublin 1, tel 878 8547, web www.jamesjoyce.ie

Here is a fine example of Dublin's Georgian architecture, with superb plasterwork ceilings by Michael Stapleton. The Centre houses temporary and permanent exhibitions, including an impression of the way the Joyces lived in Trieste, Zurich and Paris while Joyce was writing *Ulysses*, as well as an interactive computer installation on *Ulysses*, and short documentary films. The Centre also runs walking tours (see page 207) through the north inner city where Joyce spent much of his youth. See also museum in Joyce Tower, Sandycove page 213.

Open Tues–Sat 10.00–17.00 *Admission* €5, students/senior citizens €3, walking tours €10, students/senior citizens €8

Kilmainham Gaol Inchicore Road, Dublin 8, tel 453 5984, web www.heritageireland.ie

Since 1796, generations of Irish revolutionaries were incarcerated here along with the city's criminals. As a vivid and riveting slice of Irish history the Gaol is unbeatable, and all the more shocking because it was in use right up until 1924. Famous movies have been filmed here, including the seminal *Italian Job*—remember Noel Coward sashaying down the central iron staircase? For those who want an insight into one of the most important events in Irish history, a collection of documents relating to the Easter Rising of 1916 is on view, with a notable focus on the role of women in the revolution. Informative, moving, sometimes disturbing.

Open April–Sept Mon–Sun 09.30–18.00 (last admission at 17.00), Oct–March Mon–Sat 09.30–17.30 (last admission at 16.00), Sun 10.00–18.00 (last admission at 17.00) *Admission* (by guided tour only) adult €6.00, student €2.00, senior €4.00, child €2.00, family €14.00; group rates available (groups must be booked in advance)

Wheelchair access.

Municipal Gallery of Modern Art (see Hugh Lane Gallery, page 199)

Quiet moments

National Gallery of Ireland Merrion Sq West and Clare St, Dublin 2, tel 661 5133, web www.nationalgallery.ie.

In recent years, the Gallery's outstanding collection of Irish and international art has been given an expanded space in a purpose-built building on Clare St which is so stunningly designed that it's worth a visit in itself; it is a prime example of the best of modern architecture, bright, airy, elegant and simple. The permanent collection includes such unmissable masterpieces as Caravaggio's *The Taking of Christ*, Jack B. Yeats's *Grief*, and William Orpen's *The Holy Well*, and there are frequent temporary exhibitions of paintings and sculptures on loan from elsewhere. The Gallery holds drawing classes for both children and adults, hosts concerts, and has an excellent café. A real treasure. Great art bookshop, too.

Open Mon–Sat 09.30–17.30 (except Thurs 09.30–20.30), Sun 12.00–17.30 *Admission* free

National Museum of Ireland

The national museum is divided into three distinct sites across the city (and one in Castlebar, Co Mayo), see www.museum.ie. As of this writing, the Natural History Museum on Merrion St is closed until further notice, but there are still two open in Dublin:

Archaeology and History Kildare St, Dublin 2, tel 677 7444

Varied collection of artefacts dating from 7000 BC to the 20th century. The exhibition of prehistoric gold is stunning, as are the outstanding examples of Celtic and mediaeval art.

Open Tues–Sat 10.00–17.00, Sun 14.00–17.00 *Admission* free

Decorative Arts and History Collins Barracks, Benburb St, Dublin 7, tel 677 7444

Set in the beautifully crisp architecture of a renovated army barracks, the permanent national decorative arts and history collection contains artefacts from Ireland's domestic, social, economic and military history. Here you will find an array of everyday items and curiosities from elegant silver and glassware to weaponry and costumes. Throughout the year, the museum runs imaginatively-themed lecture and exhibition programmes. Although not situated right in the city centre, the easy access by bus and the Luas Red line, an excellent courtyard café and a car park make this a convenient museum to visit.

Getting there Museum stop Luas Red line; Dublin Bus nos 90, 25, 25A *Open* Tues–Sat 10.00–17.00, Sun 14.00–17.00 *Admission* free. Wheelchair access.

Number Twenty-Nine 29 Lr Fitzwilliam St, Dublin 2, tel 702 6165, email numbertwentynine@esb.ie.

A 1794 Georgian house restored with great care to give an impression of how life would have been lived there in the late 18th and early 19th centuries. It contains a fine collection of Georgian furniture, glass, ceramics and costumes. Visitors are shown a short video before a guided tour giving insight into the life of both the servants and the bourgeoisie in the period 1790–1820.

Open Tues–Sat 10.00–17.00, Sun 14.00–17.00. Group visits by special arrangement. *Admission* adult €6; students, senior citizens €3; children under 16 free

Royal Hibernian Academy (RHA) Gallagher Gallery 15 Ely Place, Dublin 2, tel 661 2558, web www.royalhibernianacademy.com

Recently refurbished, the RHA Gallagher Gallery is a large, bright, airy space for the display of contemporary and 20th-century Irish and international art. Three of its galleries display curated exhibitions, while the fourth, the Ashford Gallery, is devoted exclusively to works by artists without commercial representation in Dublin, its purpose being to promote the sale of their work. The RHA's Annual Exhibition, every year during the summer, displays work by members of the Academy as well as other artists, and is always a treat for art-lovers.

Open Mon–Sat 11.00–19.00, Sun 14.00–17.00 *Admission* free. Limited wheelchair access.

Science Gallery Trinity College, Pearse St, Dublin 2, tel 896 4091, web www.sciencegallery.ie

A unique and exciting venue for exhibitions showing off up-to-the minute scientific research and, in particular, fusions of science and the arts. There is no permanent exhibition, but new temporary exhibitions come to the gallery every few weeks; even in the gaps in between exhibitions, the gallery café remains open, with its selection of scientific magazines for visitors to read.

Open hours vary with each exhibition; check website for details. On Mondays the Gallery is always closed, but the café is open from 10.00 to 17.00. *Admission* free except for special events

Temple Bar Gallery and Studios 5–9 Temple Bar, Dublin 2, tel 671 0073

Mixed media gallery specialising in cutting-edge art by living artists, including sculpture, painting, photography, installations, and film. It provides exhibition space as well as studios for working artists, and also holds superb experimental exhibitions such as first shows by promising newcomers. Spacious, attractive, and accessible. *Open* Tues–Sat 11.00–18.00 (Thurs 19.00) *Admission* free. Wheelchair access.

Trinity College Dublin, **Old Library/Book of Kells** Trinity College, Dublin 2, tel 608 2320/2308

Trinity's central location makes it one of Dublin's most easily accessible artistic and historic showpieces. Between the extraordinary architecture, the sculptures and the contents of some of the buildings, it really is a visual treat from one end to the other. While you're walking around look out for the sculpture by contemporary artists, for example: *Cactus*, by the American artists Alexander Calder, in Fellow's Square, or *Sphere with Sphere*, by Arnaldo Pomodoro, in front of the Berkeley Library. The Long Room (Ireland's oldest library) contains a superb collection of manuscripts and early printed books, the most famous being *The Book of Kells*. If possible, visit the Long Room early in the day, or you could end up queuing for quite a while.

Open Mon–Sat 09.30–17.00; Sun (May–Sept) 09.30–16.30; Sun (Oct–Apr) 12.00–16.30 *Admission* adult €9.00, students/seniors €8.00, family (2 adults and up to 4 children) €18.00, children under 12 free.

Tours and trips

City walks and tours

Guided walking tours

The best, cheapest and greenest way to get a feel for the city is to see it on foot. There are several publications available in bookshops or through the tourist offices which suggest routes to walk around the city but, as it is such a small area, these are not really necessary unless you have a special interest. Generally, a good map is all you need. People are usually friendly when approached and asked for directions, even if they cannot always help you. And if you're lucky, you won't be told 'Ah now—if I was going there, I wouldn't start from here.'

If you have a particular interest in history or literature, however, or if you just feel like taking a guided walking tour, the following are a few we recommend. All the tours below take wheelchair users, but can't always guarantee that the routes taken will be 100 per cent wheelchair friendly (that, after all, is the job of Dublin City Council), so best to call if you have any queries. Tickets for most of the tours are available from Dublin Tourism offices as well as directly from the guide; the **Dublin Tourism Centre** is on Suffolk St, Dublin 2, and there is another city centre tourist office at 14 Upr O'Connell St, Dublin 1. Concession prices are usually available for students, seniors, the unemployed and people with disabilities.

Another option, if you have the technology, is to download one of Dublin Tourism's free iWalks, narrated by historian and artist Pat Liddy. The podcasts, complete with maps, cover such topics as Georgian Dublin, Castles & Cathedrals and Medieval & Viking Dublin, and there's even one on *Ulysses*—see www.visit-dublin.com/iwalks.

1916 Rebellion Walking Tour tel 086 858 3847, web www.1916rising.com

The 1916 armed rebellion against the British was a brief and bloody affair (particularly for civilians). It took just over a week for the British to divert soldiers from the trenches in France to heavy-handedly crush the Rising, as it is often called. One of the most celebrated Dublin tours, this lives up to its reputation, taking in scenes from the rebellion that laid the foundations for Irish independence. Guides Lorcan Collins and Conor Kostick have even turned the tour into a bestselling book, *The Easter Rising*, published by O'Brien Press.

Times March–Oct Mon–Sat 11.30, Sun 13.00; Nov–Feb group bookings only

Duration Takes about 2 hrs

Meet at The International Bar, 23 Wicklow St, Dublin 2

Tickets €12 bought on the day or in advance from Dublin Tourism. Groups of more than 10 should book in advance.

Dublin Literary Pub Crawl tel 670 5602 (general)/087 263 0270 (credit card booking), web www.dublinpubcrawl.com

A light-hearted guided tour by two actors who perform humorous extracts from Dublin's best-known writers and, in true style, visit a selection of pubs on the way.

Times April–Oct Mon–Sat 19.30, Sun 12.00, 19.30; Nov–March Thurs–Sat 19.30, Sun 12.00, 19.30

Duration Takes about 2 hrs 15 min

Meet upstairs in The Duke pub, 9 Duke St, Dublin 2

Tickets €13, concessions €11 at The Duke from 19.00 on the day or in advance from Dublin Tourism. Or book by phone or online. The tour is wheelchair accessible except for the initial meeting upstairs in The Duke.

Historical Walking Tours of Dublin tel 087 688 9412/087 830 3523, web www.historicalinsights.ie

Funny and informative, these are conducted by history graduates of Trinity College and cover the major features of Irish history from Dublin's development right up to the present day. As well as the main 'greatest hits' tour, there are special tours dealing with more specific subjects for group bookings (the **food tour** in particular is great fun, with cheese and oyster tasting at the Temble Bar Market). Details for the main tour are below.

Times May–Sept Mon–Sun 11.00, 15.00; April & Oct Mon–Sun 11.00; Nov–March Fri–Sun 11.00

Tours and trips

Duration Takes about 2 hrs
Meet at the Front Gate of Trinity College, Dublin 2
Tickets €12, concessions €10 from the tour guide or in advance from Dublin Tourism. Or book online. Under-14s free. Email for group bookings.

James Joyce Centre 35 Nth Great George's St, Dublin 1, tel 878 8547, web www.jamesjoyce.ie

The Joyce Centre offers three interesting Joyce-themed jaunts around the city, all starting from the centre itself: a general one for non-Joyceans (the Circular Tour); one dealing with Joyce's popular book of short stories (the *Dubliners* Tour); and one dealing with *Ulysses* (the Footsteps of Leopold Bloom Tour). Check the website schedule or contact the centre to see which tours are on and when. If you can't make the set times you can arrange another time with the centre for a minimum charge of €40 (covering up to four people). Around Bloomsday (16 June), the centre runs special events and tours.

Times May–Sept Tues, Thurs, Sat 11.00, 14.00; Oct–April Sat 11.00, 14.00
Duration All tours around 75–90 min
Tickets €10, concessions €8 from the centre

The South Wall (or the Great South Wall or South Bull Wall) is an 18th-century breakwater built to improve navigation of the Liffey; it lies west of Ringsend and makes for a spectacular walk on a fine day. You can stroll right out to the red Poolbeg Lighthouse way out in Dublin Bay, from where you can survey the city and its surrounds from a unique perspective. Walking along the wall can be disconcerting, with perfectly calm water on one side and the choppy sea on the other. In high tides it almost feels as though you're walking on water. The South Wall faces the later-constructed Bull Wall or North Bull Wall, notable as it was designed by Captain William Bligh of the *Bounty* mutiny fame.

Getting there There is no public transport to the South Wall but there is car parking and public access just beyond Poolbeg Generating Station (Dublin's main power station, known as the Pigeon House—a landmark in itself with its two tall smokestacks).

Tours and trips

Guided bus tours

If you are only in Dublin for a short stay or if the weather puts
you off walking, there are a couple of bus tours which will still
give you a reasonable feel for the city's sights.

Dublin Bus City Tour tel 703 3028, web www.dublinsightseeing.ie
This is a hop-on, hop-off trip around the city's main sites, including the
zoo, galleries and museums, and the Guinness Storehouse. The ticket
is valid all day so you have the option to get off at any of the 23 stops
and back on again whenever you please. As well as the live English
commentary there's a multilingual recorded commentary on every
second or third bus.
Times and departure point Every 10 min from 09.30 to 15.00, every 15
min from 15.00 to 17.00, every 30 min from 17.00 to 18.30 (last bus 17.00
Nov–Mar). Tour starts from Cathal Brugha St, around the corner from
the Dublin Bus head office on O'Connell St, but can be joined at any
point along the route—look out for the green City Tour bus stops.
Duration Takes about 1 hr 30 min
Tickets €15, concessions €13, children €6, available on the bus or from
Dublin Bus, 59 Upr O'Connell St, Dublin 1, or from Dublin Tourism. Also
available from the Bus & Rail desk at Dublin Airport and online. Internet
booking up to 1 hr before departure, with a 20 per cent discount.

Dublin City Sightseeing (Dualway) tel 605 7705/458 0054, web www.
irishcitytours.com
Another hop-on, hop-off style tour, taking the standard tourist
route past the main attractions. It's slightly more expensive than the
Dublin Bus one but as well as the live English commentary there is
a multilingual recorded commentary on all buses, plus a recorded
commentary for kids. Text script available for the hearing impaired and
some wheelchair-accessible buses (phone in advance). The **Gray Line
city tour** is operated by the same company and costs the same price,
but takes a slightly different route. The one ticket can be used on both
routes.
Times and departure point Tours start at 09.30 (09.15 April–Sept)
and the last bus leaves between 16.00 and 18.00 depending on the
season—check the time with the driver. Buses depart every 10 min or
so in the morning and every 15 min or so in the afternoon from outside

Tours and trips

Dublin Tourism, 14 Upr O'Connell St, Dublin 1, but can be picked up at any of the stops along the route.

Duration Takes about 1 hr 30 min

Tickets €15.50, concessions €13, children €7, family (2 adults, 2 children) €38, available on the bus or from Dublin Tourism, or online with a 20 per cent discount.

Ghost Bus Tour (Dublin Bus) tel 703 3028, web www.dublinsightseeing.ie

Visits haunted houses and sites around the city, sharing tales of body-snatching as well as Dracula's Dublin origins. A good laugh if you are with a group but not suitable for children.

Times and departure point Mon–Thurs 20.00; Fri 20.00, 20.30; Sat–Sun 19.00, 21.30 from Dublin Bus, 59 Upr O'Connell St, Dublin 1

Duration Takes about 2 hrs

Tickets €25 from Dublin Bus, 59 Upr O'Connell St, Dublin 1 or from Dublin Tourism. Also available from the Bus & Rail desk at Dublin Airport and online. Internet booking up to 1 hr before departure.

Rock'n'Roll, Writers Bus Tour tel 620 3929, web www.dublinrocktour.ie

A relative newcomer, this tour guides you through Ireland's rich musical legacy, from Phil Lynott to Rory Gallagher to U2, all in a real tour bus with soft leather seats and TVs. Skilfully links literary and musical history, with a bit of politics thrown in as well. Limited wheelchair access if informed in advance.

Times and departure point Departs from Westmoreland St, Dublin 2, 12.00, 14.00, 16.00, 18.00; Mar–Sept daily; Oct–Dec Wed–Sun only. Group bookings only Jan–Feb

Duration Takes about 1 hr 15 min

Tickets €15, concessions €14, available on the bus or from Dublin Tourism, or book by phone or online.

Viking Splash Tour tel 707 6000, web www.vikingsplash.ie

See historical Dublin by land and water from an amphibious World War II vehicle called a 'DUKW'. Sites include Viking, Medieval and Georgian Dublin, with a splash into the newly developed Grand Canal Docks.

Times and departure point Tours from Mar–Nov approx. Times vary depending on demand so call in advance to check; during summer usually every half hour, winter every hour and a half. Departs from St Stephen's Green North.

Duration Takes about 1 hr 15 min

Tickets €20, concessions €18, children €10, available at the departure point or from Dublin Tourism. Or book by phone or online.

Tours and trips

The highest pub in Dublin

Johnnie Fox's Glencullen, Co Dublin, tel 295 5647, web www.jfp.ie
pint of Guinness €4.60

Up in the Dublin Mountains, Johnnie Fox's likes to think of itself as 'The Highest Pub in Ireland', though it is, in fact, not. Nevertheless, we can definitively say that Johnnie Fox's is the highest pub in Dublin.

The place is famous for its seafood and its 'hooleys' (music and dancing sessions—held every night), though neither could be said to fit in the shoestring category.

The interior is a veritable museum of treasures—there are old bicycles, pots, pans and bits and bobs, decked everywhere so as to be almost comedic in their abundance. The pub was originally a farm and parts of it still feel like an old Irish barn or farmhouse. Every inch of the walls is covered in framed things; you could spend an hour just browsing and reading with a pint in your hand, as long as you don't mind stepping out of the way of waiters rushing to get food on tables and Italian women looking for the toilet.

Open Mon–Sat 11.00–23.30, Sun 12.00–23.00
How to get there Dublin Bus 44B

....

Day trips and tours out of Dublin

Because Ireland is so small, it's possible to get up early in the morning, take a bus or a train from Dublin to Galway, Cork or Belfast, have a good five to seven hours to explore the city, and then get another bus or train home for bedtime. This is by no means the ideal way to experience the atmosphere and attractions of Ireland's other cities, but it is an option if you're desperate to see more of the country and are tight on time and cash. The bus will always be your cheaper option, often vastly so—though the journeys are longer and less pleasant. For bus timetable and fare details see www.buseireann.ie or tel 836 6111; for trains: www.irishrail.ie, tel 1850 366 222.

For many writers the real Ireland is found in the wild places such as Connemara, Donegal or Kerry. Unfortunately, unless you have a car, you will often have to get private bus connections as well as the main Bus Éireann/Irish Rail services, and the journey length as well as the infrequent timetabling mean that it's really not worth the effort unless you can spend at least a full day at your destination (see also *Getting out of Dublin*, page 84).

An alternative is to go on a one-day guided bus/rail tour with Railtours Ireland, tel 856 0045, web www.railtoursireland. com. These are not especially cheap: you can see Connemara for €89 or Kerry for €109. It is also, of course, not the best way to experience the beauty of these places—you'd like to discover it for yourself. But it's an option if you're short on time and have the cash.

There are also a number of companies that run one-day bus tours to some of the standard attractions around Ireland. Both **Barratt Tours**, tel (061) 384 700/087 237 5986, web www.4tours. biz, and **Eirtrail**, tel 086 824 1124, web www.eirtrail.com, offer one-day tours from Dublin to the stupendous Cliffs of Moher. **Paddywagon** has one-day tours to the Cliffs of Moher, Blarney Castle or Giant's Causeway, amongst other places, tel 823 0822, web www.paddywagontours.com. In *Bus tours of the coast* (page 224) we have only listed tours to places close to the capital. It is, after all, cheaper and easier not to stray too far from Dublin.

Dublin Bay by DART

The choice of sights close to Dublin is wide—from gloomy tombs that predate the Pyramids to the grandeurs of 18th-century ascendancy Ireland. The simplest 'day out', though, is just to run the circuit of Dublin Bay on the DART train line, from the bleak estates of Roddy Doyle's Kilbarrack to the windy splendours of Killiney Bay. Get someone to point out Sorrento Terrace, where Neil Jordan lives. If you have about €8 million

Tours and trips

stuffed down the sofa, you can live there too.

The DART travels the length of Dublin Bay, from the seaside towns of Bray and Greystones in the south to Howth and Malahide in the north. The route takes you through some of the most historically interesting parts of the city and, on a fine day, with the glittering sea on one side and the leafy stations and historical buildings on the other, it makes a great tour. With an all-day ticket for €8.30 you can drop off at any of the little stations and visit the seaside towns. There are spectacular walks with sea views at Howth Head, Bray and Killiney.

The **coastal path from Bray to Greystones** is a beautiful walk between two Victorian seaside towns. Walk along the seaside promenade towards Bray Head, and climb to the cross at the top. Continue along a grass track that hugs the coastline and brings you to Greystones, close to the harbour area. If you walk back to Bray the round trip would take maybe two hours and is about 10km. Or you can just catch the DART back.

The **Bray Sea Life Centre** on the seafront, tel 286 6939, web www.sealifeeurope.com, is not spectacular but worth a look if you like fishies or are with the kids (admission €10.95, concessions €9.95, children €7.95). The aquarium has a children's play area as well as full wheelchair access and an accessible toilet. Appropriately enough it's beside a seafood restaurant.

Killiney is Ireland's Celebrity Central. Among those living here are Bono, The Edge, Enya, Van Morrison and Neil Jordan. Turn right when coming out of the station and head parallel to the sea, up the hill until you come to a T-junction, which is Vico Rd (the Italian-sounding names around here stem from the place's supposed resemblance to Naples). Turn right and walk for a short distance to see one of the finest views over Killiney Bay, stretching from Sorrento Terrace across to Bray. This vista appeared in the movie *Once*. If you turn left at the next T-junction and walk up the hill, you will come to Killiney village, and a short distance further on you'll find the entrance to Victoria Park, which at its highest point has an obelisk and even more incredible views.

Dalkey is an attractive village with lots of character and fine restaurants/cafés, shops, galleries and pubs. **Dalkey Castle and Heritage Centre**, tel 285 8366, web www.dalkeycastle.com, is well worth a visit from May to October, or in the week running up to Christmas, for a highly entertaining half-hour guided tour. Conducted by actors in medieval character, it's like being part of a wandering piece of performance art, and costs just €6 (last tour around 16.30 daily). The centre is open till 17.00 daily the rest of the year too, but you'll be greeted by one character rather than with the full performance.

At **Sandycove** swim in the small beach at the little harbour (safe for children) or, for the more adventurous, the **Forty Foot**, which used to be exclusively for men (and most, including clergymen, used to swim naked).

Adjacent to the Forty Foot is the **James Joyce Tower**, one of the Martellos built by the British to defend against an invasion by Napoleon. James Joyce stayed in the tower with Oliver St John Gogarty for six nights and it now houses a **Joyce museum**, tel 280 9265, open from April to September (admission €7.50, concessions €6.30, children €4.70). It's a great place to be on Bloomsday (16 June), when there are special readings and performances.

There is also a lovely **promenade walk to Dún Laoghaire Harbour** from here. Take a walk on either pier—the east pier is the more popular, which means the west pier (nearer to Salthill & Monkstown station) makes for the nicer walk. Visit Teddy's shop on nearby Windsor Terrace for the best whipped ice-cream in Dublin!

Tours and trips

Sandymount station is convenient for the RDS show-grounds where the internationally famous Dublin Horse Show is held every August. The RDS also hosts major exhibitions and concerts (see page 159).

Lansdowne Road station is right beside the oldest rugby ground in the world. The ground is being reconstructed at present, but when completed, hopefully in 2010, it will be shared between the Irish Rugby Football Union and the Football Association of Ireland, seating 50,000 for rugby and soccer internationals. It's also going to be renamed the Aviva Stadium, after an insurance company, but since Dubliners habitually still refer to their railway stations by the pre-1966 names this looks like a doubtful investment.

The entrance to the grounds of **Malahide Castle**, tel 846 2184, web www.malahidecastle.com, is less than a hundred metres to your right after exiting Malahide station. The castle belonged to the Talbot family from 1185 to 1973 and sits on 250 acres of parkland. It was here also that James Boswell's very racy 18th-century diaries were discovered, hidden in a croquet box. The history is interesting but the tour on offer a little boringly presented. If you're there during the summer buy a combi ticket and visit the **Fry Model Railway**—the largest model railway in the country. In keeping with the model theme, the magnificent doll's house **Tara's Palace** is also here, along with a couple of other attractions. Alternatively, you could skip it all and just wander around admiring the grass, trees and flowers for free.

The castle is open till 17.00 every day all year round (18.00 on Sundays from April to September); the railway only from April to September, and not on Wednesdays or on Sunday mornings. Admission to either castle or railway is €7.25, concessions €6.10, children €4.55, family (two adults and three children under 12) €21. Combined tickets €12.50, concessions €10.30, children €7.70, family €35.50. The castle is not wheelchair accessible but the model railway is and there is an accessible toilet.

Take a walk, of about two or three hours depending on your pace, from Sutton station along the coastal path/track around Howth Head to Howth Harbour, where you can catch the DART back to the city. The cliff walk is absolutely beautiful on a fine day with varied terrain and vistas. For access to the walk, turn left out of the station and, when you come to Sutton Cross, cross the junction and head onto Greenfield Rd. You'll come to a small beach after about 600m; at the end of the beach take the minor road to the right, Strand Rd, and head on for a kilometer or more, always hugging the coast, until you come to a gravel path on your right. Follow this and at the Martello Tower take the cliff path to the right and continue on the track around to Howth village, passing the Bailey Lighthouse along the way.

Howth, a famous Dublin fishing port, is a quaint village with many fine cafés, pubs and restaurants, which are particularly good for seafood, funnily enough. Turn right when you come out of the station and go past the pier to follow the beautiful (if sometimes crowded) cliff walk up Howth Head. Along the way you'll pass Balscadden House, where W. B. Yeats lived for three years.

Also deserving of a look is the **National Transport Museum**, tel 832 0427/848 0831/847 5623, web www.nationaltransportmuseum.org. Turn left out of the station and it is about 700m away; you'll see the sign for where to turn left again. The National Transport is not so much a museum as a barn crammed with old trucks and buses. That's the beauty of it, though—nothing has been sanitised or commercialised. It's operated almost entirely voluntarily, and most of the vehicles haven't even been restored because there is no money. You can see old horse-drawn carriages, steam engines, trams, ambulances, fire engines and school buses; vehicles dating from the 1880s up to 2000. It's open Saturdays, Sundays and bank holidays all year round 14.00–17.00; from June to August it's also open 10.00–17.00 Monday to Friday. Admission €3.50, children/concessions €2, family (two adults and up to five children) €9.

On your way to the Transport Barn you'll pass Howth Castle, which is not open to the public but still an impressive building. You could also take a walk up to the Deer Park Hotel and enjoy the breathtaking views of Dublin.

Further afield

If weather permits and you're into hiking, it's well worth taking at least a day to walk part of the **Wicklow Way**, a beautiful hiking route that stretches from the outskirts of south Dublin across the Wicklow Mountains, taking you past lakes, forests, old ruins and historical sites. The full walk takes about eight to ten days. For maps and more information visit www.wicklow-way.com or ask at the Dublin Tourism Centre on Suffolk St, Dublin 2.

Brú na Bóinne (The Boyne Valley) Donore, Co Meath, tel (041) 988 0300, web www.heritageireland.ie

This whole region is steeped in Irish history. The Hill of Tara is the supposed seat of Brian Boru and the ancient High Kings, and the Battle of the Boyne (1690), which secured the Protestant Ascendancy in Ireland, was fought here. But the main attraction is the extraordinary barrow tombs of Newgrange, Knowth and Dowth. Surrounded by standing stones, some more than four tonnes in weight, and decorated by mysterious spirals, lozenges and lines, these tombs are older than the Egyptian pyramids and Stonehenge. At dawn on the 21st of December, the shortest day of the year, the first rays of sunlight strike precisely into the very heart of the ancient tomb of Newgrange, as they have done for over five thousand years.

Admission to the tombs is only through the visitor centre and with a guided tour. Newgrange and Knowth can both be visited but there is no access to Dowth. For conservation reasons, the number of visitors is restricted—so access to Newgrange and Knowth themselves is not even totally guaranteed, particularly in summer, unless you are on an organised tour (such as one of the bus tours below) that includes admission. There is no wheelchair access to the tombs (blame the builders) but the centre with an exhibition and tearooms is fully accessible, including accessible toilets.

Open Feb–April daily 09.30–17.30; May 09.00–18.30; June–mid-Sept 09.00–19.00; mid–end Sept 09.00–18.30; Oct 09.30–17.30; Nov–Jan 09.00–17.00

Admission There are four different price schemes, depending on how much you want to see. Admission to the visitor centre and the exhibition, which includes a full-scale replica of the Newgrange chamber and a model of Knowth, is €2.90 for adults, €2.10 for seniors and €1.60 for students/children. There isn't really much point in coming all this way, though, unless you're also going to visit Newgrange itself: adults €5.80, seniors €4.50, children/students €2.90.

Getting there Take a bus from Busáras, Store St, Dublin 1 to Drogheda, or a suburban train from Connolly Station, Dublin 1 to Drogheda, and then a Bus Éireann shuttle bus (no 163) to the visitor centre. Alternatively, Over the Top Tours offer a shuttle bus that goes direct from Dublin to Brú na Bóinne at €18 return—Freephone 1800 42 42 52, tel 860 0404/087 259 3467, web www.overthetoptours.com (entrance to Newgrange is guaranteed but you pay in yourself). Or, you could go on an **organised tour** with any of a number of companies. We include just two below.

Bus Éireann tel 836 6111, web www.buseireann.ie This tour guarantees a visit inside Newgrange itself. On alternate days in summer it also visits other places of interest such as the Hill of Tara (see page 220) and Mellifont Abbey. In winter it always goes via the Hill of Tara to Brú na Bóinne. There's a commentary on the sights along the way, and entry to all heritage sites visited is included.

Departs from Busáras, Store St, Dublin 1 at 10.00, returning at 17.45; May–Sept daily except Fri, Oct–April Thurs & Sat only

Tickets in high season €36, concessions €30, children €25; in low season €25, concessions €22, children €17. Ten per cent online discount.

Mary Gibbons Tours tel 283 9973/086 355 1355, web www. newgrangetours.com

Award-winning tour that visits Newgrange, the Boyne Valley and the Hill of Tara, and includes entrance to the tomb.

Departs Mon–Sat all year round from a number of points in the city, including the Dublin Tourism Centre/Pizza Hut, Suffolk St, Dublin 2, at 10.15, arriving back in Dublin at around 16.30

Tickets €35, students €30

Castletown House Celbridge, Co Kildare, tel 628 8252, web www. castletownhouse.ie

The largest and most impressive Palladian-style country house in Ireland, at the end of a long avenue in the village of Celbridge about 20km west of the city. Built, incidentally, by a lawyer.

What little remains of Castletown's once immense grounds along the banks of the River Liffey can still be explored by visitors for free all year round and makes a lovely walk on a fine day.

Access to the house itself is by guided tours only, but these are well worthwhile, as much for insights into the fascinating family that once inhabited it as for the architecture and design. There are also tearooms in the house and cafés in the nearby village for refreshments.

The house is fully wheelchair accessible, with a lift to all floors, and toilets for wheelchair users are available.

Open mid-Mar–Oct Tues–Sun and bank holiday Mondays 10.30–16.45 (last tour)

Admission €4.50, concessions/children €3.50

Getting there Dublin Bus nos 67, 67A from Pearse St to Celbridge, and then a 15 min walk to Castletown

Glendalough Co Wicklow, tel (0404) 45325/(0404) 45352, web www. heritageireland.ie

The name means 'glen of the two lakes' and it is a spectacular setting for mountain walks and picnics yet only an hour from Dublin, making it ideal for a day trip. Take in the scenery and fresh air or explore the monastic settlement that lasted in this secluded spot from the 6th to the 14th century, when it was destroyed by English troops. The monuments remaining include the round tower and St Kevin's Kitchen (a church). The visitor centre, which has an exhibition and an audio-visual show, is wheelchair accessible, along with the picnic areas and toilets. So are some of the less rugged areas around the lake, but much of the park, including the monastic settlements, is not.

Visitor centre open mid-Mar–mid-Oct 09.30–17.15 (last admission); mid-Oct–mid-Mar 09.30–16.15

Admission to the visitor centre €3, seniors €2, children/students €1 (it's free to just roam around if you don't want to visit the visitor centre). Guided tours on request.

Getting there Take St Kevin's Bus, tel 281 8119, web www.glendaloughbus.com, which leaves St Stephen's Green North, Dublin 2 (opposite the Mansion House) at 11.30 daily (€20 return to Glendalough, €12 children). The last bus returning to Dublin from Glendalough is at 16.30, except on Sat, Sun and bank hols during the summer season (Mar–Sept) when it's at 17.40. Alternatively, organised tours are provided by a number of companies, including:

Bus Éireann tel 836 6111, web www.buseireann.ie
Tour of Glendalough and Powerscourt Gardens (see below). Includes entry into the Glendalough Visitor Centre and a guided tour of the monastic settlement.

Departs from Busáras, Store St, Dublin 1 at 10.00, returning at 17.45; Mar–Nov daily, Dec–Feb Wed, Fri, Sun only

Tickets in high season €36, concessions €30, children €25; in low season €25, concessions €22, children €17. Ten per cent online discount

Coach Tours of Ireland tel (044) 934 8479, web www.coachtoursofireland.com

The Wicklow Day Coach Tour includes a stop for morning coffee (not included in the price) at the Glencree Reconciliation Centre, a guided tour of the monastic site and a lunch stop at Ballykissangel (the locus of a long-running soap).

Departs daily from several points in the city including the Dublin Tourism Centre, Suffolk St, Dublin 2 at 09.00, returning to Dublin at around 17.00

Tickets €24, concessions/children €22

Wild Wicklow Tours tel 280 1899, web www.wildwicklow.ie
Includes a stop for morning coffee (not included in the price) at Avoca Handweavers and a tour of the monastic settlement.

Departs daily from several points in the city including the Dublin Tourism Centre, Suffolk St, Dublin 2 at 09.10 and Dún Laoghaire Ferry Terminal at 10.00; returns to Dublin between 17.00 and 17.30.

Tickets €28, students/children €25

Tours and trips

Hill of Tara Navan, Co Meath, tel (046) 902 5903/(041) 988 0300, web www. heritageireland.ie

The Hill of Tara is worth a visit if you are also on your way to Newgrange. This is where the ancient High Kings of Ireland supposedly sat, after they were crowned at the Lia Fáil, the Stone of Destiny atop the hill. Of late Tara has been in the news thanks to the construction of the M3 Motorway, which protestors argue runs too close to the hill and endangers the ancient site (in 2008 the World Monument Fund listed it among its 100 Most Endangered Sites in the World). There is an audio-visual show and guided tours are available on request. Limited wheelchair access.

Open daily mid-May–mid-Sept 10.00–17.00 (last admission)
Admission €3, seniors €2, children/students €1, family (2 adults with children under 18) €8
Getting there Take Bus Éireann route no 109 and get off at Tara Cross. The Hill is about a 1.5km walk from here. Or you could go on an organised tour with Bus Éireann (see page 217) or

Over the Top Tours Freephone 1800 42 42 52, tel 860 0404/087 259 3467, web www.overthetoptours.com

The Celtic Tour visits the prehistoric tomb of Fourknocks, Mellifont Abbey, Monasterboice and the Hill of Slane, as well as the Hill of Tara. Includes complimentary tea/coffee.

Departs from the Dublin Tourism Centre, Suffolk St, Dublin 2; Mon–Sat 09.00, Sun 09.30; returns at 17.30
Tickets €29, concessions €27

Irish National Stud, Japanese Gardens and St Fiachra's Garden Tully, Co Kildare, tel (045) 522 963/(045) 521 617, web www.irish-national-stud. ie

The first ever steeplechase was held in Co Cork in 1752, so it's no surprise that the Irish have an affinity for horses. There's lots to do at the National Stud: walk between the wide paddocks under shady trees, watching the horses go about their business; visit the stallion boxes; visit the horse museum and see the skeleton of Arkle, 'the greatest steeplechaser in history'. Here, his greatness lives on—in the form of a window exhibit.

If horses hold no interest for you, the Japanese Gardens offer a 'spiritual journey' through the Life of Man. Enter through the Gate of Oblivion and exit through the Gateway to Eternity, climbing the Hill of

Learning and crossing the Marriage Bridge along the way. St Fiachra's Garden reflects the environments that inspired the spirituality of the 6th and 7th centuries.

There are picnic tables, guided tours, a restaurant and a gift shop. The famous Kildare retail outlet is also nearby for those of you wanting to shop. The stud and the gardens are fully wheelchair accessible including accessible toilets.

Open mid-Feb–Dec 09.30–17.00 daily

Admission €11, concessions €8, children €6, family (2 adults and 4 children) €27

Getting there Bus Éireann no 126 goes from the Connolly Station Red line Luas stop to the National Stud Mon–Sat 09.30, with a return service leaving the stud at 15.45 (on Sunday there are two services—10.00 and 12.00 from Connolly returning at 15.00 and 17.30). Alternatively, take a train from Heuston Station, Dublin 8 to Kildare Station, and then a shuttle bus or taxi to the National Stud.

Larchill Arcadian Garden Kilcock, Co Kildare, tel 628 7354, web www. larchill.ie

A few kilometres north of Kilcock is the sole surviving example in Europe of a mid-18th-century *ferme ornée* ('ornamental farm') or Arcadian garden. It's wonderful for anyone interested in historic gardens and great fun for children too. As well as a formal walled garden, there is a 1km walk through landscaped parkland in which there are ten classical and gothic follies, among other features including an eight-acre lake and a replica of the fortress on the Rock of Gibraltar. Larchill also has one of the largest numbers of rare farm animal breeds in Ireland in its gothic model farm and a pets' corner and adventure playground for kids. The visitor centre, with tearooms and a gift shop, is wheelchair accessible, as are the toilets and the walled garden.

Open to all visitors 12.00–18.00 May bank holiday weekend (Sat–Mon), June–Aug Thurs–Sun (plus bank holiday Mondays), Sept Sat–Sun

Open to pre-booked groups only on other days May–Sept. Closed the rest of the year

Admission €7.50, children €5.50, family (2 adults and 4 children) €27.50

Getting there Bus Éireann no 115 from Busáras/Connolly Station to Kilcock; or, take Dublin Bus no 66 from Pearse St to Maynooth and then get a taxi the few kilometres to the gardens.

Tours and trips

Newbridge House and Farm Donabate, Co Dublin, tel 843 6534, email newbridgehouse@fingalcoco.com

If you are a bit of a period freak and it's a lovely day, head out to Newbridge House, unchanged since its building in 1737—have a look and then go on to Donabate Beach nearby. The house has all the original furniture and features, as well as Robert West's intricate plasterwork. A traditional farm on the grounds preserves the older species of farm animals—Kerry cows, Jacob sheep, Connemara ponies and more—and even has old farm machinery on display along with the Lord Chancellor's coach. There is a chicken incubator: it's magic to see the tiny balls of fluff peck their way out of the shells. There is a playground, a shop, a café and guided tours. This is a great trip for children or the uneducated townee who thinks Stephen's Green is, if anything, a little too rural. There is no wheelchair access to the house but limited access to the farm.

Open April–Sept Tues–Sat 10.00–17.00 (closed 13.00–14.00; last tour around 1 hr before closing), Sun and bank hol 12.00–18.00; Oct–Mar Sat, Sun and bank hol 12.00–17.00

Admission to the house (including guided tour) €7, concessions €6, children €3.50, family (2 adults and 4 children) €18; farm €3.80, concessions €2.80, children €2.50, family (2 adults and 2 children) €10

Getting there Dublin Bus nos 33, 41, 41B, 41C from Lr Abbey St to Swords, then 33B from Swords to Newbridge House; or, take a suburban train from Connolly Station, Dublin 1 to Donabate.

Powerscourt Estate Enniskerry, Co Wicklow, tel 204 6000, web www.powerscourt.ie

The demesne contains the Palladian house and formal gardens, which are often crowded but undeniably still beautiful. There's also an exhibition and an overpriced restaurant and shops. **Powerscourt Waterfall**, a couple of kilometres away, is better value, and is well worth the trip as well as or as an alternative to the house and gardens. There are toilet and picnic facilities, and a playground, but nothing else to intrude on this unspoilt scene. The 121m waterfall is the highest in Ireland and the surrounding hills and forests are great for walks. It's a great spot for barbecues too—which are allowed, but no alcohol. The picturesque village of Enniskerry offers cosy pubs and cafés to retire to after the day's activity before heading back to town.

There is partial wheelchair access to the house and gardens and an accessible toilet there too. The waterfall consists mostly of open parkland and there is an accessible toilet.

Open House and garden all year round 09.30–17.30 daily (gardens close at dusk in winter); waterfall Nov–Feb 10.30–16.00 (closed for 2 weeks prior to Christmas), Mar–April 10.30–17.30, May–Aug 09.30–19.00, Sept–Oct 10.30–17.30

Admission House and exhibition free; gardens €8, concessions €7, children €5; waterfall €5, concessions €4.50, children €3.50

Getting there Dublin Bus nos 44, 44C from Townsend St to Enniskerry village. The house and gardens are about a 10 min walk from the village and the way is signposted. The waterfall is about another hour's walk away—turn left at the entrance to the house/gardens and follow the signs. You could also go to the gardens on an organised tour. Bus Éireann's *Glendalough* tour (page 218) goes to Powerscourt Gardens, as do a couple of tours in *Bus tours of the coast* below.

Russborough House Blessington, Co Wicklow, tel (045) 865 239, web www.russborough.ie

Russborough is a truly beautiful house, with intricate plasterwork and gorgeous furniture. What really sets it apart from other Palladian homes, however, are its two collections of fine art: the Milltown collection and the Beit collection, the latter containing works by Goya, Vermeer and Rubens. Thanks to these riches the house has been robbed four times since the 1970s, including by the IRA and Dublin's infamous 'General', Martin Cahill. Most of the paintings were later recovered.

The Russborough guided tour, which lasts about an hour, is a little dour, but the house itself and the paintings are magnificent. Other attractions include a beech hedge maze and a walk around the surrounding parkland. There is also a restaurant and a gift shop.

Open May–Sept daily 10.00–18.00 (last tour around 17.00); April & Oct Sun and bank hols 10.00–18.00. Rest of year by appointment only.

Admission €10, concessions €8, children €5, family (2 adults and up to 4 children under 16) €25; maze admission €3

Getting there Dublin Bus no 65 from Eden Quay to Blessington. Russborough is just over 3km from Blessington on the Baltinglass/Tullow road.

Tours and trips

Victoria's Way Sculpture Park Roundwood, Co Wicklow, tel 281 8505, web http://homepage.eircom.net/~victoriasway

In this Enchanted Forest of Calm you will come to know the thrill of the eternal Now, the transcendent perfection of the present. On the Meditation Path through the woods, experience a peace that surpasses joy, as you travel alone . . . to the Alone.

OK—that may sound strange, but seriously, this place has a weird effect on you. Standing in a field in the Wicklow Mountains there are several eight-foot-high solid stone Hindu statues. But these aren't just ordinary Hindu statues—you have Ganesh playing the uilleann pipes or dancing to his Walkman. Other sculptures include a giant finger with 'Create or Die' written on it and the Split Man. All these are the brainchildren of one man, Victor, who commissioned the statues specially from India and Ireland. The park used to be called Victor's Way until Victor had an epiphany and realised he needed to follow his feminine side.

Victoria's Way is another world, weird and magical. If you don't go you will forever wonder what turns your life may have taken if you did.

The park can get waterlogged, so if there's been sustained heavy rain do check if it's open before you go. It's open country so it should be possible for a wheelchair user to get around with some assistance. *Open* May–Aug 12.30–18.30 daily *Admission* €2.50
Getting there Take St Kevin's Bus, tel 281 8119, web www. glendaloughbus.com, which leaves St Stephen's Green North, Dublin 2 (opposite the Mansion House) at 11.30 daily. Ask to be dropped off at the crossroads where the bus turns towards Sally Gap (about 2km from Roundwood village). Victoria's Way is 300m away, on the Roundwood road.

Bus tours of the coast

There are a number of companies that offer excursions to Wicklow, the Boyne Valley and various points of interest on the outskirts of Dublin. Here are just three of them.

Dualway tel 605 7705/458 0054, web www.irishcitytours.com
A variety of tours on offer, including to Wicklow, Newgrange, and around Dublin Bay (with a visit to Malahide Castle).

Times and departure points Newgrange tour departs from the Dublin Tourism Centre, Suffolk St, Dublin 2; all others from Dublin Tourism, 14 Upr O'Connell St, Dublin 1. Dublin Bay and Castle Tour lasts about 3 hrs 30 min; all other tours about 7 hrs.

Tickets €25–38, concessions €22–35, children €12–25 depending on the tour. Online discounts may be available.

Dublin Bus tel 703 3028, web www.dublinsightseeing.ie

The North Coast and Castle Tour includes a visit to Malahide Castle and lasts three hours. The South Coast and Gardens Tour includes a stop at Powerscourt Gardens and lasts four and a half hours. Both tours are wheelchair accessible (but note that there is no wheelchair access to Malahide Castle).

Times and departure point North Coast departs 10.00, 14.00 daily; South Coast 11.00 daily, both from Dublin Bus, 59 Upr O'Connell St, Dublin 1

Tickets €25, children €12. Online discounts available.

Over the Top Tours Freephone 1800 42 42 52, tel 860 0404/087 259 3467, web www.overthetoptours.com

Minibus tours which claim to go where the large coach tours don't. As well as the Newgrange shuttle bus and Celtic Tour listed above, Over the Top offer a Wicklow tour and a 'Mystery' tour which promises to take you to 'some of Ireland's most amazing and hidden sites'.

Times and departure points Depending on the tour, leaves around 09.00 from the Dublin Tourism Centre, Suffolk St, Dublin 2, and from O'Connell St, returning around 17.30

Tickets €28/29, concessions €25/27

Wheelchair-accessible tours

Vantastic Freephone 1800 242 703, web www.vantastic.ie

Vantastic offer wheelchair-accessible tours around Dublin City, to the Malahide Castle estate and to Dublin Zoo, as well as accessible shopping trips and tours to the National Stud/Japanese Gardens and Powerscourt/Glendalough. They cater for groups or individuals; the vehicles cater for three manual wheelchairs or two electric wheelchairs, with up to eight passengers in total. Tours available all year round but early booking is recommended—call for a quote.

The sporting life

Dublin offers much in the way of sport. Gaelic games, run by the GAA (Gaelic Athletic Association), add a whole new dimension to the world of sport, with Gaelic football and hurling attracting massive interest both playing and watching—a boon for anyone tired of the ceaseless round of the same old international sports.

Almost every sport is catered for to some extent, with a slew of boxing clubs in every suburb and regular bouts at the National Stadium. Swimming pools pepper the city, and golf clubs of both championship and amateur standard pop up all over the place, with regular tournaments of quality on show. Alternatively, if you don't find this exciting enough, there are many and varied opportunities to gamble on the event to add that extra spice. Dublin has a host of sports to offer the visitor if you are brave enough to search them out. The *Evening Herald* and the *Irish Independent* are the best for details of what's on. For details of horse and greyhound racing venues, see page 243.

Watching sport

Gaelic games

The characteristic of GAA games is the vivid speed of the play and the fluidity with which it switches from one end of the pitch to the other. **Gaelic football** is a cross between rugby and soccer, played with a round ball, encompassing the handling and kicking skills of rugby and the vision and dexterity of soccer. Players are not allowed to pick the ball up directly from the ground.

Hurling is played with long sticks made of ash wood, with players allowed to handle the sliothar (pronounced 'shlither': the ball) but again not to pick it up directly from the ground. The sliothar is made of leather and is about the same size as a cricket ball, although a great deal softer. It has cork on the inside to make it lighter and to help it to travel at speed. Hurling, when played well, has a phenomenal velocity about it and an inherent grace that makes it one of the most aesthetic and exciting field sports in the world.

Camogie is hurling for women and is similarly as fast, exciting and skilful as games come. A demanding sport to play and a thrilling one to watch, camogie is well worth investigating. Ladies' football is also the biggest growing sport in the country at the moment.

The GAA retains its special hold on the nation's attention. Every town, suburb, parish and village in the country has its own pitch and training facilities, complete with club colours and local flavour. The sport is amateur and incites high tribal passions. For that reason, it is often more rewarding to sniff out a club game where the footballers and hurlers who may never feel the glory of representing their county have the chance to revel in the attention of their parish.

The biggest club games in Dublin are generally played during the summer and autumn months at **Parnell Park** ('The Nell'), Dublin 5—this is the place to head to, practically every Saturday evening of the summer months and most Sunday afternoons during the winter.

If you decide to forego the club scene then a trip to **Croke Park**, Dublin 3, the showpiece stadium of the GAA, is wholeheartedly recommended. 'Croker' is a hugely impressive, 82,300-capacity state-of-the-art affair, complete with corporate boxes and facilities. From mid-March to the end of September the games become quite serious with regular crowds of 25,000–65,000 and then of course full houses when the finals arrive.

The real start of the Croke Park season is St Patrick's Day (17 March), when the All-Ireland club finals are played. From then on the elite county teams take centre stage, the skill level rises and the entry fees rise accordingly. Touts have been known to get anything up to €1,500 for an All-Ireland final ticket, but they are best avoided as high quality forgeries are frequently in circulation. Go during June or July when tickets are cheaper and easier to come by; the atmosphere is not as intense but you will at least get a strong taste of it. If you have trouble getting tickets for big games, try the ticket booths on match mornings on Lr Drumcondra Rd, about five minutes from Croke Park. If you do somehow manage to get a ticket to an All-Ireland final, you are in for one of the great treats in life.

A big game is usually preceded by a Minor (under-18) match, which starts at 13.00–13.30; the Senior games generally start between 15.00 and 16.00, nearly always on Sundays. You can take a bus from O'Connell St in the city centre, but on big match days you would probably make more progress walking, where fans mark an obvious route to the stadium.

Croke Park Jones's Rd, Dublin 3, tel 819 2300, web www.crokepark.ie
  Wheelchair access and accessible toilet.
  Getting there Dublin Bus nos 3, 11, 11A, 16, 16A, 41
  Admission early summer provincial game €20 stands, €15 terrace, €10 concessions; qualifier €25 stands, €15 terrace, €10–15 concessions. As the season progresses prices rise and tickets become like gold dust. Senior All-Ireland final tickets have a face value of €70 stands, €35 terrace. Children get the best deal—it's €5 whatever the match.
Parnell Park Donnycarney, Dublin 5, tel 831 2099, email info@hill16.ie
  Wheelchair access and accessible toilet.
  Getting there DART to Killester and then a 10-min walk; Dublin Bus nos 20B, 27, 27B, 42, 42A, 42B and get off at or near Donnycarney Church (Our Lady of Consolation)
  Admission €13–€15, concessions €5, children under 15 free

Rugby

A couple of times a year Dublin is invaded for the weekend by hordes of English, Scottish, Welsh, Italian or French fans for rugby internationals in the Six Nations Championship (hence the shortage of hotel beds at these times, and shocking price hikes). At the moment the matches are being held in Croke Park (see above) while Lansdowne Road Stadium is transformed into the Aviva Stadium, named after an insurance company. The new Lansdowne, which will be shared between the Irish Rugby Football Union (IRFU, web www.irishrugby.ie) and the Football Association of Ireland, is to open in 2010.

Rugby internationals tend to be special occasions—the atmosphere in the city is scarcely equalled throughout the rest of the year, only St Patrick's Day comes close. You can try your luck getting a Six Nations ticket, but only the touts ever seem to have any. If you manage to come across one then consider yourself blessed and enjoy a unique occasion in the Irish sporting calendar. The Irish rugby public always set out to have a good time regardless of the result.

The main Dublin clubs are **Clontarf**, the only major northside club, **Lansdowne**, **St Mary's**, **Old Wesley**, **Blackrock** and **Old Belvedere**. The southside clubs are based within a stone's throw of each other in Donnybrook and Ballsbridge, and Blackrock. Lansdowne have been playing in the RDS (see page 159) while Lansdowne Road is out of commission—from 2010 they will be back at the new Aviva Stadium.

The stadia should be wheelchair accessible, but the level of accessibility varies so it's wise to phone ahead and check facilities. *Admission* If you are paying more than €10 for a league game the club has some cheek. Concessions/children's prices are around €5.

The sporting life

Blackrock College RFC Stradbrook Rd, Blackrock, Co Dublin,
tel 280 0151, web www.blackrockcollegerfc.com
Getting there Dublin Bus nos 4, 4A from O'Connell St or 45 from Eden
Quay

Clontarf Rugby Club Castle Ave, Clontarf, Dublin 3, tel 833 6214,
web www.clontarfrugby.com
Getting there Dublin Bus no 130 from Lr Abbey St, Dublin 1 to Castle
Ave

Lansdowne Rugby Club Lansdowne Rd, Ballsbridge, Dublin 4,
tel 668 9300, web www.lansdownerugby.com
Getting there DART to Lansdowne Rd; Dublin Bus nos 4, 4A, 7, 7A from
O'Connell St or 45 from Eden Quay

Old Belvedere 28A Anglesea Rd, Donnybrook, Dublin 4, tel 660 3378, web
www.oldbelvedere.ie
Getting there Dublin Bus nos 4, 4A, 5, 7, 7A, 63 from O'Connell St or 45,
84 from Eden Quay

Old Wesley RFC Donnybrook, Dublin 4, tel 668 9153, web www.oldwesley.
ie
Getting there Dublin Bus nos 4, 4A, 5, 7, 7A, 63 from O'Connell St or 45,
84 from Eden Quay.

St Mary's College RFC Templeville Rd, Templeogue, Dublin 6W, tel 490
0440, web www.stmaryscollegerfc.com
Getting there Dublin Bus nos 15, 15B, 49, 65, 65B from Eden Quay or 74
from Britain Quay/Grand Canal Dock

Soccer

Soccer underwent a boom period in Ireland in the 1990s, following the success of the international team. Of course, most of the
good Irish players were creamed off by the full-time professional
leagues in England. **Bohemians, Shamrock Rovers, St Patrick's
Athletic** and **Shelbourne** are the only League of Ireland clubs
worth going to see (and you might even skip Shels, who lost
their Premier Division status in 2007). While the standard of
fare is inconsistent, it can occasionally be good value for money.
You are just as likely to be bored senseless at a nil-all draw as you
are to be enthralled by an 8- or even 9-goal thriller. The Dublin

Derby games are always worth a risk, especially those involving the teams above, who on their best days play highly entertaining football. Bohs and 'the Hoops', Shamrock Rovers, are the biggest teams, with a long-standing rivalry.

St Patrick's Athletic play in Inchicore while Shelbourne are at Tolka Park, a small yet impeccable all-seater stadium in Drumcondra. In fact, most League of Ireland grounds are completely seated. Shamrock Rovers' new ground is in Tallaght, while Bohs are at Dalymount Park in Phibsborough. All the stadia have wheelchair access and accessible toilets. *Admission* prices are around €15–20, concessions/children €5–10.

Bohemians Dalymount Park, Phibsborough, Dublin 7, tel 868 0923, web www.bohemians.ie
Getting there Dublin Bus nos 4, 10, 19, 19A, 38, 38A, 38B, 38C, 83, 120
St Patrick's Athletic Richmond Park, Emmet Rd, Inchicore, Dublin 8, tel 454 6332, web www.stpatsfc.com
Getting there Dublin Bus nos 51B, 51C, 78A from Aston Quay, Dublin 1
Shamrock Rovers Tallaght Stadium, Whitestown Way, Tallaght, Dublin 24, tel (offices in Dublin 12) 460 5948, web www.shamrockrovers.ie
Getting there Luas Red line from Connolly Station to Tallaght; Dublin Bus nos 49, 49A, 50, 54A, 56A, 65, 65B, 77, 77A
Shelbourne FC Tolka Park, Richmond Rd, Dublin 3, tel 837 5536/837 5754/836 8781, web www.shelbournefc.ie
Getting there Dublin Bus nos 3, 11, 11A, 11B, 16, 16A from O'Connell St, Dublin 1 or 41, 41B, 41C from Lr Abbey St, Dublin 1

And also
Boxing
You can see regular bouts at the 2,000-capacity **National Stadium**, the world's first purpose-built boxing stadium. Check online or in the *Evening Herald* or *Irish Independent* for details of fights.

Prices depend on the event and range from €10–50, with concessions generally a fiver less; children's tickets are usually half price.

Big fights can be seen at **The O₂** (see page 159).

National Stadium Sth Circular Rd, Dublin 8, tel 453 3371, web www.nationalstadium.ie
   Wheelchair access and accessible toilet.
   Getting there Dublin Bus nos 16, 16A, 19, 19A, 122 from O'Connell St, Dublin 1

Cricket

After our amateur national side's astonishing success in the 2007 World Cup, beating Pakistan to reach the final eight, it looked for a while like the whole country might take up cricket.

During the summer you can watch cricket in Trinity College, Dublin 2, home of the **Dublin University Cricket Club** (which once counted Samuel Beckett among its players), web www.cricket.tcdlife.ie. At the weekend during summer there are usually matches in the Phoenix Park, Dublin 8 (home of the **Phoenix Cricket Club**, web www.phoenixcricketclub.com), or at the **Leinster Cricket Club**, Observatory Lane, Rathmines, Dublin 6, tel 497 2428, web www.leinster.cc (Dublin Bus nos 15, 15A, 15B).

International matches involving Ireland are occasionally played at **Clontarf Cricket Club** (joint venue with Clontarf Rugby Club), Castle Ave, Clontarf, Dublin 3, tel 833 6214, web www.clontarfcricket.com (Dublin Bus no 130 from Lr Abbey St, Dublin 1).

For more info check out www.irishcricket.org.

The sporting life

Playing sport

Athletics

If you like nothing better than just to run, then get in touch with the **Athletic Association of Ireland**, tel 886 9933, web www.athleticsireland.ie. They should be able to give you details of your nearest club and how to get involved.

Boxing

Boxing is another mainstay of city life, particularly in the poorer inner city areas, and there is a raft of clubs to choose from. Any city centre gym should be able to give you details of how to get involved. You can also contact the **Irish Amateur Boxing Association**, tel 453 3371, web www.iaba.ie.

Cycling

Dublin has some wonderful road and mountain biking routes, particularly in the nearby Dublin and Wicklow Mountains. There are at least 30 cycling clubs in Dublin; some only do leisure cycling, but most are competitive.

Cycling Ireland is the umbrella body for the sport here, tel 855 1522, web www.cyclingireland.ie. The website lists local clubs with contact names and phone numbers. It also covers cycling for people with disabilities.

As well as weekly training spins, most cycling clubs run at least one big, marshalled leisure cycle every year. These generally have several routes and distances to suit both beginner/leisure cyclists and experienced riders. The major leisure cycle in the Dublin region is the **Wicklow 200**, held in June, see www.wicklow200.ie. It attracts 1400 riders, many from abroad.

The sporting life

If you want to be competitive, road races are held nearly every weekend during the season, see www.cyclingireland.ie and www.irishcycling.com.

Triathlon events are booming in Ireland as elsewhere, see www.triathlonireland.com for event and club listings.

For mountain bikers there is plenty of great riding in the Dublin and Wicklow Mountains. The main trail network is at Ballinastoe, near Roundwood, see www.coillteoutdoors. ie. For information on MTB clubs, events and races see www. mtbireland.com, www.madmtb.com, www.epicmtb.com and www.team-worc.com.

Bike shops are also good sources of information—**Cycleways**, 185–186 Parnell St, Dublin 1, tel 873 4748, web www.cycleways. com, has plenty of expert, friendly, knowledgeable staff.

Gaelic games

Perhaps the easiest sports to play are Gaelic games, with some 100 clubs in the Dublin area which are always on the lookout for new members. One of the latest developments to hit Gaelic games is the mushrooming of ladies' teams, with the All-Ireland ladies' football final attracting bigger and bigger crowds. There are also 41 camogie clubs around the capital.

Gaelic clubs welcome people of any talent and level, and make great efforts to teach the rudiments of the games, so places can always be found for new people. Newcomers' chances of playing for the first team may be slim but the great thing about the reserve teams is their willingness to embrace the social aspects of the game; indeed, they are more renowned as drinking clubs than breeding grounds for new talent.

The nearest Gaelic football, hurling or camogie club is never more than a few kilometres away. There is a club directory (for men) on the website of the Dublin County Board, at www.hill16.

The sporting life

ie/hill16clubs.asp, or you can search through the Club Finder at www.gaa.ie. Alternatively, all Dublin clubs are registered with **Parnell Park**, tel 831 2099, the administrative headquarters for hurling and men's football in the capital. They will be more willing to answer any inquiries or advise you on who else to get in touch with.

There are directories for **ladies' football clubs and camogie clubs** at www.dublinladiesgaelic.ie and www.dublincamogie.ie respectively. You can also call the ladies' football office on 836 3156, or for camogie call 836 4619.

Clubs vary enormously in size and scale of facilities. The bigger clubs have more teams and probably provide more effective coaching for beginners. Joining fees vary depending on the club.

If you're really fanatical about football and hurling, the magazine *Hogan Stand*, web www.hoganstand.com, is for you. A visit to the GAA Museum at Croke Park, tel 819 2323, web http://museum.gaa.ie, is also a must (see page 198).

Golf/pitch'n'putt

The quality of Irish golf courses is world-renowned, and the sport has been booming in recent years, helped no doubt by the international successes of Padraig Harrington, Paul McGinley and Darren Clarke. It's not exactly a shoestring sport but if you really want to chase a little white ball around then the par 3, 18-hole course at the **Spawell Golf Centre** may suit. You can hire whatever equipment you need to tackle their short course. If you haven't quite reached that stage yet then try their covered driving range to hone your talents, where you can vent your frustrations to your heart's content. They also have snooker and outdoor tennis, plus badminton and squash facilities and a full bar and restaurant.

The sporting life

Spawell Golf Centre Templeogue, Dublin 6W, tel 490 7990, web www. spawell.ie
  Price €9 including club hire, children/seniors €5.50; driving range €6–9 depending on the number of balls, or €5.50 before noon on weekdays for any number of balls
  Open Mon–Fri 09.00/09.30–22.00, Sat–Sun 09.00–19.00
  Getting there Dublin Bus nos 15B, 49, 65, 65B

Pitch'n'putt is the shorter and much more affordable version of golf, and there are many pitch'n'putt courses around Dublin's suburbs. It's usually 9 holes, though sometimes you may be lucky and find a 12- or 18-hole course. For beginners it's usually better to find a course with short distances (60 metres or less) to the flag. One such course is at the **Deer Park Hotel** in Howth, which has a very manageable 18-hole course with breathtaking views of the sea. If you are a U2 fan, you'll be glad to know Larry Mullen Jr lives nearby. A 12-hole course in pleasant surroundings is in **St Anne's Park**, Raheny. At St Anne's you have to bring your own equipment. Both locations also have proper golf.

Deer Park Hotel Howth, Co Dublin, tel 832 2624/832 3489, web www. deerpark-hotel.ie
  Prices Mon–Fri €3.50 before 13.00, €4.50 after; Sat, Sun and bank hol €6.30 (club hire €2.50)
  Open in winter Mon–Fri 08.00–17.00/17.30, Sat–Sun 07.00–17.00/17.30; in summer Mon–Fri 08.00–21.00, Sat–Sun 07.00–21.00
  Getting there DART to Howth; Dublin Bus no 31 from Eden Quay
St Anne's Park Raheny, Dublin 5, tel 833 1859/833 8898/222 5278 (park enquiries)
  Price €6, children €3
  Open Mon–Sat from 10.00, last tee-off time varies with light
  Getting there Dublin Bus nos 29A, 31, 32, 32B from Eden Quay

Hill walking and rock climbing

Another of the joys of Dublin is the city's close proximity to the Dublin and Wicklow Mountains. They are stunningly beautiful and very accessible but can also be dangerous: the weather can quickly change from sunny and clear to cold, wet and misty, so be sure you are well prepared and equipped.

Mountaineering Ireland, tel 625 1115, web www.mountaineering.ie, is the umbrella body for hill walking/climbing and rock climbing. For any interested climber/walker their website gives details of the nearest club that you could join.

An Óige, the Irish Youth Hostel Association, tel 830 4555, web www.anoige.ie/www.hillwalkersclub.com, is another great organisation to become involved with. Walkers meet on a Sunday morning and are brought to their (usually very scenic) destination in a minibus. Walks are classified according to their level of difficulty, so there's always one to suit all ages and fitness levels. Despite its name An Óige welcomes members of all ages and joining it is a great way to meet new people. Membership is €20 per year.

There are many hill and coastal walks adjacent to Dublin that are accessible by public transport, covering various levels of ability. From Powerscourt Waterfall (see page 222) you can access the mountains of Djouce, Warhill and Maulin that are very popular with walkers from Dublin and Wicklow. To the west of the city, buses to Old Bawn in Tallaght will lead you in the direction of Stone Cross, above Old Bawn, where you can access Seahan and Seefingin (Dublin Bus nos 77A, 77X, 49, 49A). Alternatively, take Dublin Bus no 16 to Marlay Park in Rathfarnham, Dublin 14; trails from here will bring you up the Three Rock Mountain and the start of the Wicklow Way (see page 216).

For those who want to try rock climbing, **Dalkey Quarry**, beside Killiney Hill, is the most popular rock climbing location in south Dublin and offers routes suitable for everybody from beginners to the most experienced. The quarry is only a short walk from Dalkey DART station and anyone can walk in and just start climbing—however, this is obviously not advisable if you are inexperienced. Hiring a qualified guide is a good option and this can be a great activity for groups of adults or kids—call Calvin Torrans, international mountain guide, on 087 234 3932, or email calvinguide@hotmail.com. Calvin can also be arranged for the UCD wall.

For indoor climbing the wall at the **UCD Sports Centre**, Belfield, Dublin 4, tel 716 2185/716 2145, email climbing@ucd.ie, is 30 metres tall and offers some 60 routes for all ages and abilities. You can become a member or else it costs €8 per visit. UCD is accessible by a huge number of bus routes including no 10, which goes inside the campus.

Hockey

For those wanting to get involved the **Leinster Hockey** website, www.leinsterhockey.org, has a list of clubs and contact details. The **Irish Hockey Association** has some 180 affiliated clubs and 280 affiliated schools in total and produces the newsletter *Hockey Happenings*. The IHA head office is at Newstead, UCD, Belfield, Dublin 4, tel 716 3261, web www.hockey.ie.

Rugby

Rugby clubs, like their Gaelic counterparts, are happy to accommodate new members. Whatever your level or experience they will gladly take you on. Most clubs have at least five or six adult teams and there are a good number of women's teams.

The easiest way to find your nearest club is through **Leinster Rugby**, tel 269 3224, web www.leinsterrugby.ie. There is a list of contact details for clubs on the website—click on 'Domestic

Rugby'. Joining fees range from €50 to around €200, depending on the club and level of membership.

IRFU **Tag Rugby** is a great way to get involved if you're worried about broken collarbones or having your head stood on; it also has the benefit of mixed teams of a variety of ages. For more see www.irishrugby.ie/tag.

Snooker

If snooker is your thing, there are a number of small halls to choose from. Breaks Snooker Club even caters for the snooker enthusiast 24 hours a day, 7 days a week, 365 days a year. They also have pool. CrossGuns Snooker Club in Phibsboro is the country's oldest, and also has snooker coaching—call for details.

Breaks Snooker Club 1 Whitehall Wks, Upr Drumcondra Rd, Dublin 9, tel 836 9433
   Price €10/hr
   Open 24 hrs every day of the year
   Getting there Dublin Bus no 16
CrossGuns Snooker Club Cross Guns Bridge, Phibsboro, Dublin 7, tel 830 3970, web www.crossgunssnookerclub.com
   Price €7/hr 14.00–18.00, €9/hr 18.00–23.00
   Open 14.00–23.00 daily
   Getting there Dublin Bus nos 19, 19A

Soccer

There is a huge network of soccer clubs throughout the city, ranging from the semi-professional to the outright amateur. If you believe that you have what it takes to make the grade then get on the phone to your local League of Ireland club. They'll gladly have a look at you or put you in touch with one of their feeder clubs. As well as the Premier and First divisions there's an under-20s league and a futsal league. Contact the **League of Ireland** with enquiries, tel 899 9500, web www.loi.ie.

If your interest is merely in a weekly run-out, then asking at your local pub will likely as not put you in touch with a local . . . well, 'team' may be a bit of a strong word, but certainly a group of lads who kick a ball about occasionally.

The **Leinster Senior League**, 43 Parnell Square, Dublin 1, tel 872 9426/087 967 7045, web www.lsl.ie, has a network of clubs which compete more strenuously than the pub teams, with more regular training sessions and proper 90-minute games, replete with referees! Again, though, this isn't the most serious league in the world and these teams are legendary for their ability to enjoy themselves after their games.

Swimming

Dublin is well served with **swimming pools and clubs** and the quality in general is good. The easiest place to find them is in the *Golden Pages* directory or at www.goldenpages.ie. Beware some of the more dilapidated ones which can be lax on hygiene; it is always a good idea to check the pools out before you use them.

Ireland's first Olympic-standard 50-metre pool is at the **National Aquatic Centre** in Abbotstown, Dublin 15, web www.nationalaquaticcentre.ie, which came into its own when Ireland hosted the Special Olympics in 2003. There is another 50-metre pool (and still one of only three in the country) at the **West Wood Club** in Clontarf, web http://westwood.hosting365.ie.

Swimming in the sea is obviously a very different experience from the chlorinated indoor pools. From May to September the Irish Sea is refreshing—or bracing, depending on your taste; it's warmest towards the end of the summer. The seaside spots themselves are worth a visit even if you don't swim: on clear bright days the views are magical.

One of the best sea bathing spots in Dublin is the **Forty Foot** natural pool at Sandycove, which is not tide-dependent (it even has its own website—www.fortyfoot.org). For years this was a men-only skinny-dipping area but it is now open to everybody. Do take the warnings about the backwash from the super-ferries seriously. The undertow and waves created can be frightening and dangerous. You could also swim off the sea wall at the little sandy beach at **Sandycove** when the tide is in. Another lovely place to bathe when the tide is right is **Seapoint**, which is nearer the city. You can check the current water quality of both Sandycove and Seapoint at www.dlrcoco.ie. On the northside there are fine strands at **Dollymount, Donabate, Malahide, Portmarnock** and **Portrane**.

Getting there Seapoint and Sandycove are on the DART line and are also served by Dublin Bus no 7. The northside strands are served by Dublin Bus nos 32, 32A, 32B and 130.

Tennis

Tennis Ireland, tel 884 4010, web www.tennisireland.ie, have all the information you need to find out about your nearest courts, with affiliated clubs listed on their website. The organisation's outdoor courts at the **National Tennis Centre** at DCU are free to use, though there's a charge for the indoor courts. Phoning and booking in advance is essential. You can hire racquets and buy balls there too.

What is definitely advisable, though, is to check out **Dublin City Council** courts, which are rarely completely full (except in June, during Wimbledon) and are inexpensive to use. You always have to have your own racquets and balls, and any sort of trainers will be allowed on the tarmacadam surface. Quite a few public parks have tennis courts, but check out **St Anne's Park** on the northside and **Herbert Park** on the southside for a large number of courts in good condition. You may have to phone ahead to book a court.

The sporting life

Herbert Park Ballsbridge, Dublin 4, tel 668 4364/222 5278 (park enquiries)
>*Price* €5/hr per court, concessions €2.50
>*Open* 10.00 daily till last light
>*Getting there* Dublin Bus nos 4, 4A, 7, 7A, 10, 45, 46A

St Anne's Park Raheny, Dublin 5, tel 833 1859/833 8898/222 5278 (park
enquiries)
>*Price* €5/hr per court, concessions €2.50
>*Open* 10.00 daily till last light
>*Getting there* Dublin Bus nos 29A, 31, 32, 32B from Eden Quay

Tennis Ireland/National Tennis Centre DCU, Ballymun Rd/Collins Ave,
Glasnevin, Dublin 9, tel 700 7407, email courtbookings@tennisireland.ie
>*Price* €14/hr per indoor court, outdoor courts free (racquet hire €5/hr)
>*Open* Mon–Fri 11.00–14.00, 19.00–22.00; Sat–Sun 10.00–18.00 (summer
hours may be later)
>*Getting there* Dublin Bus nos 11, 11A, 11B, 13, 13A, 19A, 40N, 46X, 116

Ten-pin bowling

The **Leisureplex** has four bowling alleys in Dublin. The true
peak time is generally 18.00 to 23.00 at weekends, but according
to Leisureplex's pricing structure peak time is after 19.00 Mon–
Thurs and after 12.00 Fri–Sun and on bank holidays.

Price Off-peak price is €35 per hour (€6.85 per game) for
up to six people, and peak is €44 per hour (€8 per game). Be
careful with pool, snooker, Q-Zar laser tag, food, drinks and
amusements here, or your visit will cost you a lot more than you
bargained for.

Leisureplex web www.leisureplex.ie
>*Open* 10.00–00.30 daily

Blanchardstown Centre, Dublin 15, tel 822 3030, email blanch@leisureplex.
ie
>*Getting there* Dublin Bus no 39

Malahide Rd, Coolock, Dublin 17, tel 848 5722, email coolock@leisureplex.ie
>*Getting there* Dublin Bus nos 27, 42, 43

Stillorgan, Co Dublin, tel 288 1656, email stillorgan@leisureplex.ie *Getting*
there Dublin Bus nos 11, 46A, 63, 84

Village Green Centre, Tallaght, Dublin 24, tel 459 9411, email tallaght@
leisureplex.ie
Getting there Dublin Bus nos 49, 65, 77, 50, 54A and Luas Red line

Gambling

Racecourses

A trip to **Leopardstown**, south Dublin, or **Fairyhouse**, 25 km
north of Dublin, can be the day of a lifetime. A crisp, bright
day of suspense and excitement will stay in your memory for
years—as will substantial losses, or gains. Other top racecourses
within spitting distance of the capital are **Punchestown** and **The
Curragh**, both in Kildare. The Punchestown Festival at the end
of April is not to be missed, and neither is the four-day Leopardstown Christmas Festival. The Curragh Irish Derby Day, on
the last Sunday of June every year, is the Irish equivalent of the
Royal Ascot, attracting crowds of 30,000 or more.

As important to some people as the horses on race days is
the sense of occasion and the chance to get dressed up. The posh
punters take the social aspect if anything more seriously than the
horses—yet the difference between horse racing in Ireland and
in other countries, notably England, is the extent of the social
mix at the races here.

Remember that racing is a whole day's entertainment. Buses
to and fro, the odd drink and flutter shouldn't bring the cost too
high if you don't go crazy. If you're lucky you'll cover your costs
with a couple of wins.

Many areas of the stadia are wheelchair accessible and there
are accessible toilets, but it's no harm to phone in advance and
check exactly which features are accessible—sometimes, for

example, use of a lift will have to be arranged in advance to get to the restaurant.

The Curragh Co Kildare, tel (045) 441 205, web www.curragh.ie
   Admission generally €15, concessions €7.50; Irish Derby Day €40, concessions €25
   Getting there train from Heuston Station, Dublin 8 to Kildare Station and free shuttle bus to racecourse; special buses on race days from Busáras, Store St, Dublin 1
Fairyhouse Ratoath, Co Meath, tel 825 6167, web www.fairyhouseracecourse.ie
   Admission generally €15, concessions €10
   Getting there Bus Éireann no 105 from Beresford Place, Dublin 1 to Ratoath; special buses on race days from Busáras, Store St, Dublin 1
Leopardstown Racecourse Leopardstown, Dublin 18, tel 289 0500, web www.leopardstown.com
   Admission generally €15, concessions €10; Christmas Festival €25, concessions €15. Ten per cent online discount off general admission charge
   Getting there Dublin Bus nos 63, 114; special buses on race days from Busáras, Store St, Dublin 1
Punchestown Naas, Co Kildare, tel (045) 897 704, web www.punchestown.com
   Admission €30 daily for the festival, reserved seating in the enclosure €40
   Getting there Bus Éireann no 126 to Naas; special buses during the festival from Busáras, Store St, Dublin 1

Going to the dogs

Greyhound racing, or 'the dogs', is to a respectable horse racing meeting what a weekly bric-a-brac market is to high street chic: cheaper, rougher, smellier, but often more exciting. This is certainly because the races are so fast and furious (between 30 seconds and one minute). What's more you can bet quite small amounts without the bookies sulking. Unless you are a seasoned dog expert it is pretty acceptable just to choose a number between one and six, and plump €1 on the dog in question. With bars at the track many punters even miss the actual races.

At both **Shelbourne Park** and **Harold's Cross** there are a multitude of counters at which you can bet inside, and an equal number of TV monitors from which to view the races themselves. They have bars on different levels and even serve dinner, taking bets at your table. Both stadia are wheelchair accessible and have accessible toilets.

The walk (just over 1km) from Trinity College down Pearse St towards Shelbourne Park in Ringsend, is interesting in a gritty Republican kind of way—past Pearse's birthplace, the Widow Scallan's pub, and Boland's Mills where de Valera defended the city in 1916 from troops coming along the coast from Dún Laoghaire. Turn right into Sth Lotts Rd for the track.

Harold's Cross Greyhound Stadium 151 Harold's Cross Rd, Dublin 6W, tel 497 1081, web www.igb.ie/harolds-cross
   Admission €10, concessions €5, children (under 12) €3
   Open Mon, Tues, Fri; gates open 18.30, first race 19.55
   Getting there Dublin Bus nos 16, 16A, 19A, 49, 54A
Shelbourne Park Sth Lotts Rd, Ringsend, Dublin 4, tel 668 3502, web www.igb.ie/shelbourne-park
   Admission €10, concessions/children €5
   Open Wed, Thurs, Sat; gates open 18.30, first race 19.55
   Getting there Dublin Bus nos 2, 3

Bookmakers

The bookie's shop is somewhere that your mother always hoped you would never go. It can seem a little grim, and is certainly a mostly male environment. You can either revel in the slightly seedy ambiance, or just place your bet and watch the race in the pub nearby (there will always be a pub near a bookie's).

It really doesn't matter which chain or independent shop you go to. Finding them is not a problem in the city centre and they are also doted around the suburbs; **Paddy Power** and **Ladbrokes** are two of the biggest chains. Opening hours are irregular: they open when there is something to bet on. Summer opening hours are generally 10.00–21.00 and winter 10.00–16.30.

The really exciting thing about the bookie's as opposed to course betting is that you can bet on absolutely anything. If the shop doesn't offer odds on which team will win the ski-down-a-mountain-on-a-baking-tray at the Winter Olympics, then a couple of phone calls by them and they will take your bet. Finding obscure things to bet on can be quite amusing in itself (will there be snow on Christmas Day? is the most common of the unusual bets).

Ireland at its most trusting and its most cunning, its cheapest and its most lavish, its most naive and its most desperate, at its grimiest and its most splendid, is all to be found in the bookies' shops and racecourses of Dublin. As a shortcut to the heart of the nation, it's not a bad start.

Dublin's villages

Dublin still has a few self-contained spots where old-fashioned village life goes on. These neighbourhoods have a flavour of their own and are well worth discovering if you are here on a long stay or even looking for a place to live.

From the Liberties to Kilmainham

One of the oldest and most interesting neighbourhoods in the city is known as the Liberties. It stretches roughly from St Patrick's Cathedral west to Kilmainham. They are so called because the area was outside the old Dublin wall and so out of the city's jurisdiction. Home of the Guinness Brewery since 1759 and once settled by a prosperous community of Huguenots, it has gone seriously downhill since the 19th century.

Understandably, this part of town has become the city's antique trade centre, and the clutter of small shops, markets and bric-à-brac vendors dotted around **Francis St** and **Meath St** serve both the serious collector market and the junk junkies for miles around. Most welcome browsers, too. You can also come to the vendors on Meath St and **Thomas St** for very cheap basics: deodorant, washing powder, toilet rolls, as well as cheap clothes and accessories.

For foodies, one place not to miss is the **Gallic Kitchen** on Francis St, tel 454 4912, web www.gallickitchen.com, a top patisserie where you can take away all manner of sweet and savoury tarts to munch on your way. Pub culture is well represented here, with a host of traditional examples bearing historical names. And then there is **Vicar Street** (see page 159), the hip, glass-fronted café-style bar and venue on Thomas St (easy to identify

Dublin's villages

by the colourful street sculpture outside), which attracts a young music crowd from all over the city.

Moving down Thomas St, past the beautifully restored **St Catherine's Church** (1769), onto James's St, you'll find the temple to Dublin's most famous export, the Guinness Brewery. The brewery itself has long been closed to tourists but the Guinness experience can still be enjoyed by visitors at their super high-tech **Guinness Storehouse** visitor centre around the corner (see page 199). Entry is not especially cheap but worth it for the view you get over the city with your complimentary pint from the sky-high Gravity Bar at the end of the tour.

Nearby Kilmainham is rich in another kind of culture. Here, the **Irish Museum of Modern Art** (see page 200) has been housed since 1991 in the Royal Hospital (1680–86), a former home for retired soldiers and Ireland's finest example of 17th-century architecture. Across the street, **Kilmainham Gaol** (see page 201), opened first in 1796 and famous for its associations with the leaders of the 1916 Rising. The jail is now open to the public and operates as a museum.

Ringsend and surrounds

Once a charming fishing village and a popular bathing place for Dubliners, Ringsend flourished for almost 200 years as the principal packet boat station in Ireland for all traffic with Britain. It went into serious decline, however, in the early part of the 19th century, after the service was transferred to Howth and **Dún Laoghaire** (then Kingstown), leaving Ringsend without its principal source of income.

For visitors to the area, a spectacular walk on a fine day is the length of the **South Wall** (see page 207).

In the village itself, several of the pubs serve traditional pub fare, including the best of them, the **Oarsman**, just beside the bridge. Closer to the city on the Ringsend Rd, **Ocean**, a modern minimalist café/bar/restaurant affair in the ground floor of the Charlotte Quay complex (see page 126), is worth a visit for a chilled-out pint overlooking the canal basin. The best place for food in the area (although unfortunately it is only for takeaway) is the **Good Food Kitchen & Store** in Gordon St, tel 668 4514. It's tucked away in the warren of little streets between Barrow St (where the Grand Canal Dock DART Station is; the area is nicknamed 'Google Land' by Dubliners thanks to the company's presence there) and South Lotts Rd; the Good Food Kitchen serves soups, salads, wraps and all kinds of goodies made with top-quality ingredients for reasonable prices—a real treat in a surprising location. It's open from about 06.00 but closes at 15.00.

The nearby seaside village of Sandymount, now a very upmarket suburb, is also a good spot for walks beside **Sandymount Strand**; when the tide is out you can walk out to the horizon (in the 1920s the strand was a suggested site of Dublin airport!). You'll find good food or a pint in one of the pubs around the quaint village green. Look out for W. B. Yeats' birthplace on the Green.

In the early 19th century **Sandymount Castle** was an interesting but modest house. However, travelling in Italy its then owner boasted to his aristocratic Italian friends about the castle he lived in. Imagine his horror when months after his return to Ireland one of those friends announced his intention to make a visit. In a panic the owner erected the castellations we can now see on the roof, and lo! Sandymount had a castle!

Dublin's villages

The modern village: Dublin's Docklands

In the mid-1990s the Government decided to completely rede-
velop Dublin's Docklands, some 1,300 acres of land on either
side of the River Liffey. Since then the regeneration has been
utterly transforming this part of the city, making it vibrant and
trendy and something of a symbol of the New Ireland.

South of the river, between Pearse St and Sir John Rogerson's
Quay, lies **Grand Canal Square**, designed by American land-
scape architect Martha Schwartz. From a distance the giant red
glowsticks sticking out of the ground look somewhat tacky, but
stand among them on a darkening evening and it does feel just a
little bit magical.

The main attractions are on the north side of the river,
stretching from the Custom House to The O_2 arena. The International Financial Services Centre is here, as is the National
College of Ireland. There are farmers' markets, Christmas
markets, theatre performances and festivals. For the past few
years the **Docklands Maritime Festival** has hosted a fleet of tall
ships that the public can board and explore for free, attracting
130,000 visitors in 2008 over the June bank holiday weekend.

The *Jeannie Johnston* replica famine ship is moored at North
Wall Quay, near Rowan Gillespie's famine sculptures, which
dramatically recall a terrible time for the country.

The state-of-the-art, 14,000-seater venue **The O_2** (see
page 159)—the largest indoor venue in the country—opened
in December 2008 on North Wall Quay, replacing the Point
Theatre. You can even get ferry trips up the Liffey to The O_2 on
certain concert nights. Check out the websites **www.liffeyferry.
com**, tel 473 4342, and **www.liffeyrivercruises.com**, tel 473 4082,
for more info. Costs are €2.50 each way to cross the river and €5
each way to travel from Custom House Quay up to The O_2.

Capel St, Parnell St, Moore St

The northside is hailed as keeper of the true Dublin character and nowhere is that character—both old and new—more evident than on Capel St, Parnell St and Moore St. From the north quays Capel St feeds into Parnell St off which runs the famous Moore St market. From O'Connell Bridge walk west until you see Nealon's pub; turn right and you're on Capel St. The first thing that hits you is the sheer number of sex shops—Holy Ireland, where are you? But there are also several great pubs, chief among them the relatively new (but staunchly traditional) **McNeill's**, (see page 122) which is also a music shop. There are a number of music shops here, charity shops, good **cafés** and bakeries. Drag queen **Miss Panti's gay bar** (see page 22) is here, along with a camping store and a Polish supermarket.

Parnell St has become Dublin's unofficial Chinatown, though you will also find Korean wholesalers; an African hairstylists and hair accessories store; an African food shop and restaurant; and other **ethnic shops and restaurants**, all frequented by the locals (Chinese, Korean, Nigerian, Polish). With the Georgian splendour of Nth Great George's St and the **James Joyce Centre** (see page 201) off it, Parnell St is both part of Irish history and a slice of modern Dublin life.

The cheap fruit and veg barrow traders of Moore St are still around, now competing with a host of Asian and African vendors and shops. There is a halal food store, an Afro-Caribbean supermarket, a Chinese supermarket, along with too many mobile phone/laptop repair shops and knicknack stores to count, both in the **Moore St Mall** and on the street itself. In the mall there is also a Polish bookstore and Charity Hair Studio, where you can get dreadlocks and African styling done.

Dublin's villages

Index